A Routledge Literary Sourcebook on

The Poems of John Keats

Few modern critics would dispute Keats's status as one of the great English poets and many consider his *Lamia, Isabella, The Eve of St. Agnes, and other Poems* as the most important single volume of verse to be published during the Romantic period. Perhaps more importantly, he remains one of the most popular poets of any era.

This Routledge Literary Sourcebook offers an introduction to his life, contexts and work, and to the wealth of critical responses to his poetry. A section on Contexts offers a sketch of Keats's brief but crowded life, a glossary of important acquaintances, a chronology and excerpts from key letters. The second section of the Sourcebook, Interpretations, combines a survey of criticism with reprinted critical texts – ranging from very mixed early responses to more recent essays. This is followed by a selection of Key Poems, all introduced and extensively annotated by the editor, with reference to documents found in the previous sections. The volume concludes with a discussion of the various editions of Keats and offers a helpful guide to further reading.

John Strachan's refreshingly clear guidance and a wealth of reprinted material make this the ideal starting point for anyone wishing to make their own reading of the poems of John Keats.

John Strachan is Reader in English at the University of Sunderland. His editions of Romantic period poetry and prose include *Parodies of the Romantic Age* (1999), *British Satire 1785–1840* (2003) and Leigh Hunt's *Poetical Works* (2003).

Routledge Literary Sourcebooks

Series Editor: Duncan Wu, St Catherine's College, Oxford University

Also available are Routledge Literary Sourcebooks on:
E. M. Forster's *A Passage to India* edited by Peter Childs
Mary Wollstonecraft's *A Vindication of the Rights of Woman* edited by Adriana Craciun
William Shakespeare's *Othello* edited by Andrew Hadfield
William Shakespeare's *King Lear* edited by Grace Ioppolo
Henrik Ibsen's *Hedda Gabler* edited by Christopher Innes
Mary Shelley's *Frankenstein* edited by Timothy Morton

Forthcoming titles are:
William Shakespeare's *The Merchant of Venice* edited by Susan Cerasano
Herman Melville's *Moby-Dick* edited by Michael J. Davey
The Poems of W. B. Yeats edited by Michael O'Neill
Harriet Beecher Stowe's *Uncle Tom's Cabin* edited by Debra J. Rosenthal

For further details on this series, see www.literature.routledge.com/rls

A Routledge Literary Sourcebook on

The Poems of
John Keats

Edited by John Strachan

Routledge
Taylor & Francis Group
New York   London

For Ben Colbert and Hilary Weeks

821.7 KEA STR

3087848

LEEDS TRINITY UNIVERSITY

First published 2003
by Routledge
11 New Fetter Lane, London EC4P 4EE

Simultaneously published in the USA and Canada
by Routledge
29 West 35th Street, New York, NY 10001

Transferred to Digital Printing 2008

Routledge is an imprint of the Taylor & Francis Group, an informa business

Selection and editorial matter © 2003 John Strachan

British Library Cataloguing in Publication Data
A catalogue record for this book is available from the British Library

Library of Congress Cataloging in Publication Data
A Routledge literary sourcebook on the poems of John Keats / edited by John Strachan.
    p. cm.—(Routledge literary sourcebooks)
Includes bibliographical references and index.
1. Keats, John, 1795–1821—Criticism and interpretation—Handbooks, manuals, etc.
I. Strachan, John (John R.)   II. Series
  PR4837 .R59 2003
  821'.7—dc21
                                                            2002153226

ISBN 13: 978-0-415-23478-8 (pbk)

Contents

2: Interpretations

3: Key Poems

4: Further Reading

Series Editor's Preface

The Routledge Literary Sourcebook series has been designed to provide students with the materials required to begin serious study of individual literary works, all in a single volume. This includes an overview of the critical history of the work, including extracts from important critical debates of recent decades, and a selection of key passages from the text itself. Volume editors provide introductory commentaries and annotation for the reader's guidance. These handy books provide almost everything most students will need for the contextual and critical overview of literature expected in schools and universities today.

This aim is reflected in the structure of each Sourcebook. Section 1, 'Contexts', provides biographical data in the form of an author chronology and contemporary documents relating to the author and his or her work. In Section 2, 'Interpretations', the editor assembles extracts from the most influential and important criticism throughout the history of the work. In some cases this includes materials relating to performances or adaptations. The third section, 'Key Passages', gathers together the essential episodes from the literary text connected by editorial commentary and annotation so as to relate them to ideas raised earlier in the volume. The final section offers suggestions for further reading, including recommended editions and critical volumes.

Annotation is a key feature of this series. The editor's annotations appear as footnotes at the bottom of the relevant page, along with any notes which are part of the reprinted text. Any reprinted notes are prefaced by the author's name in square brackets, e.g. [Robinson's note]. All other notes have been added by the volume editor.

Routledge Literary Sourcebooks offer the ideal introduction to single literary works, combining primary and secondary materials, chosen by experts, in accessible form.

Duncan Wu

Acknowledgements

I am grateful to the series editor of the Routledge Literary Sourcebooks, Duncan Wu, whose suggestion it was that I edit this volume, and who has been very helpful in its preparation. I am indebted to Jane Moore for her advice and support. I would also like to thank Liz Thompson and Sünje Redies at Routledge.

I am grateful to the copyright holders for permission to quote extracts from the following books:

John Jones, 'The Feel I Have' from *John Keats's Dream of Truth* (Chatto & Windus, London, 1969, copyright Curtis Brown London).

Marjorie Levinson, *Keats's Life of Allegory: The Origins of a Style* (Blackwell, Oxford, 1988).

Jerome J. McGann, 'Keats and the Historical Method in Literary Criticism' © Jerome J. McGann 1985. Reprinted from *The Beauty of Inflections: Literary Investigations in Historical Method and Theory* by Jerome J. McGann (1985) by permission of Oxford University Press.

Anne K. Mellor, 'Ideological Cross-Dressing: John Keats/Emily Brontë', copyright 1993, from *Romanticism and Gender*. Reproduced by permission of Routledge, Inc., part of the Taylor & Francis Group.

Nicholas Roe, 'Apollo's Touch' © Nicholas Roe 1997. Reprinted from *John Keats and the Culture of Dissent* by Nicholas Roe (1997) by permission of Oxford University Press.

Stuart M. Sperry, 'The Great Odes' from *Keats the Poet*. Copyright © 1973 by Princeton University Press, new afterword © 1994 by Princeton University Press. Reprinted by permission of Princeton University Press.

Helen Vendler, 'Ode to a Nightingale', reprinted by permission of the publisher from *The Odes of John Keats* by Helen Vendler, Cambridge, Mass: The Belknap Press of Harvard University Press. Copyright © 1983 by the President and Fellows of Harvard College. Poems are quoted from *Poems of John Keats* edited by Jack Stillinger, The Belknap Press of Harvard University Press, 1982. Letters are quoted from *Letters of John Keats*, edited by Hyder E. Rollins, Harvard University Press, 1958.

Earl R. Wasserman, *The Finer Tone: Keats' Major Poems*, pp. 66-83 © 1953. Reprinted by permission of Johns Hopkins University Press.

Daniel P. Watkins, 'History, Self and Gender in Ode to Psyche' from *Keats and History*, ed. Nicholas Roe (Cambridge University Press, 1995).

Susan J. Wolfson, 'Keats and Gender Criticism' from *The Persistence of Poetry: Bicentennial Essays on Keats*, eds Robert Ryan and Ronald A. Sharp (University of Massachusetts Press, Amherst, 1998). *The Persistence of Poetry* is copyright 1998 by the University of Massachusetts Press.

Every effort has been made to trace and correspond with copyright holders. If any have been inadvertently overlooked, the publishers will be pleased to make the necessary arrangements at the earliest opportunity.

Introduction

'Oh for ten Years, that I may overwhelm/Myself in poesy' wrote John Keats in October 1816, the month of his twenty-first birthday. Keats, recently qualified as an apothecary, had decided to abandon his medical career, and the poem in which these lines occur, 'Sleep and Poetry', shows him self-consciously devoting himself to a more uncertain calling, that of a poet. It may be that the modesty of Keats's wish for 'ten Years' reflects an awareness of the possibility of his life being a short one (Keats was nine when his mother died of tuberculosis), but, either way, his prayer was not to be granted. Nonetheless, in the short period left to him (just under four and a half years), Keats served his literary apprenticeship well; by 1819, the year in which he composed the majority of the poems for which he is remembered ('The Eve of St. Agnes', 'La Belle Dame Sans Merci', the great odes, 'Lamia' and the fragmentary 'The Fall of Hyperion'), he was capable of one of the most remarkable outbursts of creativity in English literary history. Few modern critics would dispute Keats's status as one of the greatest English poets. That said, this current critical consensus compares starkly with Keats's early reputation, which was contentious, with enthusiastic praise co-existing with the sourest condemnation. To his contemporaries, Keats was a controversial figure: to some, socially presumptuous, politically unsound, even indecent; to others a precocious talent snuffed out by illness or, more fancifully, the vicious attacks of antagonistic critics. And neither was the poet's achievement effortlessly realised. Though idolatrous Victorian admirers sometimes viewed his verse as the sublime outpourings of untutored genius, Keats had to work hard at becoming a poet, fusing natural talent with laborious poetic experimentation. Keats borrowed from, imitated and eventually assimilated a host of influences (Leigh Hunt, Wordsworth, Coleridge, Spenser, Dante, Boccaccio, Milton and Shakespeare) in his progress from the early, often fumbling, poetic efforts to the remarkable accomplishment of his 1820 collection *Lamia, Isabella, The Eve of St. Agnes, and other Poems*, a book which, perhaps, has only the *Lyrical Ballads* of 1798 to rival it as the most important single volume of verse to be published during the Romantic period.

This Sourcebook provides the student reader of Keats with the critical tools needed to approach the poet's work. It combines comprehensively annotated texts of Keats's major poetry with a detailed account of, and extracts from, the criticism which that poetry has received: from early reviews through to scholarship published in the late 1990s. The first section of the book, Contexts, offers a biographical sketch of Keats, a chronology of his short but eventful life and key contemporary documents, principally from the poet's remarkable correspondence (which is itself frequently taught alongside the verse on university syllabuses). Keats's letters, the critical documents most important to the study of his poetry, show his literary ideas developing and sketch important philosophical ideas which inform his verse.

Section 2, Interpretations, begins with a Critical History of Keats's poetry, a detailed account of the ways in which that poetry has been read and understood from the publication of the earliest reviews to the literary criticism of today. It tracks the development of Keats's literary reputation from the contentious figure which the poet cut to his contemporaries to the twentieth-century recipient of a mass of scholarly attention. This discursive account of Keatsian criticism is followed by two critical anthologies which contain readings of the poet's work published between 1816 and 1998. Early Critical Reception engages with the contemporary controversies surrounding the publication of Keats's work, extracting from early reviews such as the notorious onslaughts in *Blackwood's Edinburgh Magazine* (see pp. 34–6) and the *Quarterly Review* (see p. 34) and the vigorous defence of the poet mounted in the liberal press. It also includes later nineteenth-century assessments: William Howitt's rhapsodic Victorian eulogy of Keats (see pp. 42–3) and Matthew Arnold's attempt to offer a corrective response to such uncritical hero-worship (see pp. 43–4). Modern Criticism extracts from more recent Keatsian scholarship, and offers substantial and representative passages from some of the most important critical work on Keats's poetry. Whilst its emphasis is upon Keatsian studies post-1970, the subsection also tracks the progress of work on the poet throughout the twentieth century as a whole.

Section 3, Key Poems, offers texts of Keats's most frequently studied poetry (the poet's reputation rests upon a fairly small body of work, all of which is included in this volume). Each poem is extensively annotated and is furnished with an extended introductory headnote which provides a critical history of that poem (paying particular attention to the critics discussed in Interpretations). These summarise modern critical opinion on each poem, introducing the reader to ongoing debates about, for example, *Hyperion* or 'Ode to a Nightingale'; whereas Interpretations deals with general debates about Keats, this section guides the reader through critical readings of individual poems. The book's final section, Further Reading, provides a list of recommended editions of Keats's poetry and letters, and a short, selected bibliography of essential critical work on the poet.

In sum, this book combines an edition of Keats's major poetry with a history of the reception of the poet's work. It gathers together in accessible form the critical documents necessary for the study of Keats's extraordinary poetic achievement.

1

Contexts

Contextual Overview

Introduction

Attempting to study the poetry of Keats without a knowledge of the contexts in which his verse was produced is an activity of limited value. And, setting academic enquiry aside, the pleasure to be found in reading Keats's work is also deepened and enriched by a knowledge of his short but eventful life, of the literary and political quarrels in which his work participated, and of the correspondence in which he formulated his ideas about the nature of art and the imagination. Consequently, this section addresses Keats's life and literary contexts. It consists of a short biography and a list of Keats's friends and contemporaries. This will be followed by a chronology and, in the Contemporary Documents section, a selection from the poet's important letters.

The Life of John Keats

John Keats was born in London on 31 October 1795, the son of a livery stable manager at the Swan and Hoop in Finsbury, North London. The 'humble' nature of his antecedents has frequently been overstated, by antipathetic critic and partisan alike; Keats's maternal grandfather owned the Finsbury inn and other property, and it was the early deaths of his mother and father and a resulting, almost interminable, court case concerning the Keats children's inheritance which blighted what would have otherwise been a fairly prosperous bourgeois upbringing. And although J. G. Lockhart jeered in *Blackwood's Edinburgh Magazine* in 1818 that Keats was an upstart 'Cockney' ignoramus who lacked the classical education appropriate to a poet, Keats's schooling at the progressive Enfield School in North London was by no means rudimentary. That said, his school career was certainly shorter than that of many of his poetical peers, and nor did Keats have the university education of the likes of Byron, Coleridge and Wordsworth. Instead, he left school at the age of fifteen to be prepared for a practical rather than an intellectual career, as apprentice to Thomas Hammond, an apothecary-surgeon of Edmonton, London.

Keats seems to have begun writing verse in 1814, possibly as an occasional diversion from his immersion in the unpleasant realities of the daily routine with Hammond and, later, the grim wards of Guy's Hospital where he continued his medical training. The pivotal year in Keats's brief life was 1816. His first published work, the sonnet 'O Solitude! if I must with thee dwell', appeared in the *Examiner* in May, and during the summer, after completing examinations which licensed him to practise as an apothecary, Keats decided to devote himself to the profession of poetry. In October 1816, he wrote what is generally seen as his first important poem, 'On First Looking into Chapman's Homer' (pp. 79–82), and met his poetic and political hero, Leigh Hunt. The indefatigably sociable Hunt was an important figure in Keats's personal and poetic development, publishing him in his journals, the *Examiner* and the *Indicator*, and introducing him to other talented young men: the painter Benjamin Robert Haydon and the poets Shelley and J. H. Reynolds (in December 1816 Hunt published the first appreciation of Keats's work in an *Examiner* article, the 'Young Poets' (pp. 33–4), which grouped Keats alongside Shelley and Reynolds). Keats, like Hunt, had a talent for friendship and such men as Hunt, Reynolds, Benjamin Bailey, Charles Cowden Clarke, Richard Woodhouse, Charles Armitage Brown and Joseph Severn provided him with an emotional and literary support system, notably during the personal and financial difficulties of his last two years. And Keats was also fortunate in the strength of his familial ties, being particularly close to his brothers George and Tom (in late 1816 he moved with his brothers to Cheapside in the City of London). Keats's friends and family, and later his fiancée, Fanny Brawne, were the principal sounding board for the development of his ideas about poetry, politics and the nature of the imagination, both in conversation and in the poet's enduring and remarkable letters, a body of correspondence which has little to equal it in English literary history. The critical and philosophical concepts which inform Keats's poetry (negative capability, the notion of the poet as chameleon, the chamber of maiden-thought, the vale of soul-making and so on) were all developed in his letters.

By March 1817, Keats had produced his first, somewhat uneven, collection of verses, *Poems*, published by C. and J. Ollier, and in the following month he was contracted by the firm of Taylor and Hessey to write a long mythological romance, *Endymion*, which appeared in April 1818. Though *Endymion* was badly received, and has had few unqualified admirers since its first appearance, it was an important part of Keats's poetic apprenticeship, clearing the path to the remarkably productive period which began in September 1818, which was perhaps the most notable month in Keats's life. On the negative side, it saw *Endymion* savagely noticed by John Wilson Croker in the high Tory *Quarterly Review* (p. 34). To the *Quarterly*, Keats was a camp-follower of the politically subversive circle around Hunt, and Croker's attack was as much political as literary. However, it also included important literary and personal events: Keats met Fanny Brawne for the first time (by Christmas Day he had reached an 'understanding' with her and by the autumn of 1819 they were officially engaged) and his poetic *annus mirabilis*, the so-called 'great year' of intense and sustained poetic creativity which lasted until September of the following year, began as he started work on his mythological, Miltonic epic *Hyperion* (pp. 96–118). On the first of December 1818, Keats moved to Charles Armitage Brown's house in Hampstead, only to see this new beginning coincide, on the very same day, with the death of his brother Tom from consumption. Tom's death was acutely traumatic for Keats. Whilst the psychobiographical claim that it prompted him into the poetic triumphs of early to mid-1819 (on the grounds that his brother's demise concentrated the poet's mind upon his own mortality) are perhaps overly simplistic, it is undeniable that Keats's bereavement underpins to some extent the profound meditations upon death, sickness and sorrow in the great odes and, later, 'The Fall of Hyperion'. Between January and May 1819, Keats produced romances, odes and lyrics of the highest quality. January saw the composition of 'The Eve of St. Agnes' (pp. 119–34) and the following month 'The Eve of St. Mark'. Between February and April he wrote 'Isabella; or, The Pot of Basil' (pp. 86–96) and in April 'La Belle Dame Sans Merci' (pp. 134–8). In April and May 1819, Keats composed his remarkable series of 'spring odes': the 'Ode to Psyche' (pp. 140–5), 'Ode to a Nightingale' (pp. 145–50), 'Ode on a Grecian Urn' (pp. 150–6) and the 'Ode on Melancholy' (pp. 156–8). Between June and September he completed 'Lamia' (pp. 158–72) and worked on the unfinished *'The Fall of Hyperion. A Dream'* (pp. 176–86). The 'great year' was completed on 19 September with the composition of 'To Autumn' (pp. 173–6), and Keats wrote little poetry of note after completing the lyric.

By late 1819, John Keats's emotional equilibrium had left him. He was deeply anxious about the troubles experienced by his brother George and his wife in America and was plagued by money worries which led him to consider a career as a literary journalist and precluded the possibility of marriage to Fanny Brawne, for whom he was tormented by erotic feeling. And in February 1820, Keats suffered a severe haemorrhage which indicated the onset of consumption ('my death warrant' as he stoically labelled it). Following the publication in July of *Lamia, Isabella, The Eve of St. Agnes, and other Poems*, Keats left England for Italy in mid-September 1820 in the vain hope that a Mediterranean climate might help his health. He arrived in Rome on 15 November but was very soon incapacitated by illness (Keats wrote no poetry in Italy and his final letter dates from 30 November 1820). At 11 p.m. on 23 February 1821, Keats died at the Piazza di Spagna in Rome. He was buried three days later in the city's English Cemetery.

Keats's Friends and Contemporaries

Benjamin Bailey (1791–1853): clergyman and friend of Keats.
Fanny Brawne (1800–65): Keats's fiancée.
Charles Armitage Brown (1786–1842): merchant, author and friend of Keats.
George Gordon, Lord Byron (1788–1824): poet.
Charles Cowden Clarke (1787–1877): friend and son of Keats's headmaster at Enfield School. Introduced Keats to Leigh Hunt.
Samuel Taylor Coleridge (1772–1834): poet.

John Wilson Croker (1780–1857): poet, Tory politician and author of the
Quarterly Review's attack on *Endymion*.

Charles Wentworth Dilke (1789–1864): civil servant, journalist and friend of
Keats.

Benjamin Robert Haydon (1786–1846): painter, diarist and friend of Keats.

William Hazlitt (1778–1830): radical critic and essayist.

James Augustus Hessey (1785–1875): publisher, with John Taylor, of *Endymion*
and *Lamia, Isabella, The Eve of St. Agnes, and other Poems*.

James Henry Leigh Hunt (1784–1859): poet, essayist and radical journalist.
Keats's friend and patron.

Francis Jeffrey (1773–1850): critic, lawyer and editor of the *Edinburgh Review*.

John Gibson Lockhart (1794–1854): Tory journalist and a principal contributor
to *Blackwood's Edinburgh Magazine*.

Charles Ollier (1788–1859): publisher, with his brother James, of Keats's Poems.

John Hamilton Reynolds (1794–1852): poet, journalist and solicitor.

Joseph Severn (1793–1879): painter and friend. Nursed Keats in his final illness.

Percy Bysshe Shelley (1792–1822): poet and friend of Keats.

John Taylor (1781–1864): publisher, with James Hessey, of *Endymion* and
Lamia, Isabella, The Eve of St. Agnes, and other Poems.

Richard Woodhouse, Jr (1788–1834): lawyer, philologist and friend of Keats.

William Wordsworth (1770–1850): poet.

Chronology

1795
- Born 31 October in Finsbury, London, the first child of Thomas Keats, livery stable manager at the Swan and Hoop, and Frances Keats (née Jennings)

1797
- 28 February, birth of Keats's brother George

1798
- 18 November, birth of brother Tom

1803
- 3 June, birth of sister Fanny; August, Keats begins to attend the Reverend John Clarke's school at Enfield

1804
- 15 April, Thomas Keats dies from injuries sustained in a fall from his horse; 27 June, Frances Keats marries again, to William Rawlings, and Keats and his siblings move to their grandparents' house in Lower Edmonton

1810
- March, Frances Keats Rawlings dies of tuberculosis; July, Richard Abbey and John Nowland Sandall are appointed guardians to the Keats children

1811
- Keats leaves Enfield School; apprenticed at Edmonton to Thomas Hammond, apothecary and surgeon

1814
- Begins to write poetry: first known poem is his 'Imitation of Spenser', written most probably in the early part of the year

1815

- 2 February, writes a sonnet in celebration of Leigh Hunt's release from prison; 1 October, becomes a student at Guy's Hospital

1816

- John Nowland Sandall dies, leaving Richard Abbey as the Keats children's sole guardian; 5 May, Keats's first published work, the sonnet 'O Solitude! if I must with thee dwell', is printed in Leigh Hunt's *Examiner*; 25 July, completes examinations which license him to practise as an apothecary; October, writes 'On First Looking into Chapman's Homer' and meets Leigh Hunt, Benjamin Robert Haydon and John Hamilton Reynolds; November, moves with his brothers to 76, Cheapside; 1 December, is praised, with Percy Bysshe Shelley and J. H. Reynolds, in Hunt's *Examiner* article on the 'Young Poets', in which 'On First Looking into Chapman's Homer' is published for the first time; December, meets Shelley at Hunt's house, writes 'Sleep and Poetry' and 'I stood tiptoe', and Haydon takes a life mask of Keats

1817

- March, his first volume, *Poems*, published by C. and J. Ollier; Keats moves to Hampstead, views the Elgin Marbles; October, the first of *Blackwood*'s attacks on the 'Cockney School of Poetry' published; 22 November, writes to Benjamin Bailey of 'the holiness of the Heart's affections and the truth of Imagination – What the imagination seizes as beauty must be truth'; 21 December, writes of 'negative capability' to his brothers George and Tom; 28 December, attends Haydon's 'immortal dinner' with Wordsworth, Charles Lamb and others

1818

- January–February, attends William Hazlitt's lectures on the English poets; 3 March, attends Hazlitt's lecture 'On the Living Poets'; April, publication of *Endymion. A Poetical Romance* by Taylor and Hessey; 3 May, writes to Reynolds comparing Milton with Wordsworth and setting out his notion of the 'chamber of maiden thought'; *c.* 28 May, attends the marriage of George Keats to Georgiana Wylie; September, *Endymion* is savagely noticed in the *Quarterly Review*, Keats meets Fanny Brawne, begins so-called 'great year' of intense and sustained poetic creativity and begins to compose *Hyperion*; 27 October, writes to Woodhouse of the 'Poetical character . . . that sort of which, if I am anything, I am a Member; that sort distinguished from the Wordsworthian or egotistical sublime . . . It has no character – it enjoys light and shade . . . What shocks the virtuous philosopher, delights the chameleon Poet'; 1 December, moves to Charles Armitage Brown's house in Hampstead, and Tom Keats dies from consumption the same day; 25 December, reaches 'an understanding' with Fanny Brawne.

1819

- January, writes 'The Eve of St. Agnes'; February, writes 'The Eve of St. Mark'; February/March–April, writes 'Isabella; or, The Pot of Basil'; April writes 'La Belle Dame Sans Merci' and abandons *Hyperion*; 21–30 April, writes 'Ode to Psyche'; May, writes the 'Ode to a Nightingale', the 'Ode on a Grecian Urn' and the 'Ode on Melancholy'; June–September, composes 'Lamia'; July–September, works on 'The Fall of Hyperion. A Dream'; 19 September, writes 'To Autumn'

1820

- February, suffers a severe tubercular haemorrhage, his 'death warrant'; July, publication of *Lamia, Isabella, The Eve of St. Agnes, and other Poems*; 18 September, leaves England for Italy with the artist Joseph Severn; 15 November, arrives in Rome; 30 November, writes his last surviving letter

1821

- 23 February, dies of consumption in Rome at his lodgings, No. 26 Piazza di Spagna; 26 February, is buried in the English Cemetery in Rome

Contemporary Documents

Introduction

Keats's entertaining and illuminating letters rank highly in the history of English literary correspondence. And, just as significantly, those letters provide the most vital context to the study of his poetry and should be read alongside it. In them, Keats developed philosophical and critical concepts which inform his verse: negative capability, the chamber of maiden-thought, the vale of soul-making, the chameleon poet and so on. This sub-section offers a selection of Keats's most important letters (taken from Hyder Edward Rollins's 1958 edition, *The Letters of John Keats, 1814–1821*). It concludes with a poignant letter from Leigh Hunt, written, though Hunt did not know as much, after the poet's death.

From letter from **Keats to Benjamin Bailey**, 22 November 1817

> This letter is Keats's first significant prose meditation upon themes which inform many of his most important letters and much of his poetry: the imagination, the relationship between beauty and truth, and the question of identity, especially poetic identity.

[. . .] I wish you knew all that I think about Genius and the Heart—and yet I think you are thoroughly acquainted with my innermost breast in that respect or you could not have known me even thus long and still hold me worthy to be your dear friend. In passing however I must say of one thing that has pressed upon me lately and encreased my Humility and capability of submission and that is this truth—Men of Genius are great as certain ethereal Chemicals operating on the Mass of neutral intellect—by they have not any individuality, any determined Character. I would call the top and head of those who have a proper self Men of Power—

But I am running my head into a Subject which I am certain I could not do justice to under five years s[t]udy and 3 vols octavo—and moreover long to be talking about the Imagination—so my dear Bailey do not think of this unpleasant affair if possible—do not—I defy any ha[r]m to come of it—I defy—I'll shall write to Crips this Week and reque[s]t him to tell me all his goings on from time to time by Letter whererever I may be—it will all go on well—so dont because you have suddenly discover'd a Coldness in Haydon suffer yourself to be teased. Do not my dear fellow.

O I wish I was as certain of the end of all your troubles as that of your momentary start about the authenticity of the Imagination. I am certain of nothing but of the holiness of the Heart's affections and the truth of Imagination—What the imagination seizes as Beauty must be truth—whether it existed before or not—for I have the same Idea of all our Passions as of Love they are all in their sublime, creative of essential Beauty—In a Word, you may know my favourite Speculation by my first book and the little song I sent in my last—which is a representation from the fancy of the probable mode of operating in these Matters. The Imagination may be compared to Adam's dream—he awoke and found it truth. I am the more zealous in this affair, because I have never yet been able to perceive how anything can be known for truth by consequitive reasoning—and yet it must be—Can it be that even the greatest Philosopher ever arrived at his goal without putting aside numerous objections—However it may be, O for a Life of Sensations rather than of Thoughts! It is 'a Vision in the form of Youth' a Shadow of reality to come— and this consideration has further conv[i]nced me for it has come as auxiliary to another favorite Speculation of mine, that we shall enjoy ourselves hereafter by having what we called happiness on Earth repeated in a finer tone and so repeated—And yet such a fate can only befall those who delight in sensation rather than hunger as you do after Truth—Adam's dream will do here and seems to be a conviction that Imagination and its empyreal reflection is the same as human Life and its spiritual repetition. But as I was saying, the simple imaginative Mind may have its rewards in the repeti[ti]on of its own silent Working coming continually on the spirit with a fine suddenness—to compare great things with small—have you never by being surprised with an old Melody—in a delicious place—by a delicious voice, fe[l]t over again your very speculations and surmises at the time it first operated on your soul—do you not remember forming to yourself the singer's face more beautiful than it was possible and yet with the elevation of the Moment you did not think so—even then you were mounted on the Wings of Imagination so high—that the Prototype must be here after—that delicious face you will see—What a time! I am continually running away from the subject—sure this cannot be exactly the case with a complex Mind—one that is imaginative and at the same time careful of its fruits—who would exist partly on sensation partly on thought—to whom it is necessary that years should bring the philosophic Mind—such an one I consider your's and therefore it is necessary to your eternal happiness that you not only drink this old Wine of Heaven which I shall call the redigestion of our most ethereal Musings on Earth; but also increase in knowledge and know all things. [. . .]

From letter from **Keats to George and Tom Keats**,
21 December 1817

> This is the most famous of Keats's letters, containing as it does his summary
> account of his most important critical formulation, 'negative capability'. Keats
> had recently annotated his copy of *Paradise Lost* thus: 'What creates the
> intense pleasure of not knowing? A sense of independence, of power, from the
> fancy's creating a world of its own by the power of probabilities.' In the letter,
> Keats returns to the subject of 'not knowing', in his willingness to embrace,
> where necessary, the state of remaining in 'uncertainties, mysteries, doubts'
> rather than 'irritabl[y] reaching after fact and reason'. Walter Jackson Bate's
> interpretation of the negative capability passage is reprinted on **pp. 50–1**
> below.

[. . .] I spent Friday evening with Wells & went the next morning to see *Death
on the Pale horse*. It is a wonderful picture, when West's age is considered: But
there is nothing to be intense upon; no women one feels mad to kiss; no face
swelling into reality, the excellence of every Art is its intensity, capable of
making all disagreeables evaporate, from their being in close relationship with
Beauty & Truth—Examine King Lear & you will find this exemplified
throughout; but in this picture we have unpleasantness without any momen-
tous depth of speculation excited, in which to bury its repulsiveness—The pic-
ture is larger than Christ rejected—I dined with Haydon the sunday after you
left, & had a very pleasant day, I dined too (for I have been out too much
lately) with Horace Smith & met his two Brothers with Hill & Kingston &
one Du Bois, they only served to convince me, how superior humour is to wit
in respect to enjoyment—These men say things which make one start, without
making one feel, they are all alike; their manners are alike; they all know
fashionables; they have a mannerism in their very eating & drinking, in their
mere handling a Decanter—They talked of Kean & his low company—Would I
were with that company instead of yours said I to myself! I know such like
acquaintance will never do for me & yet I am going to Reynolds, on
Wednesday—Brown & Dilke walked with me & back from the Christmas
pantomime. I had not a dispute but a disquisition with Dilke, on various
subjects; several things dovetailed in my mind,' & at once it struck me, what
quality went to form a Man of Achievement especially in Literature & which
Shakespeare possessed so enormously—I mean *Negative Capability*, that is when
man is capable of being in uncertainties, Mysteries, doubts, without any irritable
reaching after fact & reason—Coleridge, for instance, would let go by a fine
isolated verisimilitude caught from the Penetralium of mystery, from being
incapable of remaining content with half knowledge. This pursued through
Volumes would perhaps take us no further than this, that with a great poet the
sense of Beauty overcomes every other consideration, or rather obliterates all
consideration. [. . .]

From letter from **Keats to John Hamilton Reynolds**, 3 February 1818

This letter sees Keats repudiating two of the most significant influences upon his previous work and aspiring to a 'great and unobtrusive' Shakespearian sensibility. Both Hunt and, most particularly, Wordsworth are 'obtrusive', that is overly egotistical, poets. Underpinning Keats's phraseology is Hazlitt's lecture, 'On Shakespeare and Milton', which he had heard at the Surrey Institution on 27 January, in which the essayist had compared Wordsworth, with his 'morbid feelings and devouring egotism', with Shakespeare, who 'was the least of an egoist that it was possible to be'. In Keats's letter of 21 December 1817, the poet had praised Shakespeare as the supreme example of negative capability, and here he abandons Wordsworth and Hunt and pledges poetic allegiance to 'the old poets'.

[. . .] It may be said that we ought to read our Contemporaries, that Wordsworth &c. should have their due from us, but for the sake of a few fine imaginative or domestic passages, are we to be bullied into a certain Philosophy engendered in the whims of an Egotist—Every man has his speculations, but every man does not brood and peacock over them till he makes a false coinage and deceives himself— Many a man can travel to the very bourne of Heaven, and yet want confidence to put down his halfseeing. Sancho will invent a Journey heavenward as well as any body. We hate poetry that has a palpable design upon us—and if we do not agree, seems to put its hand in its breeches pocket. Poetry should be great & unobtrusive, a thing which enters into one's soul, and does not startle it or amaze it with itself but with its subject.—How beautiful are the retired flowers! how would they lose their beauty were they to throng into the highway crying out, 'admire me I am a violet! dote upon me I am a primrose!' Modern poets differ from the Elizabethans in this. Each of the moderns, like an Elector of Hanover governs his petty state, & knows how many straws are swept daily from the Causeways in all his dominions & has a continual itching that all the Housewives should have their coppers well scoured: the antcients were Emperors of vast Provinces, they had only heard of the remote ones and scarcely cared to visit them,—I will cut all this—I will have no more of Wordsworth or Hunt in particular—Why should we be of the tribe of Manasseh, when we can wander with Esau? why should we kick against the Pricks, when we can walk on Roses? Why should we be owls, when we can be Eagles? Why be teased with 'nice Eyed wagtails', when we have in sight 'the Cherub Contemplation'?—Why with Wordsworths 'Matthew with a bough of wilding in his hand' when we can have Jaques 'under an oak &c'—The secret of the Bough of Wilding will run through your head faster than I can write it—Old Matthew spoke to him some years ago on some nothing, & because he happens in an Evening Walk to imagine the figure of the old man—he must stamp it down in black & white, and it is henceforth sacred— I don't mean to deny Wordsworth's grandeur & Hunt's merit, but I mean to say we need not be teazed with grandeur & merit—when we can have them uncontaminated & unobtrusive. Let us have the old Poets, & robin Hood [. . .]

From letter from **Keats to John Hamilton Reynolds**, 3 May 1818

Whether he was striking a pose of idolatry or antipathy, thinking about
Wordsworth tended to bring out the best in Keats's critical writing. Here,
prompted by a rereading of 'Tintern Abbey', Keats develops an extended simile
of human life as a 'mansion of many apartments'. After the first, 'infant or
thoughtless chamber', we encounter 'the chamber of maiden thought', whose
'pleasant wonders' serve only, and ultimately, to convince us that 'the world is
full of misery and heartbreak, pain, sickness, and oppression'. Keats then com-
pares, adversely, Milton's thought with Wordsworth's; testimony not to
Wordsworth's mental superiority but to what Keats labels the 'grand march of
intellect' evident in human history, a theme which is a principal theme of the
epic poem which he began in September 1818, Hyperion.

[. . .] I will return to Wordsworth—whether or no he has an extended vision or a
circumscribed grandeur—whether he is an eagle in his nest, or on the wing—And
to be more explicit and to show you how tall I stand by the giant, I will put down
a simile of human life as far as I now perceive it; that is, to the point to which I say
we both have arrived at—Well—I compare human life to a large Mansion of
Many Apartments, two of which I can only describe, the doors of the rest being
as yet shut upon me—The first we step into we call the infant or thoughtless
Chamber, in which we remain as long as we do not think—We remain there a long
while, and notwithstanding the doors of the second Chamber remain wide open,
showing a bright appearance, we care not to hasten to it but are at length imper-
ceptibly impelled by the awakening of the thinking principle—within us—we no
sooner get into the second Chamber, which I shall call the Chamber of Maiden-
Thought, than we become intoxicated with the light and the atmosphere, we see
nothing but pleasant wonders, and think of delaying there for ever in delight:
However among the effects this breathing is father of is that tremendous one of
sharpening one's vision into the heart and nature of Man—of convincing ones
nerves that the World is full of Misery and Heartbreak, Pain, Sickness and
oppression—whereby This Chamber of Maiden Thought becomes gradually
darken'd and at the same time on all sides of it many doors are set open—but all
dark—all leading to dark passages—We see not the ballance of good and evil. We
are in a Mist—We are now in that state—We feel the 'burden of the mystery.' To
this point was Wordsworth come, as far as I can conceive, when he wrote 'Tintern
Abbey' and it seems to me that his Genius is explorative of those dark Passages.
Now if we live, and go on thinking, we too shall explore them, he is a Genius and
superior [to] us, in so far as he can, more than we, make discoveries, and shed a
light in them—Here I must think Wordsworth is deeper than Milton—though I
think it has depended more upon the general and gregarious advance of intellect,
than individual greatness of Mind—From the Paradise Lost and the other Works
of Milton, I hope it is not too presuming, even between ourselves to say, his
Philosophy, human and divine, may be tolerably understood by one not much

advanced in years. In his time englishmen were just emancipated from a great superstition—and Men had got hold of certain points and resting places in reasoning which were too newly born to be doubted, and too much opposed by the Mass of Europe not to be thought etherial and authentically divine—who could gainsay his ideas on virtue, vice, and Chastity in Comus, just at the time of the dismissal of Cod-pieces and a hundred other disgraces? who would not rest satisfied with his hintings at good and evil in the Paradise Lost, when just free from the inquisition and burning in Smithfield? The Reformation produced such immediate and great benefits, that Protestantism was considered under the immediate eye of heaven, and its own remaining Dogmas and superstitions, then, as it were, regenerated, constituted those resting places and seeming sure points of Reasoning—from that I have mentioned, Milton, whatever he may have thought in the sequel, appears to have been content with these by his writings—He did not think into the human heart, as Wordsworth has done—Yet Milton as a philosopher, had sure as great powers as Wordsworth—What is then to be inferr'd? O many things—It proves there is really a grand march of intellect—it proves that a mighty providence subdues the mightiest Minds to the service of the time being, whether it be in human Knowledge or Religion [. . .]

Letter from **Keats to Richard Woodhouse**, 27 October 1818

In his 3 February 1818 letter to Reynolds, Keats had condemned Wordsworth as an 'egotist'. Here the poet returns to the subject of poetic egotism in his famous distinction between the 'poetical character' of which he, himself, was 'a member' and the Wordsworthian 'egotistical sublime'. Keats's brand of poet, who enters empathetically into other people's natures and beings, is a poetic 'chameleon' with 'no identity' and 'no self' of his own.

My dear Woodhouse,

Your Letter gave me a great satisfaction; more on account of its friendliness, than any relish of that matter in it which is accounted so acceptable in the 'genus irritabile' The best answer I can give you is in a clerklike manner to make some observations on two principle points, which seem to point like indices into the midst of the whole pro and con, about genius, and views, and achievements, and ambition cœtera. 1st as to the poetical character itself, (I mean that sort of which, if I am anything, I am a member; that sort distinguished from the wordsworthian or egotistical sublime; which is a thing per se and stands alone) it is not itself—it has no self—it is every thing and nothing—It has no character—it enjoys light and shade; it lives in gusto, be it foul or fair, high or low, rich or poor, mean or elevated—It has as much delight in conceiving an Iago as an Imogen. What shocks the virtuous philosop[h]er, delights the camelion Poet. It does no harm from its relish of the dark side of things, any more than from its taste for the bright one; because they both end in speculation. A poet is the most unpoetical of any thing in existence; because he has no Identity—he is continually in for—and filling some other body—The Sun, the Moon, the Sea and Men and Women who are creatures of impulse are poetical and have about them an unchangeable attribute—the poet has none; no identity—he is certainly the most unpoetical of all God's Creatures. If then he has no self, and if I am a Poet, where is the Wonder that I should say I would write no more? Might I not at that very instant [have] been cogitating on the Characters of saturn and Ops? It is a wretched thing to confess; but is a very fact that not one word I ever utter can be taken for granted as an opinion growing out of my identical nature—how can it, when I have no nature? When I am in a room with People if I ever am free from speculating on creations of my own brain, then not myself goes home to myself: but the identity of every one in the room begins so to press upon me that, I am, in a very little time, annihilated—not only among Men; it would be the same in a Nursery of children. I know not whether I make myself wholly understood: I hope enough so to let you see that no dependence is to be placed on what I said that day.

In the second place I will speak of my views, and of the life I purpose to myself—I am ambitious of doing the world some good: if I should be spared that may be the work of maturer years—In the interval I will assay to reach to as high a summit in Poetry as the nerve bestowed upon me will suffer. The faint conceptions I have of Poems to come brings the blood frequently into my forehead—All I hope is that I may not lose all interest in human affairs—that the solitary indifference I feel for applause even from the finest Spirits, will not blunt any acuteness of vision I may have. I do not think it will—I feel assured I should write from the mere yearning and fondness I have for the Beautiful, even if my night's labours should be burnt every morning and no eye ever shine upon them. But even now I am perhaps not speaking from myself; but from some character in whose soul I now live. I am sure however that this next sentence is from myself. I feel your anxiety, good opinion, and friendliness, in the highest degree, and am

Your's most sincerely
John Keats

From journal-letter from **Keats to George and Georgiana Keats**, 16 April 1819

This portion of Keats's journal-letter to his brother and sister-in-law, which he wrote between 24 February and 3 May 1819, demonstrates the playful side of the poet's correspondence in its brisk portrait of Coleridge's conversation.

[. . .] Last Sunday I took a Walk towards highgate and in the lane that winds by the side of Lord Mansfield's park I met Mr Green our Demonstrator at Guy's in conversation with Coleridge—I joined them, after enquiring by a look whether it would be agreeable—I walked with him a[t] his alderman-after dinner pace for near two miles I suppose In those two Miles he broached a thousand things—let me see if I can give you a list—Nightingales, Poetry—on Poetical sensation—

Metaphysics—Different genera and species of Dreams—nightmare—a dream accompanied by a sense of touch—single and double touch—A dream related— First and second consciousness—the difference explained between will and Volition—so many metaphysicians from a want of smoking the second consciousness—Monsters—the Kraken—Mermaids—southey believes in them— southeys belief too much diluted—a Ghost story—Good morning—I heard his voice as he came towards me—I heard it as he moved away—I had heard it all the interval—if it may be called so. He was civil enough to ask me to call on him at Highgate Good Night! It looks so much like rain I shall not go to town to day; but put it off till tomorrow [. . .]

From journal-letter from **Keats to George and Georgiana Keats**, 21 April 1819

Later in the journal-letter, Keats writes his important meditation (John Jones calls it 'the finest thing he wrote outside his poetry' – see **pp. 51–3**) on the 'vale of Soul-making', in which he 'sketch[es] a system of salvation' which, unlike Christianity, 'does not affront our reason and humanity'. Christianity is derivative of ancient philosophies, a 'Scheme of Redemption' with no more intrinsic validity than Hinduism or Zoroastrianism. Attributing the existence of evil to original sin, it offers empty promises of eventual supernatural salvation ('What a little circumscribe[d] notion!'). Instead, Keats offers a humanistic account of individual 'redemption' in which the ubiquitous experience of suffering is ultimately an educative force: 'Do you not see how necessary a world of pains and troubles is to school an intelligence and make it a soul, a place where the heart must feel and suffer in a thousand diverse ways?'
   The passage is also significant inasmuch as its themes inform the odes which Keats was to write over the next few weeks. By 30 April, Keats had written the 'Ode to Psyche' (a name that means 'soul'), in which he vows to be Psyche's 'priest, and build a fane¹/In some untrodden region of my mind'. Daniel P. Watkins's interpretation of this passage is extracted on **pp. 66–9** below. Furthermore, the letter's attention to a 'world of pains and troubles' anticipates the preoccupations of the 'Ode on a Grecian Urn', the 'Ode on Melancholy' and, most particularly, the 'Ode to a Nightingale'.

[. . .] The common cognomen of this world among the misguided and superstitious is 'a vale of tears' from which we are to be redeemed by a certain arbitrary interposition of God and taken to Heaven—What a little circumscribe[d] straightened notion! Call the world if you Please 'The vale of Soul-making' . . . how then are Souls to be made? . . . to have identity given them—so as to possess

---

1   A temple.

a bliss peculiar to each ones individual existence? How, but by the medium of a world like this? . . . I will call the *world* a School instituted for the purpose of teaching little children to read—I will call the *human heart* the *horn Book* used in that School—and I will call the *Child able to read*, the Soul made from that *school* and its *hornbook*. Do you not see how necessary a World of Pains and troubles is to school an Intelligence and make it a soul? A Place where the heart must feel and suffer in a thousand diverse ways! Not merely is the Heart a Hornbook, It is the Minds Bible, it is the Minds experience, it is the teat from which the mind or intelligence sucks its identity—As various as the Lives of Men are—so various become their souls, and thus does God make individual beings, Souls, Identical Souls of the sparks of his own essence—This appears to me a faint sketch of a system of Salvation which does not affront our reason and humanity—I am convinced that many difficulties which christians labour under would vanish before it—There is one wh[i]ch even now Strikes me—the Salvation of Children—In them the Spark or intelligence returns to God without any identity—it having had no time to learn of, and be altered by, the heart—or seat of the human Passions—It is pretty generally suspected that the chr[i]stian scheme has been copied from the ancient persian and greek Philosophers. Why may they not have made this simple thing even more simple for common apprehension by introducing Mediators and Personages in the same manner as in the hethen mythology abstractions are personified—Seriously, I think it probable that this System of Soul-making—may have been the Parent of all the more palpable and personal Schemes of Redemption, among the Zoroastrians, the Christians and the Hindoos. For as one part of the human species must have their carved Jupiter; so another part must have the palpable and named Mediator and saviour, their Christ, their Oromanes and their Vishnu—If what I have said should not be plain enough, as I fear it may not be, I will but you in the place where I began in this series of thoughts—I mean, I began by seeing how man was formed by circumstances—and what are circumstances?—but touchstones of his heart—? and what are touch stones—but proovings of his hearrt?—and what are proovings of his heart but fortifiers or alterers of his nature? and what is his altered nature but his soul?—and what was his soul before it came into the world and had These provings and alterations and perfectionings?—An intelligence—without Identity—and how is this Identity to be made? Through the medium of the Heart? And how is the heart to become this Medium but in a world of Circumstances? [. . .]

From letter from **Leigh Hunt to Joseph Severn**, February 1821

Early in the month after Keats's death, Leigh Hunt, as yet unaware of the poet's demise, wrote to Severn in a poignant and moving letter which serves as a touching, if unwitting, oration to the poet's memory.

[. . .] how often I thought of Keats, and with what feelings. Mr Brown tells me he is comparatively calm now, or rather quite so. If he can bear to hear of us, pray tell him,—but he knows it already, and can put it into better language than any man. I hear that he does not like to be told that he may get better; not is it to be wondered at, considering his firm persuasion that he shall not recover. He can only regard it as a puerile thing, and an insinuation that he cannot bear to think that he can die. But if his persuasion should happen to be no longer so strong upon him, or if he can now put up with such attempts to console him, tell him of what I still (upon my honour, Severn) think always, that I have seen too many instances of recovery from apparently desperate cases of consumption not to be in hope to the very last. If he cannot bear this, tell him—tell that great poet and noble-hearted man—that we shall all bear his memory in the most precious part of our hearts, and that the world shall bow their heads to it, as our loves do. Or if this, again, will trouble his spirit, tell him that we shall never cease to remember and love him; and that the most sceptical of us has faith enough in the high things that nature puts into our heads to think all who are of one accord in mind or heart are journeying to one and the same place, and shall unite somewhere or other again, face to face, mutually conscious, mutually delighted. Tell him he is only before us on the road, as he was in everything else; or whether you tell him the latter or no, tell him the former, and add that we shall never forget that he was so, and that we are coming after him. [. . .]

2

Interpretations

Critical History

The following essay deals with the critical history of Keats's poetry as a whole; the critical and reception history of the individual poems included in Section 3, Key Poems, is discussed in the headnote to each poem. Cross-references to articles and books extracted in Early Critical Reception and Modern Criticism are shown in bold.

Three central and interdependent themes resound through Keats's poetry: the relationship between the ideal world of art and the human world of suffering, the nature of poetry itself and, throughout, an attention to pre-Christian mythology. And this poet who was so preoccupied with myth was himself subject to myth-ologising, arguably from the publication of his poem *Endymion* in 1818 and, most certainly, after his death in Rome on 23 February 1821. *Endymion* was much influenced by Keats's early hero (and, later, mentor) Leigh Hunt, the poet and editor of the radical journal the *Examiner*, and his volume was caught in the cross-fire between the Hunt circle and the Tory wits of *Blackwood's Edinburgh Magazine* and the *Quarterly Review*. The poet's 'lower-class' background, his febrile eroticism and his liberal politics would have been enough to prompt vitriol from the contemporary Tory reviews, but his association with the so-called 'Cockney School' of Hunt exacerbated matters and the journalistic *contretemps* over Keats's work was as much a political quarrel as a poetical one. From the right Keats was condemned as a politically subversive social upstart whilst the liberal camp, with which the poet explicitly identified himself, eulogised his power and promise and condemned the malignity of attacks by government sycophants. To John Wilson Croker of the *Quarterly*, Keats was an 'insane' camp-follower of Hunt and 'Cockney poetry' (p. 34), whilst to J. G. Lockhart of *Blackwood's*, principal contributor of a series of ferocious articles 'On the Cock-ney School of Poetry', 'Johnny Keats' was a man tempted away from the humble, if respectable, trade of apothecary and 'reduced to a state of insanity' by poetic over-indulgence. 'Back to the shop, Mr John' urges Lockhart spitefully, if amus-ingly (pp. 34–6). On the other hand, to Hunt and his friends and acolytes Keats was a 'young aspirant' to 'the English Muse' (Hunt, pp. 33–4), 'a young and powerful writer' (J. H. Reynolds, pp. 37–8) and the 'muses' son of promise'

(Cornelius Webb). After Keats's death, the mythologising of the poet's reputation continued apace, with Shelley's elegy *Adonais* (1821), great though it is, offering a misleading account of a 'writer of the highest genius' who was slain by the *Quarterly*, his consumption attributable 'to the rupture of a blood-vessel in the lungs' prompted by Croker's anathemas (p. 41).

By the mid-Victorian period, Keats's poetic stock had risen considerably and his reputation grew amongst readers other than liberal avant-gardists. When his friend Joseph Severn, who had nursed Keats in his death-throes, returned to England in 1838 after a seventeen-year absence, he noted with surprise that the fame of 'dear Keats' 'was not only well established, but was increasing from day to day'. Though Leigh Hunt had done a great deal to preserve Keats's reputation after his death, it was the publication of Richard Monckton Milnes's *Life, Letters, and Literary Remains of John Keats* (1848)[1] which prompted much of the increase of interest in the poet during the mid-century. That said, to a significant degree it was Keats's biography, the story of a prodigious talent cut down in his youth, which lay behind this upsurge in attention. For Matthew Arnold, writing in 1853, Keats was 'one whose exquisite genius and pathetic death render him for ever interesting' (pp. 43–4). By the 1850s, the positive myth-makers had triumphed over the Tory demonisers in their celebration of the doomed, ethereal poet killed, in Byron's words, 'by an Article'.[2] Though Monckton Milnes had emphasised Keats's 'manly' fortitude and imaginative vigour and George Keats had declared that his brother had been 'the very soul of manliness and courage', a somewhat feminised version of the poet prevailed, prompted in part by Shelley's notion of Keats as a 'delicate and fragile' figure and Hazlitt's less admiring references to his 'effeminacy of style' and 'deficiency in masculine energy' (p. 42). Even the partisan W. M. Rossetti declared that Keats's inferior verse possessed a 'morbid tone, marking want of manful thew and sinew'. His best poetry, on the other hand, possessed an 'exquisite' and 'sensuous' imagination, and this notion of Keats, celebrated by Rossetti and criticised by Matthew Arnold, tended to preoccupy the Victorian imagination. This 'unworldly' aesthete, Oscar Wilde's 'Priest of Beauty slain before his time',[3] was generally seen as a figure too preoccupied with dreaming and the worlds of art and beauty to have much to say about contemporary English life and politics. For example, Stopford A. Brooke, writing in 1907, declared that Keats has 'no vital interest in the present, none in man as a whole, none in the political movement of human thought'.[4] The Pre-Raphaelites prized the sensual and other-worldly beauty of Keats's poetry; Rossetti, who considered Keats's poetry 'the highest point of romantic

1 Richard Monckton Milne's, *Life, Letters, and Literary Remains of John Keats*, 2 vols, London: E. Moxon, 1848.
2 In *Don Juan*, vol. 5 of *The Complete Poetical Works*, ed. Jerome J. McGann, Oxford: Clarendon Press, 1986, p. 483.
3 In *Poems and Poems in Prose*, vol. 1 of *The Complete Works of Oscar Wilde*, ed. Bobby Fong and Karl Beckson, Oxford: Oxford University Press, 2000, p. 234.
4 Stopford A. Brooke, *Studies in Poetry*, Duckworth, 1907.

imagination', revelled in its supposed lack of external significance: 'The Eve of St. Agnes' 'means next to nothing, but means that little so exquisitely'.

By the turn of the twentieth century, Keats's reputation was secure. In 1925, just over a hundred years after the poet's death, John Middleton Murry published his *Keats and Shakespeare*, which is in large part a rhapsodic eulogy to Keats's greatness. Of the 'Ode to a Nightingale', Murry writes: 'Keats' poetic mastery at this moment can be compared with nothing in English literature save Shakespeare's in his maturity. Keats was twenty-three. How was this miracle – for indeed it is nothing less – accomplished? That question can never be wholly answered.'[5] Though such near-idolatrous enthusiasm would have seemed almost deranged to Keats's contemporary decriers (and, indeed, Murry's very title would have struck early reviewers such as J. G. Lockhart as ludicrous), by the early twentieth century Keats had become an English classic worthy of comparison with the 'greatest' of them all. Murry's book is part of a long and distinguished twentieth-century tradition of work on Keats, both biographical and critical. Though the critic Sidney Colvin had worried in 1917[6] that, given the huge amount of work on Keats that had appeared in the century since the publication of his *Poems*, there might be little left to add, critical labour on the poet has increased in volume ever since. H. W. Garrod's *Keats* (1926) was perhaps the most notable study to be published between the wars, a book which reminded the world of the poet's 'revolutionary sympathies, of his Huntian or Wordsworthian politics' (pp. 45–6). On the other hand, it is the formal qualities of Keats's work which preoccupy M. R. Ridley's 1933 *Keats's Craftsmanship: A Study in Poetic Development*,[7] a provocative and detailed study of Keats's poetic development. Other contemporaneous studies, such as Clarence DeWitt Thorpe's *The Mind of John Keats* (1926)[8] and Claude Lee Finney's *The Evolution of Keats's Poetry* (1936),[9] offered important accounts of the sources of, and poetic influences upon, Keats's work.

There was no shortage of Keatsian scholarship during the post-war period. The standard edition of Keats's letters dates from 1958, Hyder Edward Rollins's *The Letters of John Keats, 1814–1821* (from which the extracts in the Contexts section are taken), whilst the most notable work of criticism published during the 1950s was Earl R. Wasserman's *The Finer Tone: Keats's Major Poems* (1953). Wasserman's bejewelled and elaborate readings of Keats's poems as allegories of the 'dimensionless mystery beyond our mortal vision' now seem somewhat tendentious and over-extended (pp. 47–9). They provoked Jack Stillinger in his important 1961 essay, 'The Hoodwinking of Madeline: Scepticism in "The Eve of

---

5 John Middleton Murry, *Keats and Shakespeare: A Study of Keats' Poetic Life from 1816 to 1820*, London: Oxford University Press, Humphrey Milford, 1925, p. 131.
6 Sidney Colvin, *John Keats: His Life and Poetry, his Friends, Critics, and After-fame*, London: Macmillan, 1917.
7 M. R. Ridley, *Keats's Craftsmanship: A Study in Poetic Development*, Oxford: Clarendon Press, 1933.
8 Clarence DeWitt Thorpe, *The Mind of John Keats*, New York: Oxford University Press, 1926.
9 Claude Lee Finney, *The Evolution of Keats's Poetry*, Cambridge, Mass.: Harvard University Press, 1936.

St. Agnes" ',[10] to repudiate both uncritical, rhapsodic salutes to the sensuousness and beauty of Keats's poetry and what he saw as the over-elaborate metaphorical readings of 'allegorical' critics such as Wasserman. Whilst the New Criticism of the 1940s and 1950s paid comparatively little attention to the Romantic poets, Keats's work was addressed, notably in its use of irony and paradox, as in the close readings by Cleanth Brooks in such essays as 'Keats's Sylvan Historian: History without Footnotes' (1947) (pp. 46–7). The New Critical approach to Keats had a vigorous afterlife in Helen Vendler's 1983 study *The Odes of John Keats*, a book which, though it has been criticised for its inattention to social and political context, offers impressive and sustained formal close readings of the odes (pp. 60–2). A preoccupation with form and an attention to irony and paradox also informs the Yale School's attention to Keats in Paul de Man's deconstructionist account[11] and Geoffrey H. Hartman's meditation upon the nature of Keatsian poetics in his 1975 essay 'Poem and Ideology: A Study of Keats's "To Autumn" '.[12] In a series of books,[13] their colleague Harold Bloom offered a psychoanalytically charged variant of the source and influence hunting evident in the pre-war work of the likes of Finney and Thorpe. For Bloom, Keats was engaged in a literary form of Oedipal strife with his great predecessors such as Shakespeare, Milton and Wordsworth, and struggled with the power of the great English poets, who, Bloom argued, threatened to overwhelm his own poetic voice rather than, as more orthodox critics of influence have had it, informing it. For example, in *A Map of Misreading* (1975), Bloom writes that the 'first of his great odes, the *Ode to Psyche* ... struggles with the shadows of Milton and Wordsworth, but not to win a blessing, as Shelley does. Keats is concerned rather with clearing an imaginative space for himself'. Before boarding the cart of high literary theory, Bloom had written on Keats in *The Visionary Company* (1961, revised 1971), a sophisticated introduction to the Romantic poets which remains valuable.[14]

The 1960s saw the publication of three major biographies of Keats, by Walter Jackson Bate, Robert Gittings and Aileen Ward. Ward's engaging *John Keats: The Making of a Poet* (1963)[15] had the misfortune to appear in the same year as Bate's magisterial *John Keats* (1963), which remains the standard life. Bate's book combines biography with perceptive literary criticism and is arguably the most valuable single book on Keats (pp. 50–1). Gittings's full biography *John Keats* (1968) complements his useful account of the poet's *annus mirabilis*, *John Keats:*

10 Jack Stillinger, 'The Hoodwinking of Medeline: Scepticism in "The Eve of St. Agnes" ', *Studies in Philology*, 58, 1961, pp. 533–55.
11 In his 'Introduction' to *The Selected Poetry of Keats*, New York: New American Library, 1966.
12 Geoffrey H. Hartman, 'Poem and Ideology: A Study of Keats's "To Autumn" ', in *The Fate of Reading and Other Essays*, Chicago, Ill.: University of Chicago Press, 1975, pp. 124–46.
13 *The Anxiety of Influence: A Theory of Poetry*, New York: Oxford University Press, 1973, *A Map of Misreading*, New York: Oxford University Press, 1975 and *Poetry and Repression: Revisionism from Blake to Stevens*, New Haven, Conn.: Yale University Press, 1976.
14 Harold Bloom, *The Visionary Company: A Reading of English Romantic Poetry*, Ithaca, NY: Cornell University Press, 1st edn 1961, rev. edn 1971.
15 Aileen Ward, *John Keats: The Making of a Poet*, London: Secker & Warburg, 1963.

The Living Year (1954).[16] In the same period, three British critics offered brilliant if highly individualistic studies of Keats: John Bayley, John Jones and Christopher Ricks. Bayley's 'Keats and Reality' (1962) declares that the 'most decisive ingredient [of Keats's poetry] is vulgarity' (pp. 49–50) whilst Jones's *John Keats's Dream of Truth* (1969) offers a detailed study of Keats's 'sensual humanism' (pp. 51–3). Ricks's 1974 *Keats and Embarrassment* builds on Bayley's work in its account of the importance of embarrassment to 'the shape of [Keats's] imagination' (pp. 56–7). Also dating from the early 1970s is Stuart Sperry's *Keats the Poet* (1973), which remains a landmark volume in modern Keatsian criticism, a study of Keats's preoccupation with the poetic imagination and the nature of poetry which stresses the indeterminacy of meaning evident in that poetry (pp. 55–6).

If the 1960s, which saw the publication of the lives by Bate, Gittings and Ward, was the decade of Keatsian biographical scholarship, the 1970s was the decade of Keatsian textual scholarship, with the appearance of three valuable editions of Keats's poetry. Jack Stillinger's *The Poems of John Keats* (1978)[17] replaced Garrod's *The Poetical Works of John Keats*[18] as the standard scholarly edition of Keats, and remains so to this day. Though Stillinger's scrupulous textual edition does not concern itself with explanatory footnotes, the 1970s also saw the publication of heavily annotated editions of the poet's work: John Barnard's *John Keats: The Complete Poems* (1973)[19] and, most comprehensive, Miriam Allott's *The Poems of John Keats* (1970).[20]

Following the biographical labours of the 1960s, Keats enjoyed an upsurge of critical interest. Indeed, the sheer volume of recent work on Keats has been demonstrated by Jack Stillinger, who in 1999 produced a list of no fewer than 'fifty-nine interpretations' of a single poem, 'The Eve of St. Agnes', published since the 1970s.[21] Much of the critical focus in contemporary work on Keats is ideological, focusing upon gender, politics and class, part of the wider 'turn to history' evident in Romantic studies as a whole from the 1980s onwards and the contemporaneous expansion of feminist readings of literary history. Much fine work has been published since the critical schools of historicism ('New Historicist' or otherwise) and feminism turned their attention to Keats in the late 1970s. This is not to imply, of course, that feminist criticism is not political in its focus or that historically focused writing on Keats ignores sexual politics. There is much overlap between gender-based criticism and ideologically focused scholarship; critics such as Marjorie Levinson (in *Keats's Life of Allegory* (1988), pp. 62–4) or Daniel P. Watkins (in *Keats's Poetry and the Politics of the Imagination* (1989)[22]) fuse both methods. Nonetheless, for the sake of clarity, I shall treat the two

---

16 Robert Gittings, *John Keats*, London: Heinemann, 1968 and *John Keats: The Living Year, 21 September 1818 to 21 September 1819*, London: Heinemann 1954.
17 Jack Stillinger (ed.), *The Poems of John Keats*, Cambridge, Mass.: Harvard University Press, 1978.
18 H. W. Garrod (ed.), *The Political Works of John Keats*, Oxford: Clarendon Press, 1st edn 1939, 2nd edn 1958.
19 John Bernard (ed.), *John Keats: The Complete Poems*, Harmondsworth: Penguin, 1973.
20 Miriam Allott (ed.), *The Poems of John Keats*, London: Longman, 1970.
21 Jack Stillinger, *Reading The Eve of St. Agnes: The Multiples of Complex Literary Transaction*, New York: Oxford University Press, 1999.
22 Daniel P. Watkins, *Keats's Poetry and the Politics of the Imagination*, Rutherford, NJ: Fairleigh Dickinson University Press, 1989.

methods separately, beginning with historicist criticism. It important to note that there is nothing new in reading Keats's poetry in political terms. The poet's contemporaries, as we have seen, saw his work as deeply ideological, and earlier twentieth-century critics such as Garrod and Thorpe and later sociopolitical critics such as Carl Woodring (in *Politics in English Romantic Poetry* (1970), pp. 53–5) have engaged with Keats's politics. That said, formalist enquiry (i.e. criticism which attends to the style and structure of a poem rather than to any 'external' contexts) tended to predominate for much of the century, and it is undeniable that Jerome J. McGann's 1979 New Historicist essay 'Keats and the Historical Method in Literary Criticism' (pp. 57–60) prompted an important series of politically charged accounts of Keats. This sociohistorical criticism is perhaps best exemplified in the 1986 special issue of *Studies in Romanticism*, edited by Susan Wolfson, on 'Keats and Politics', Levinson's forcefully argued *Keats's Life of Allegory*, Watkins's Marxist study *Keats's Poetry and the Politics of the Imagination* and Nicholas Roe's two important books, the edited essay collection *Keats and History* (1995), represented here by Daniel P. Watkins's 'History, Self, and Gender in "Ode to Psyche"' and his 1997 monograph *John Keats and the Culture of Dissent*. Levinson apart, much of this criticism takes issue with McGann. Whilst 'Keats and the Historical Method' accuses the poet of acting in ideological bad faith in attempting to escape from historical circumstance, critics such as Roe or Jeffrey N. Cox, in his *Poetry and Politics in the Cockney School* (1998), are more positive in their assessment and insist upon Keats's deeply held commitment to liberal politics. The work for which Keats is principally remembered contains little overtly political content in the manner of Shelley's 'The Mask of Anarchy' or Coleridge's 'Poems of Political Recantation', and historicist criticism, as in Roe's account of the 'Ode to a Nightingale' (pp. 69–72) or Cox's study of the 'Ode on a Grecian Urn' (pp. 74–5), is often most interesting in its teasing out of the ideological significance of work which does not appear at first glance to be political.

Keats has also been much debated in gender criticism over the last decade or so, in a body of work which has offered suggestive new ways of thinking about the poet. That said, once again this involves a latter-day return to the critical preoccupations of Keats's contemporaries: Hazlitt thought the chief 'fault of Mr Keats's poems was a deficiency in masculine energy of style' and even Keats's indefatigable admirer Hunt found the character of Hyperion 'effeminate'. Much nineteenth-century criticism addressed the notion of Keats's masculinity, and underpinning some of this work is a sense, to borrow Susan Wolfson's term, of the poet's 'feminised' imagination. Whilst Hazlitt sees Keats's 'effeminacy' as a weakness, feminist readers of the 1970s such as Adrienne Rich and Erica Jong celebrated this aspect of the poet in their gendered account of the concept of negative capability. Rich explicitily identifies women's 'tremendous powers of intuitive identification and sympathy with other people' with Keatsian 'negative capability'.[23] Jong writes in 1973 that 'feminism means empathy. And empathy is

---

23 *Adrienne Rich's Poetry*, ed. Barbara Charlesworth Gelpi and Albert Gelpi, New York: W. W. Norton & Co. Inc., 1975, p. 115.

akin to the quality Keats called "negative capability" – that unique gift for projecting oneself into other states of consciousness' However, subsequent feminist criticism has focused upon what Anne K. Mellor labels 'Keats's ambivalent attitude toward gender'. This issue, and the history of gendered thinking about the poet, is usefully addressed in Susan Wolfson's article 'Keats and Gender Criticism' (1998). The work of Wolfson, Mellor and Marlon B. Ross has been instrumental in drawing gender criticism towards the centre of academic debate on Keats. Writing in his influential essay 'Beyond the Fragmented Word: Keats at the Limit of Patrilineal Language' (1990), Ross contends that Keats's *Hyperion* testifies to his desire 'to assert not just [his] coming into manhood but also his coming into discursive power', a power 'which define[s] poetic maturity in terms of patriarchal culture'.[24] Ross is representative of a group of contemporary Keatsians who argue that there is clear evidence of misogynistic tendencies in the poet's work. For example, Daniel P. Watkins's 1995 essay 'History, Self, and Gender in "Ode to Psyche" ' argues that the poet has a 'masculinist poetic strategy'. The same point has been made by Margaret Homans in 'Keats Reading Women: Women Reading Keats' (1990) and Karen Swann in her 1988 essay 'Harassing the Muse'.[25] For Homans, Keats demonstrates a 'resentment of [women's] real and imagined power over him and [a] compensatory wish to assert his own masculine authority'.[26] On the other hand, Mellor's *Romanticism and Gender* (1993), though it does not exempt Keats entirely from the charge of masculinism, is more positive, seeing the poet as an 'ideological cross-dresser' who was able to embrace some aspects of what she calls 'feminine Romanticism' (pp. 64–6). Similarly, Wolfson's 'Keats and Gender Criticism' traces the ambiguities inherent in the poet's position: Keats's 'overall syntax of gender is more zig-zag than linear, and the total story more indeterminate than definitive' (pp. 72–4).

Critical interest in Keats shows no sign of abating, and, indeed, the bicentenary of Keats's death in 1995 prompted a number of valuable critical reappraisals of the poet: collections of essays,[27] special numbers of learned journals,[28] and so on. It remains to be seen how the twenty-first century will deal with Keats, but the critical preoccupation with his work will doubtless continue and mutate into fascinating new forms, testimony to the poet's continuing hold on the critical consciousness.

24 Marlon B. Ross, 'Beyond the Fragmented Word: Keats at the Limit of Patrilineal Language', in Laura Claridge and Elizabeth Langland (eds), *Out of Bounds: Male Writers and Gender(ed) Criticism*, Amherst, Mass.: University of Massachusetts Press, 1990, pp. 110–31.
25 Karen Swann, 'Harassing the Muse', in Anne K. Mellor (ed.), *Romanticism and Gender*, Bloomington, Ind.: Indiana University Press, 1998, pp. 81–92.
26 Margaret Homans, 'Keats Reading Women: Women Reading Keats', *Studies in Romanticism*, 29, 1990, pp. 34–70.
27 Nicholas Roe (ed.), *Keats and History*, Cambridge: Cambridge University Press, 1995; Michael O'Neill (ed.), *Keats: Bicentary Readings*, Edinburgh: Edinburgh University Press for the University of Durham, 1997; Robert Ryan and Ronald A. Sharp (eds), *The Persistence of Poetry: Bicentennial Essays on Keats*, Amherst, Mass.: University of Massachusetts Press, 1998.
28 No fewer than five journals of Romantic studies devoted issues to Keats during the bicentenary year.

Early Critical Reception

Introduction

Though it is always instructive to examine a poet's early reception, it is especially so in the case of John Keats. Keats is, after all, the poet who was supposedly, in Shelley and Byron's ill-informed accounts, killed by a savage notice in the *Quarterly Review*. Such a notion is mistaken, but it is true that Keats's work, for political as much as aesthetic reasons, was very roughly treated at its first appearance. Setting aside Keats's modern status as an established classic and studying contemporary reviews reveals a contentious, troubling and controversial figure whose work and reputation were caught up in some of the most significant literary and political quarrels of the post-Napoleonic period.

The first notice of Keats was Leigh Hunt's 'The Young Poets', published in the *Examiner* in December 1816, which brackets him with John Hamilton Reynolds and Percy Bysshe Shelley as poets of great promise (pp. 33–4). However welcome such early attention might have been, Hunt's patronage was to prove a double-edged sword and Keats became irredeemably associated in the public eye with Hunt and, to use the *Quarterly*'s cruel but effective nickname, the 'Cockney School'. Keats was caught in the crossfire between the radical grouping around the *Examiner* and Tory reviews such as the *Quarterly* and *Blackwood's Edinburgh Magazine* which specialised in vitriolic personal abuse of their ideological opponents. J. W. Croker of the *Quarterly* wrote of the 'insanity' of Keats's poetry (p. 34), whilst J. G. Lockhart of *Blackwood's* attacked the poet as a politically seditious upstart, an ill-educated 'maniac' who presumed to write mythological verse without any first-hand knowledge of the classical languages (pp. 34–6). These spiteful, if compelling, attacks prompted defences of Keats by both radical critics (Reynolds (pp. 37–8), and Hunt again (p. 40)) and the Whig grandee Francis Jeffrey, the editor of the *Edinburgh Review* (p. 38). After Keats's death, Shelley's preface to *Adonais* pays tribute to the poet whilst simultaneously peddling the myth of his final illness being prompted by Croker's anathemas (p. 41). Byron and Hazlitt take a different line on Keats from their radical peers. Hazlitt sees his poetry as being characterised by an 'effeminacy of style' (p. 42), whilst Byron, in several witty but acerbic tirades, also uses sexual metaphor, as in his jesting reference to 'Johnny' Keats 'f-gg-g his *Imagination*' (pp. 39–40).

The subsection concludes with two Victorian assessments, by William Howitt and Matthew Arnold. Howitt encapsulates the rhapsodical tone of certain Victorian criticism, in his celebration of Keats as the 'highest and divinest of God's messengers to earth' (pp. 42–3). Whilst critics such as Howitt and W. M. Rossetti rejoiced in the exquisite and sensuous nature of Keats's work, Arnold faulted many of the poems and letters as the production of 'a merely sensuous man' (pp. 43–4). For Arnold, the important Keatsian writings are the product of a different side of the poet, the 'intellectual' and 'tough-minded' man. Interestingly, it is Romantic period rather than Victorian criticism which has greater critical resonance today; the debates about the poet's politics and his sexual identity which resound through the earliest critical writing are those which have dominated Keatsian criticism since the 1980s.

From **Leigh Hunt, 'The Young Poets'**, *Examiner*, 1 December 1816

The first published notice of Keats's poetry. Hunt presents Keats, alongside Shelley and Reynolds, as a promising new member of the 'new school' of poetry which was currently effecting a 'revolution in our literature', replacing the school of Pope.

The object of the present article is merely to notice three young writers, who appear to us to promise a considerable addition of strength to the new school [. . .]

The last of these young aspirants whom we have met with, and who promise to help the new school to revive Nature and

To put a spirit of youth in every thing, –

is, we believe, the youngest of them all, and just of age. His name is JOHN KEATS. He has not yet published any thing except in a newspaper; but a set of his manuscripts was handed us the other day, and fairly surprised us with the truth of their ambition, and ardent grappling with Nature. In the following Sonnet there is one incorrect rhyme, which might easily be altered, but which shall serve in the mean time as a peace-offering to the rhyming critics. The rest of the composition, with the exception of a little vagueness in calling the regions of poetry 'the realms of gold', we do not hesitate to pronounce excellent, especially the last six lines. The word swims is complete; and the whole conclusion is equally powerful and quiet; [Hunt quotes 'On First Looking into Chapman's Homer'.]

We have spoken with the less scruple of these poetical promises, because we are not really in the habit of lavishing praises and announcements, and we have no fear of any pettier vanity on the party of young men, who promise to understand human nature so well.

From **John Wilson Croker's review of** *Endymion*, *Quarterly Review* (1818)

First published in the high Tory *Quarterly Review* (dated April 1818 but not published until September 1818). This is the opening of the review, which Shelley and others erroneously blamed for Keats's death.

Reviewers have sometimes been accused of not reading the works which they affected to criticise. On the present occasion we shall anticipate the author's complaint, and honestly confess that we have not read his work. Not that we have been wanting in our duty – far from it – indeed, we have made efforts almost as superhuman as the story itself seems to be, to get through it; but with the fullest stretch of our perseverance, we are forced to confess that we have not been able to struggle beyond the first of the four books which of this Poetic Romance consists. We should extremely lament this want of energy, or whatever it may be, on our parts, were it not for one consolation – namely, that we are no better acquainted with the meaning of the book through which we have so painfully toiled, than we are with that of the three with which we have not looked into.

It is not that Mr Keats (if that be his real name, for we almost doubt that any man in his senses would put his real name to such a rhapsody,) it is not, we say, that the author has not powers of language, rays of fancy, and gleams of genius – he has all these; but he is unhappily a disciple of what has been somewhere called Cockney poetry; which may be defined to consist of the most incongruous ideas in the most uncouth language.

Of this school, Mr Leigh Hunt, as we observed in a former number, aspires to be the hierophant [. . .] This author is a copyist of Mr Hunt; but he is more unintelligible, almost as rugged, twice as diffuse, and ten times more tiresome and absurd than his prototype, who, though he impudently presumed to seat himself in the chair of criticism, and to measure his own poetry by his own standard, yet generally had a meaning. But Mr Keats had advanced no dogmas which he was bound to support by examples; his non-sense therefore is quite gratuitous; he writes it for its own sake, and being bitten by Mr Leigh Hunt's insane criticism, more than rivals the insanity of his poetry.

From **John Gibson Lockhart (writing as 'Z.'), 'The Cockney School of Poetry, No. IV'**, *Blackwood's Edinburgh Magazine*, August 1818

Keats's friend Benjamin Bailey had inadvertently provided Lockhart with the personal details about Keats used so effectively in this onslaught.

Of Keats,
The muses' son of promise, and what feats
He yet may do, etc.
    (Cornelius Webb)

Of all the manias of this mad age, the most incurable, as well as the most common, seems to be no other than the metromanie. The just celebrity of Robert Burns and Miss Baillie has had the melancholy effect of turning the heads of we know not how many farm-servants and unmarried ladies; our very footmen compose tragedies, and there is scarcely a superannuated governess in the island that does not leave a roll of lyrics behind her in her bandbox.

To witness the disease of any human understanding, however feeble, is distressing – but the spectacle of an able mind reduced to a state of insanity is of course ten times more afflicting. It is with such sorrow as this that we have contemplated the case of Mr John Keats. This young man appears to have received from nature talents of an excellent, perhaps even of a superior order – talents which, devoted to the purposes of any useful profession, must have rendered him a respectable, if not an eminent citizen. His friends, we understand, destined him to the career of medicine, and he was bound apprentice some years ago to a worthy apothecary in town.

But all has been undone by a sudden attack of the malady to which we have alluded. Whether Mr John had been sent home with a diuretic or composing draught to some patient far gone in the poetical mania, we have not heard. This much is certain: that he has caught the infection, and that thoroughly. For some time we were in hopes that he might get off with a violent fit or two, but of late the symptoms are terrible. The frenzy of the *Poems* was bad enough in its way, but it did not alarm us half so seriously as the calm, settled, imperturbable drivelling idiocy of *Endymion*. We hope, however, that in so young a person, and with a constitution originally so good, even now the disease is not utterly incurable. Time, firm treatment, and rational restraint, do much for many apparently hopeless invalids – and if Mr Keats should happen, at some interval of reason, to cast his eye upon our pages, he may perhaps be convinced of the existence of his malady, which in such cases is often all that is necessary to put the patient in a fair way of being cured [. . .]

It is time to pass from the juvenile *Poems* to the mature and elaborate *Endymion: A Poetic Romance*. The old story of the moon falling in love with a shepherd, so prettily told by a Roman classic, and so exquisitely enlarged and adorned by one of the most elegant of German poets, has been seized upon by Mr John Keats, to be done with as might seem good unto the sickly fancy of one who never read a single line either of Ovid or of Wieland. If the quantity, not the quality, of the verses dedicated to the story is to be taken into account, there can be no doubt that Mr John Keats may now claim Endymion entirely to himself.

To say the truth, we do not suppose either the Latin or the German poet would be very anxious to dispute about the property of the hero of the 'Poetic Romance'. Mr Keats has thoroughly appropriated the character, if not the name. His

Endymion is not a Greek shepherd loved by a Grecian goddess; he is merely a young Cockney rhymester dreaming a fantastic dream at the full of the moon. Costume, were it worthwhile to notice such a trifle, is violated in every page of this goodly octavo. From his prototype Hunt, John Keats has acquired a sort of vague idea that the Greeks were a most tasteful people, and that no mythology can be so finely adapted for the purposes of poetry as theirs. It is amusing to see what a hand the two Cockneys make of this mythology: the one confesses that he never read the Greek tragedians, and the other knows Homer only from Chapman – and both of them write about Apollo, Pan, nymphs, muses and mysteries as might be expected from persons of their education. We shall not, however, enlarge at present upon this subject, as we mean to dedicate an entire paper to the classical attainments and attempts of the Cockney poets.

As for Mr Keats' *Endymion*, it has just as much to do with Greece as it has with 'old Tartary the fierce'. No man whose mind has ever been imbued with the smallest knowledge or feeling of classical poetry or classical history, could have stooped to profane and vulgarize every association in the manner which has been adopted by this 'son of promise'. Before giving any extracts, we must inform our readers that this romance is meant to be written in English heroic rhyme. To those who have read any of Hunt's poems, this hint might indeed be needless; Mr Keats has adopted the loose, nerveless versification and Cockney rhymes of the poet of Rimini.[2] But in fairness to that gentleman, we must add that the defects of the system are tenfold more conspicuous in his disciple's work than in his own. Mr Hunt is a small poet, but he is a clever man. Mr Keats is a still smaller poet, and he is only a boy of pretty abilities, which he has done everything in his power to spoil [. . .]

We had almost forgot to mention that Keats belongs to the Cockney School of Politics, as well as the Cockney School of Poetry.

It is fit that he who holds *Rimini* to be the first poem should believe *The Examiner* to be the first politician of the day. We admire consistency, even in folly. Hear how their bantling has already learned to lisp sedition. [Z. quotes *Endymion*, iii. 1–23.] And now good morrow to 'the muses' son of promise'; as for 'the feats he yet may do', as we do not pretend to say, like himself, 'Muse of my native land am I inspired', we shall adhere to the safe old rule of pauca verba.[3] We venture to make one small prophecy: that his bookseller will not a second time venture £50 upon anything he can write. It is a better and a wiser thing to be a starved apothecary than a starved poet; so back to the shop Mr John, back to 'plasters, pills, and ointment boxes', etc. But for heaven's sake, young Sangrado,[4] be a little more sparing of extenuatives and soporifics in your practice than you have been in your poetry.

---

2 Leigh Hunt's *The Story of Rimini* (1816).
3 Few words.
4 After a character in Alain-René Le Sage's *Gil Blas* (1715–35), an ignorant pretender to medical knowledge.

From **John Hamilton Reynolds's defence of Keats**, *Alfred, West of England Journal and General Advertiser*, 6 October 1818

First published, anonymously, in the Exeter newspaper, the *Alfred, West of England Journal and General Advertiser* on 6 October 1818. Here Keats's friend, the poet John Hamilton Reynolds, defends him from J. W. Croker's venomous tirade in the *Quarterly*. Reynolds suspected that the editor of the *Quarterly*, the Tory satirist William Gifford, was responsible for the review, and he argues that it was motivated by political animus rather than offering dispassionate literary analysis. Being praised by the liberal editor of the *Examiner*, Leigh Hunt, was a 'dangerous compliment' to Keats and had led to the rough handling of the poet in the Tory press. Reynolds goes on to compare Keats's poetry favourably with that of Lord Byron. Sharing Keats's view of the egotistical sublime, Reynolds damns Byron for his 'egotism' and praises Keats for not 'obtrud[ing] his person before you' in his poetry.

We have met with a singular instance, in the last number of the *Quarterly Review*, of that unfeeling arrogance, and cold ignorance, which so strangely marked the minds and hearts of Government sycophants and Government writers. The Poem of a young man of genius, which evinces more natural power than any other work of this day, is abused and cried down [. . .] We have read the Poetic Romance of *Endymion* (the book in question) with no little delight; and could hardly believe that it was written by so young a man as the preface infers. Mr Keats, the author of it, is a genius of the highest order; and no one but a Lottery Commissioner and Government pensioner (both of which Mr William Gifford, the Editor of the *Quarterly Review*, is) could, with a false and remorseless pen, have striven to frustrate hopes and aims, so youthful and so high as this young Poet nurses [. . .] Reviewers are creatures 'that stab men in the dark': young and enthusiastic spirits are their dearest prey [. . .]

The cause of this unmerciful condemnation which has been passed on Mr Keats is pretty apparent to all who have watched the intrigues of literature, and the wily and unsparing contrivances of political parties. This young and powerful writer was noticed, some little time back in the *Examiner*; and pointed out by its editor, as one who was likely to revive the early vigour of English poetry. Such a prediction was a fine, but dangerous compliment, to Mr Keats: it exposed him instantly to the malice of the *Quarterly Review*. Certain it is, that hundreds of fashionable and flippant readers, will henceforth set down this young Poet as a pitiable and nonsensical writer, merely on the assertions of some single heartless critic, who has just energy enough to despise what is good, because it would militate against his pleasantry, if he were to praise it.

The genius of Mr Keats is peculiarly classical; and, with the exception of a few faults, which are the natural followers of youth, his imaginations and his language have a spirit and an intensity which we should in vain look for in half the popular poets of the day [. . .] Mr Keats has none of [Byron's] egotism – this daring selfishness, which is a stain on the robe of poesy – His feelings are full, earnest, and original, as those of the olden writers were and are; they are made for all time, not for the drawing-room and the moment. Mr Keats always speaks of, and describes nature, with an awe and a humility, but with a deep and almost breathless affection. – He knows that Nature is better and older than he is, and he does not put himself on an equality with her. You do not see him, when you see her. The moon, and the mountainous foliage of the woods, and azure sky, and the ruined and magic temple; the rock, the desert, and the sea; the leaf of the forest, and the embossed foam of the most living ocean, are the spirits of his poetry; but he does not bring them in his own hand, or obtrude his person before you, when you are looking at them. Poetry is a thing of generalities – a wanderer amid persons and things – not a pauser over one thing, or with one person. The mind of Mr Keats, like the minds of our older poets, goes round the universe in its speculations and its dreams. It does not set itself a task. The manners of the world, the fictions and the wonders of other worlds, are its subjects.

From **Francis Jeffrey's review of Endymion and Lamia, Isabella, The Eve of St. Agnes, and other Poems**, Edinburgh Review, August 1820

First published, unattributed, in the Edinburgh Review, XXXIV, August 1820. The Edinburgh, founded in 1802, was the leading Whig periodical of the age. The review is by the journal's founding editor, Francis Jeffrey. Jeffrey was no avant-gardist, and had launched several attacks on the 'new school' of poetry, most notably in his notorious review of Wordsworth's The Excursion (1814), which had begun with the forthright declaration 'This will never do'. But he was considerably more sympathetic to John Keats's Endymion and Lamia volumes and 'the genius they display[ed]'. Jeffrey's generous review was published too late for it to be appreciated by Keats.

We have never happened to see either of these volumes till very lately – and have been exceedingly struck with the genius they display, and the spirit of poetry which breathes through all their extravagance. That imitation of our older writers, and especially of our older dramatists, to which we cannot help flattering ourselves that we have somewhat contributed, has brought on, as it were, a second spring in our poetry; – and few of its blossoms are either more profuse of sweetness or richness in promise, than this which is now before us. Mr Keats, we understand, is still a very young man; and his whole works indeed, bear evidence enough of the fact. They are full of extravagance and irregularity, rash attempts at originality, interminable wanderings, and excessive obscurity. They manifestly require, therefore, all the indulgence that can be claimed for a first attempt: – but we think it no less plain that they deserve it; for they are flushed all over with the rich lights of fancy, and so coloured and bestrewn with the flowers of poetry, that even while perplexed and bewildered in their labyrinths, it is impossible to resist the intoxication of their sweetness, or to shut our hearts to the enchantments which they so lavishly present.

From **Lord Byron's letters to John Murray**, 1820

Unlike his friend Shelley, Byron was no admirer of Keats. To some extent, Byron's ire was attributable to his admiration for his great satirical predecessor Pope; his first mention of Keats was in a March 1820 letter which dismissed the poet's attack on Pope in 'Sleep and Poetry' ('an ominous title'). The same letter also identifies Keats as an insignificant camp-follower of the school of Wordsworth and Southey ('a tadpole of the Lakes'), and his subsequent, acerbically witty, if unfair, epistolary attacks on the poet make the same charge against Keats that he had made in the 'Dedication' to *Don Juan* (1818): that the 'Lakers' were solipsistic, self-obsessed and preoccupied with their imaginations to the exclusion of all else. In his letters to Murray, Byron couches his attack on Keats in the most extreme terms, caricaturing the poet's concern with the literary imagination as a a form of 'mental masturbation'. After Keats's death, his brother George indignantly declared that 'John was the soul of manliness and courage, and as much like the Holy Ghost as *Johnny Keats*'.

12 August

[. . .] Here are Johnny Keats's *p-ss* a-bed poetry [. . .] There is such a trash of Keats and the like upon my tables, that I am ashamed to look at them [. . .] No more Keats, I entreat: – flay him alive; if some of you don't, I must skin him myself: there is no bearing the drivelling idiotism of the Mankin. [. . .]

4 September

[. . .] The *Edinburgh* praises Jack Keats or Ketch, or whatever his names are: why, his is the *Onanism* of Poetry – something like the pleasure an Italian fiddler extracted out of being suspended daily by a Street Walker in Drury Lane. This went on for some weeks: at last the Girl went to get a pint of Gin – met another, chatted too long, and Cornelli was *hanged outright before she returned*. Such like is the trash they praise, and such will be the end of the *outstretched* poesy of this miserable Self-polluter of the human mind. [. . .]

9 September

[. . .] Mr Keats, whose poetry you enquire after, appears to me what I have already said: such writing is a sort of mental masturbation – he is always f-gg-g his *Imagination*. I don't mean he is *indecent*, but viciously soliciting his own ideas into a state, which is neither poetry nor any thing else but a Bedlam vision produced by raw pork and opium. [. . .]

18 September

[. . .] Of the praises of that little dirty blackguard Keats in the *Edinburgh* [. . .] Why don't they praise Solomon's *Guide to Health*?[5] it is better sense and as much poetry as Johnny Keates. [. . .]

From **Leigh Hunt's review of *Lamia, Isabella, The Eve of St. Agnes, and other Poems*,** the *Indicator*, 2 and 9 August 1820

First published in Leigh Hunt's the *Indicator* on 2 and 9 August 1820. Leigh Hunt's two-penny weekly, published between October 1819 and March 1821, though short-lived, is estimable, notable for some of Hunt's finest essays and for the first publication of Keats's 'La Belle Dame Sans Merci' which appeared on 10 May 1820. Here the *Indicator*'s editor returns to the subject of his former protégé. Keats is now no longer a promising poet; he has achieved poetic mastery: 'Mr Keats undoubtedly takes his seat with the oldest and best of our living poets'.

The *Hyperion* is a fragment – a gigantic one, like a ruin in the desert, or the bones of a mastodon. It is truly of a piece with its subject, which is the downfall of the elder gods [. . .]

Mr Keats's versification sometimes reminds us of Milton in his blank verse, and sometimes of Chapman both in his blank verse and rhyme; but his faculties, essentially speaking, through partaking of the unearthly aspirations and abstract yearnings of both these poets, are altogether his own. They are ambitious, but less directly so. They are more social, and in the finer sense of the word, sensual, than either. They are more coloured by the modern philosophy of sympathy and natural justice. *Endymion*, with all its extraordinary powers, partook of the faults of youth, though the best ones; but the reader of *Hyperion* and these other stories would never guess that they were written at twenty.[6] The author's versification is now perfected, the exuberances of his imagination restrained, and a calm power, the surest and loftiest of all power, takes place of the impatient workings of the younger god within him. The character of his genius is that of energy and voluptuousness, each able at will to take leave of the other, and possessing, in their union, a high feeling of humanity not common to the best authors who can less combine them. Mr Keats undoubtedly takes his seat with the oldest and best of our living poets.

---

5   The *Guide to Health* (1795), by the quack doctor Samuel Solomon, went through many editions in this period.

6   Hunt exaggerated Keats's youth. The poet began *Hyperion* in the month before his twenty-third birthday.

From **Percy Bysshe Shelley's preface to *Adonais*,** 1821

First published in *Adonais: An Elegy on the Death of John Keats, Author of Endymion, Hyperion, etc* (Pisa: privately printed, 1821). Shelley's elegy to Keats was published in July 1821. The poem, in Spenserian stanzas, laments Keats under the name of Adonais, the Greek god of beauty and fertility. It begins thus:

> I weep for Adonais—he is dead!
> O, weep for Adonais! though our tears
> Thaw not the frost which binds so dear a head!
> And thou, sad Hour, selected from all years
> To mourn our loss, rouse thy obscure compeers,
> And teach them thine own sorrow, say: 'With me
> Died Adonais; till the future dares
> Forget the Past, his fate and fame shall be
> An echo and a light unto eternity!'

Adonais was prefaced by a discursive preface, extracted below, which proved influential in its (inaccurate) account of Keats's death, claiming that the poet's mortal illness was the direct result of a haemorrhage caused by the *Quarterly*'s antipathetic review of *Endymion*. The Tory reviewers, according to Shelley, have a pen 'dipped in consuming fire'. Shelley was not an unqualified admirer of Keats, and his preface admits that he was antipathetic to the poet's earlier work: it is *Hyperion* which proves that Keats will take his place in the poetic pantheon.

It is my intention to subjoin to the London edition of this poem, a criticism upon the claims of its lamented object to be classed among the writers of the highest genius who have adorned our age. My known repugnance[7] to the narrow principles of taste on which several of his earlier compositions were modelled, prove, at least that I am an impartial judge. I consider his fragment of *Hyperion*, as second to nothing that was ever produced by a writer of the same years [. . .]

The genius of the lamented person to whose memory I have dedicated these unworthy verses, was not less delicate and fragile than it was beautiful: and where canker-worms abound, what wonder, if its young flower was blighted in the bud? The savage criticism on his *Endymion*, which appeared in the *Quarterly Review*, produced the most violent effect on his susceptible mind; the agitation thus originated ended in the rupture of a blood-vessel in the lungs; a rapid consumption ensued, and the succeeding acknowledgements from more candid critics, of true greatness of his powers, were ineffectual to heal the wound thus wantonly inflicted.

---

7 '*Hyperion* promises for him that he is destined to become one of the first writers of the age. – His other things are imperfect enough, & what is worse written in the bad sort of style which is becoming fashionable among those who fancy that they are imitating Hunt & Wordsworth' (Shelley to Marianne Hunt, 29 October 1820).

From **William Hazlitt, 'On Effeminacy of Character'**, *Table Talk*, 1821–2

Though Hazlitt was a personal friend of Keats, and although his criticism was deeply influential upon the poet's thought, the essayist had reservations about Keats's poetry. His most positive reference is found in his essay 'On Reading Old Books', which offers a glancing reference to 'the beautiful and tender images of "The Eve of St. Agnes"'. However, Hazlitt's considered judgement in *Table Talk* laments the poet's deficiency of 'masculine energy'.

I cannot help thinking that the fault of Mr Keats's poems was a deficiency in masculine energy of style. He had beauty, tenderness, delicacy, in an uncommon degree, but there was want of strength and substance. His *Endymion* is a very delightful description of the illusions of a youthful imagination, given up to airy dreams – we have flowers, clouds, rainbows, moonlight, all sweet sounds and smell, and Oreads and Dryads[8] flitting by – but there is nothing tangible in it, nothing marked or palpable – we have none of the hardy spirit or rigid forms of antiquity. He painted his own thoughts and character; and did not transport himself into the fabulous and heroic ages. There is a want of action, of character, and so far, of imagination, but there is exquisite fancy. All is soft and fleshy, without bone or muscle. We see him in the youth, without the manhood of poetry. His genius breathed 'vernal delight and joy'. – 'Like Maia's son he stood and shook his plumes,' with fragrance filled. His mind was redolent of spring. He had not the fierceness of summer, nor the richness of autumn, and winter he seemed not to have known, till he felt the icy hand of death![9]

From **William Howitt, *Homes and Haunts of the Most Eminent British Poets*, 1847**

Howitt's florid prose exemplifies a certain kind of enraptured Victorian response to Keats, offering an unworldly poet possessed of 'celestial gifts' and slain by the perfidies of 'base criticism'. It should be noted that Howitt takes pains to absolve Keats from the charge of effeminacy made by Hazlitt and others.

---

8   Mountain-nymphs and wood-nymphs.
9   In 1824, Hazlitt retuned to the subject of Keats in his *Select British Poets*:

Mr Keats is also dead. He gave the greatest promise of genius of any poet of his day. He displayed extreme tenderness, beauty, originality, and delicacy of fancy: all he wanted was manly strength and fortitude to reject the temptations of singularity in sentiment and expression. Some of his shorter and later pieces, are, however, as free from faults as they are full of beauties.

Of the class of swift but resplendent messengers by whom these ministrations [i.e. of God] are performed, neither ours nor any other history can furnish a specimen more beautiful than John Keats. He was of feeling and 'imagination all compact'. His nature was one pure mass of the living light of poetry. On this world and its concerns he could take no hold, and they could take none on him. The worldly and the worldly wise could not comprehend him, could not sympathize with him. To them his vivid orgasm of the intellect was madness; his exuberance of celestial gifts was extravagance; his unworldliness was effeminacy; his love of the universal man, and not of gross distinctions of pride and party, was treason. As of the highest and divinest of God's messengers to earth, they cried 'Away with him, he is not fit to live'; and the body, that mere mist-like, that mere shadow-like body, already failing before the fervency of his spiritual functions, fell, 'faded away, dissolved', and disappeared before the bitter frost-wind of base criticism.

From **Matthew Arnold, 'John Keats'**, in T. H. Ward (ed.), *English Poets,* 1880

First published as a critical introduction to the selections from Keats in *English Poets,* 'John Keats', by the poet and critic Matthew Arnold (1822–88), offers a corrective to contemporary worshippers of Keats such as Howitt. Arnold is particularly antipathetic towards those who celebrate Keats's sensuality; adopting Keats's distinction in his letter to Benjamin Bailey of 22 November 1817, he will have a Keats who is a poet of 'thoughts' rather than of 'sensations'. Arnold repudiates those 'who worship [Keats], and would have the world worship him too as the poet of [the] sensuous strain'. Arnold has no time for 'that imagined sensuous weakling', and offers instead a version of the poet as a 'tough-minded' man whose best work is possessed of 'flint and iron'. Useful riposte to idolatry as this might be, Arnold's position has been itself repudiated by twentieth-century critics such as John Jones[10] and Christopher Ricks, who offer important reinterpretations of the importance of 'sensuousness' to Keats's work (**pp. 51–3** and **pp. 56–7**).

No one can question the eminency, in Keats's poetry, of the quality of sensuousness. Keats as a poet is abundantly and enchantingly sensuous; the question with some people will be, whether he is anything else. Many things may be brought forward which seem to show him as under the fascination and sole domination of sense, and desiring nothing better. There is the exclamation in one of his letter: 'O for a life of sensations rather than thoughts!'. There is the thesis, in another, 'that with a great Poet the sense of Beauty overcomes every other consideration, or rather obliterates all consideration' [...] Character and self-control [...] so

---

10 Jones says of Arnold's essay: 'whereas Arnold's documentation of sensuousness is ample, that of the *poetical* virtue of flint and iron is almost non-existent' (*John Keats's Dream of Truth* (London: Chatto & Windus, 1969), p. 33).

necessary for every kind of greatness, and for the great artist, too, indispensable, appear to be wanting [. . .] They are wanting also to the Keats of the letters to Fanny Brawne [. . .] 'My sweet Fanny, will your heart never change? My love, will it? I have no limit now to my love' [. . .] one is tempted to speak even as *Blackwood* or the *Quarterly* were in the old days wont to speak; one is tempted to say that Keats's love-letter is the love-letter of a surgeon's apprentice [. . .] The sensuous strain Keats had, and a man of his poetic powers could not, whatever his strain, but show his talent in it. But he has something more, and something better. We who believe Keats to have been by his promise, at any rate, one of the very greatest of English poets [know] that Keats had flint and iron in him, that he had character; that he was, as his brother George says, 'as much like the Holy Ghost as *Johnny Keats*', – as that imagined sensuous weakling, the delight of the literary circles of Hampstead [. . .]

The truth is that 'the yearning passion for the Beautiful', which was with Keats, as he himself truly says, the master-passion, is not a passion of the sensuous or sentimental poet. It is an intellectual or spiritual passion [. . .] [Keats] has made himself remembered, and remembered as no merely sensuous poet could be; and he has done it by having 'loved the principle of beauty in all things'.

Modern Criticism

Introduction

This subsection builds upon the above Critical History of Keats's poetry by reprinting extracts from some of the most notable twentieth-century Keatsian scholarship. Whilst it includes some earlier criticism, its principal focus is upon work published since the 1960s, thereby providing the reader with an up-to-date knowledge of the state of contemporary Keatsian criticism.

From **H. W. Garrod, *Keats*,** Oxford: Oxford University Press, 1926, pp. 68–73

Heathcote William Garrod (1878–1960) was the most notable Keatsian scholar of the inter-war period. His *The Poetical Works of John Keats* (1939) remained the standard scholarly edition of the poet's work until the publication of Jack Stillinger's *The Poems of John Keats* in 1978, and his monograph *Keats* (1926) remains a valuable critical study. Here Garrod, who paid more attention to Keats's politics than most of the poet's twentieth-century critics before the 1970s, reads *Hyperion* as an 'epic of the revolutionary Idea'. The unfinished poem remains an 'indeterminate allegory', open to a number of different interpretations: political, philosophical, literary and mythological. Perhaps, Garrod speculates, the need to stabilise the poem's significance caused Keats to abandon it, leaving it a suggestive fragment which refuses to yield up a single clear meaning.

I have spoken already of Keats' early revolutionary sympathies, of his Huntian or Wordsworthian politics. I said that these sympathies went deeper, and lasted longer, than is usually recognised. Keats, I said, is more the child of the Revolutionary Idea than we commonly suppose. That is true, even in politics. But the Revolutionary Idea is neither wholly, nor primarily, political. Of the multifarious manifestations of this idea Keats undertook to write, what no other of the romantics essayed, the epic. So at least I conceive *Hyperion* – as, under allegoric forms, the epic of the Revolutionary Idea. In history, as in mythology, the Revolutionary Idea begins when children refuse any longer to be eaten by their parents. There is that in nature which will not be eaten by custom; and there is that in poetry which will not be eaten by prose; and whether what happens be figured as Jove deposing Saturn, or the French Revolution dethroning the Ancien Regime, Apollo ousting Hyperion, or Wordsworth dispossessing Pope, or, again, beauty dispossessing order, imagination replacing reason, matters hardly at all; in each event the same causes operate. Somewhat thus, I take it, Keats conceived his epic of the Revolutionary Idea. Exactly how he had it in mind to distribute the emphasis, ingenuity may be harmlessly exercised in guessing; but if Keats himself stopped because he did not know how to go on, it would be nothing out of nature, and perhaps, indeed, out of nature if it were otherwise [. . .]

I will not say that *Hyperion* remains, and was bound to remain, the fragment that it is, merely because Keats cannot bring himself to point the moral which he has so far drawn. That fear of himself, that uneasiness, operates. But it is part of a wider perplexity. I should prefer to conceive that Keats, pursuing his epic of the Revolutionary Idea, trailing, as he went, clouds of indeterminate allegory, was held by that death-shriek, or birth-shriek, of his own Apollo; that he was startled into misgiving; that some disquiet of the creating imagination assailed him; that he felt himself brought up sharply against the need of defining the need of clarifying his own conception. What truly was this god, who thus dies into life? and into what order of life does this dying in fact conduct him?

From **Cleanth Brooks, 'Keats's Sylvan Historian; History without Footnotes'**, in *The Well-Wrought Urn: Studies in the Structure of Poetry*, New York: Reynal & Hitchcock, 1947, pp. 139–52

> The American scholar Cleanth Brooks (1906–94), who taught at Yale University, was one of the most notable New Critics of the post-war period. New Criticism addressed, in Brooks's words, 'the structure of poetry', focusing, in detailed close readings, on a poem as 'a thing in itself'. Rather than appealing to external literary contexts, be they political, sexual or social, poems are treated as self-contained verbal icons. In this extract from 'Keats's Sylvan Historian', Brooks attends to the vexed question of the meaning of the famous last two lines of the 'Ode on a Grecian Urn', arguing that their significance 'can be derived from the context of the poem itself': '"Beauty is truth, truth beauty" has precisely the same status, and the same justification as Shakespeare's "Ripeness is all". It is a speech "in character" and supported by a dramatic context.'

The recognition that men and maidens are frozen, fixed, arrested, has, as we have already seen, run through the second, third, and fourth stanzas as an ironic undercurrent. The central paradox of the poem, thus, comes to conclusion in the phrase, 'Cold Pastoral'. The word 'pastoral' suggests warmth, spontaneity, the natural and the informal as well as the idyllic, the simple and the informally charming.

What the urn tells is a 'flowery tale', a 'leaf-fringed legend', but the 'sylvan historian' works in terms of marble. The urn itself is cold, and the life beyond life which it expresses is life which has been formed, arranged. The urn itself is a 'silent form', and it speaks, not by means of statement, but by 'teasing us out of thought'. It is as enigmatic as eternity is, for, like eternity, its history is beyond time, outside time, and for this reason bewilders our time-ridden minds: it teases us [. . .]

The marble men and women lie outside time. The urn which they adorn will remain. The 'Sylvan historian' will recite its history to other generations. What will it say to them? Presumably, what it says to the poet now: that 'formed experience', imaginative insight, embodies the basic and fundamental perception of man and nature. The urn is beautiful, and yet its beauty is based – what else is the poet concerned with? – on an imaginative perception of essentials. Such a vision is beautiful but it is also true. The sylvan history presents us with beautiful histories, but they are true histories, and it is a good historian.

Moreover, the 'truth' which the sylvan historian gives is the only kind of truth which we are likely to get on this earth, and, furthermore, it is the only kind that we have to have. The names, dates, and special circumstances, the wealth of data, these the sylvan historian quietly ignores. [But] mere accumulation of facts – a point our own generation is only beginning to realize – are meaningless. The sylvan historian does better than that: it takes a few details and so orders them that we have not only beauty but insight into essential truth. Its 'history', in short, is a history without footnotes. It has the validity of myth – not myth as a pretty but irrelevant make-belief, and idle fancy, but myth as a valid perception into reality.

So much for the 'meaning' of the last lines of the 'Ode'.

From **Earl R. Wasserman, *The Finer Tone: Keats' Major Poems*,** Baltimore, Md.: Johns Hopkins University Press, 1953, pp. 68–81

The Finer Tone, by Earl Reeves Wasserman (1913–73), who taught at Johns Hopkins University, was the most notable example of the allegorical criticism of Keats which enjoyed a post-war critical vogue. Such criticism offered what Wasserman called 'symbolic readings' of the poet's work; The Finer Tone interprets Keats's major poems, romances and odes alike, as allegories of the 'dimensionless mystery beyond our mortal vision'. That said, its ornate interpretations have generally been seen as tendentious and over-elaborate by more recent Keatsian scholars. Here Wasserman reads 'La Belle Dame Sans Merci' in terms of 'the three coexistent themes that dominate Keats's deepest meditations and profoundest system of values: the oxymoronic heaven's bourne towards which his spirit yearned; the pleasure thermometer which he conceived of as the spiritual path to that goal; and the self-annihilation that he understood to be the condition necessary to that journey'.

The first three stanzas, which make dramatic the subsequent narrating and excite a symbolic reading, introduce nine precisely balanced stanzas containing the main narrative (4–12). [. . .] There is nothing in Keats's ballad even suggesting the frequent interpretation that the fairy's child is responsible for the knight's expulsion from the elfin grot; only his own inherent attribute of being mortal causes his magic withdrawal [. . .] The vision of the mortal-immortal can only entice mortal man towards heaven's bourne; it cannot aid him in his aspirations or preserve his vision, which must inevitably be shattered. By this fair enchantment mortal man can only be 'tortured with renewed life'.

It is in this sense that la belle dame is sans merci, without tenderness; this is a description of what provokes man's aspirations, rather than an evaluation of it. Like the lady of the tradition of courtly love, she is the ideal whom the lover must pursue but whom he can never possess; and hence he is doomed to suffer her 'unkindness', which is her nature although not her fault. Only the inherent meanness of man's dreams, then, draws him back from heaven's bourne, for, instead of being visionary penetrations into that final essence which is beauty-truth, they are only of mutable things. Aspire though he will, the stings of human neighborhood envenom all [. . .]

The knight's inherent weakness in being unable to exclude from his visions the self-contained and world-bound mortality dissipates the ideal into which he has entered momentarily [. . .] The elfin grot once again becomes the cold hill side which is the physical, mutable world, where the knight has been all the while, but which, by means of his visionary insight, took on the magic splendor of the elfin grot, the mystery within the mutable. The vision had momentarily transfigured a real thing into an 'ethereal' thing. Exactly so, it was the poet's vision that transformed the marble embroidery on the Grecian urn into the unchanging vitality of a realm without space, time and identity; and the shattering of that vision once again froze the immortality of passion into cold, motionless marble. With the dissipation of the vision in the ballad and with the consequent return to the cold, physical world, the ladder of intensities which the knight had ascended to reach the ethereal world now crumbles beneath him: love has gone, 'the sedge has wither'd from the lake', and 'no birds sing'. Love, song, and nature fade and disappear as the knight's capacity for the passionate intensity for fellowship with essence becomes enervate and he returns to normal human weakness.

Now that the knight has been awakened from his dream by the stings of human neighborhood, he is as pale, death-pale, as the kings, princes, and warriors, for he now shares their mortality. Being mortal, his very existence is a progress towards death, and death therefore is in his nature, although in the elfin grot existence, being without time, is without death. Indeed, Keats originally wrote, 'I see *death*'s lily on thy brow [. . .] And on thy cheek *death*'s fading rose'. By withdrawing from the elfin grot, the Knight has also become a Man of Power [see p. 137]; the withdrawal is the act of reassuming his own self-contained identity, and thus he is 'alone', being his own isolated self. His aloneness is the opposite of a fellowship with essence which absorbs the proper self, that self which is cut off from its selfless origin in heaven. At heaven's bourne there can be no aloneness because there are no individual selves, no proper identities [. . .] Earthly life, then, is a spiritual solitude overcast with the pallor of death, and a denial of the 'honey wild, and manna dew,' the heaven-sent food which is life's proper pith; all mortal living is a movement towards the sacrificial altar. 'Living,' therefore, must be a biding of one's time, a meaningless exhausting of one's mortal lease, since man is only a temporary resident in this world. The elfin grot being truly his home ethereal, mortal man, in the solitude of his self, can only 'sojourn here [. . .] palely loitering,' on the cold hill side of the world. And the unfinished, hovering quality of the metrics of each stanzaic close ('And no birds sing,' 'On the cold hill's side') perfectly reinforces the aimless solitude with which Keats is investing mortal life [. . .]

The structural pattern of the main narrative stanzas (4–12) is, then, as precisely balanced as that of the 'Ode on a Grecian Urn.' In the ode the first two stanzas trace the ascent to a perception of the frieze as a timeless, spaceless, selfless realm of endless vitality; the last two, the descent from this realm, bring the poem back to the condition from which it started. And the central stanza both depicts the oxymoronic nature of this area and introduces the chemicals for its destruction. Correspondingly, the first four stanzas (4–7) of the main narrative in the ballad lead toward the oxymoronic elfin grot; the last four (9–12), away from it. And the central stanza (8) both admits the knight into the elfin grot and motivates the dissolution of the vision, for in this stanza the knight takes it upon himself to shut the 'wild wild eyes' of the mystery. In the ode, the heaven's bourne of the frieze is dispelled by a force within the poet himself, the unavoidable recollection of the mortal world; in the ballad, a force within the mortal knight – not an act of the fairy's child – causes him to shut out the wild mystery of the ideal.

From **John Bayley, 'Keats and Reality'**, in *Proceedings of the British Academy*, XLVIII, London: Oxford University Press, 1962, pp. 98–105

Its most decisive ingredient is vulgarity. What is real in his poetry is also what is vulgar; indeed, 'Keats and Vulgarity' would perhaps be the proper title for this lecture. He is, happily, the most vulgar of poets; he is vulgar not as a man but as a poet – vulgarity is his poetry's 'material sublime'. It goes down into the root and sinew of his poetic language; it is not just a surface genteelism, as in words like 'dainty'; or in cockney spellings ('exhalt', 'ear' for 'hear', &c.), but vulgarity in the heroic sense [. . .] It is the true commonness which in German is called *Das Gemeine*, a word which weightily subsumes and generalizes the more local and general senses of English [. . .] Keats's poetic personality is magnificently *gemein*. In it the earth reveals the rift of ore; it turns what might appear mean and embarrassing into what is rich and *disconcerting*: for at his most characteristic Keats always disconcerts [. . .] Keats is most fully his poetic self, most wholly involved in what he is writing, when he is, in the usual and technical sense, 'bad', or on the edge of 'badness'. One might say that the full reality of his poetry is revealed in the presence of this badness; the poetry needs it. Its greatness, its heavy truth, is profoundly involved with badness and cannot exist without it.

My use of the word 'bad' here begs as many questions as my borrowing of *gemein*, and both are more easily demonstrated than defined. The clue is, I repeat, that Keats's language seems right only for him [. . .] He describes Isabella after Lorenzo's disappearance as

> Spreading her perfect arms upon the air
> And on her low couch murmuring 'Where, O where'.

In most poets such an epithet would be merely vacuous – in Dryden a routine insensibility, in Hunt a routine archness (it is applied in *The Story of Rimini*, to Francesca's waist) – but is it not, in Keats, immensely moving? [. . .] *Hyperion* is, so to speak, not bad enough, too full of hard-won decorum. Keats distrusted art, because 'human nature' was finer as he felt, but perhaps more because his nature was spontaneously artful. The sad dilemma of his genius is that when he tries to express reality he becomes abstract; when he turns towards the discipline of art he became Parnassian. In *Hyperion* both things occur and Keats knew it [. . .] He stifles his personality in order to make the necessary calculations for the major philosophical poem, the playing up, or playing down, of 'beauties' to enhance the paragraphing and the overall effect. *Hyperion* thus becomes the prototype of what might be called *romantic correctness*.

From **Walter Jackson Bate, *John Keats*,** London: Chatto & Windus, 1963, pp. 249–50

John Keats, by Walter Jackson Bate (b. 1918), Professor of English (Emeritus) at Harvard University, remains the standard life of the poet. It combines biography with criticism, offering detailed readings of the poetry and of Keats's key critical concepts. This is Bate's account of the concept of negative capability.

[W]e could paraphrase these famous sentences as follows. In our life of uncertainties, where no one system or formula can explain everything [. . .] what is needed is an imaginative openness of mind and heightened receptivity to reality in its full and diverse concreteness. This, however, involves negating one's own ego. Keats's friend Dilke, as he said later, 'was a Man who cannot feel that he has a personal identity unless he has made up his Mind about every thing. The only means of strengthening one's intellect is to make up ones mind about nothing – to let the mind be a thoroughfare for all thoughts [. . .] Dilke will never come at truth as long as he lives; because he is always trying at it'. To be dissatisfied with such insights as one may attain through this openness, to reject them unless they can be wrenched into a part of a systematic structure of one's own making, is an egotistic assertion of one's own identity. The remark 'without any irritable reaching after fact and reason' is often cited as though the pejorative words are 'fact and reason' and as though uncertainties were being preferred for their own sake. But the significant word, of course, is 'irritable'. We should also stress 'capable' – 'capable of being in uncertainties, Mysteries, doubts' without the 'irritable' need to extend our identities and rationalize our 'half knowledge'. For a 'great poet' especially, a sympathetic absorption in the essential significance of his object (caught and relished in that active cooperation of the mind in which the emerging 'Truth' is felt as 'Beauty,' and in which the harmony of the human imagination and its object is attained) 'overcomes every other consideration' (considerations that an 'irritable reaching after fact and reason' might otherwise itch to pursue). Indeed, it goes beyond and 'obliterates' the act of 'consideration' – of deliberating, analyzing, and piercing experience together through 'consequitive reasoning'.

From **John Jones, *John Keats's Dream of Truth*,** London: Chatto & Windus, 1969, pp. 14–31

Beginning by explicitly repudiating Matthew Arnold's condemnation of the sensuous side of Keats's work, John Jones (b. 1924) offers a detailed study of the poet's 'sensual humanism'. Keats's emotional life – which prompted a visceral queasiness in Arnold – is for Jones an important shaping force upon his poetry, and his sensuality is a positive influence: a poem such as 'Isabella' works by 'squeezing the last sensuous drop out of each phase in turn'. And this sensuality, rather than detracting from the powerful humanism of the poet's work (as Arnold has it), actually lies at the core of that vision. For Jones, 'Isabella' is as concerned as the great odes are with the relationships between art, life and death. The poem is no morbid fantasy and its strength lies in Keats's empathy and fellow-feeling with those in extremity. Thus Isabella's cherishing of her dead lover's head and her immuring it in a garden pot 'declares life's total dependence upon death in a sudden knife-flash premonition of the greatest of all his poems, the ode *To Autumn*'. 'The emphasis of Keats's treatment is not, despite appearances, perverse,' argues Jones, and Isabella's attentions to Lorenzo's 'fast-mouldering head' are part of Keats's life-affirming, humanistic and 'marvelously sane' vision.

The most striking example, though by no means his best work, is a revolting story taken from Boccaccio, 'Isabella' [. . .] The girl Isabella has a lover who is tricked from her by his enemies and murdered and secretly buried. She sets out with her old nurse, finds the grave, digs down to the body and cuts off the head which she takes home and hides in the bottom of a garden-pot; and she

> cover'd it with mould, and o'er it set
> Sweet basil –

hoping thus to have the head by her always, and cherish it undisturbed. The centre of horror is the exhuming of the corpse:

> Soon she turn'd up a soiled glove, whereon
>   Her silk had play'd in purple phantasies,
> She kiss'd it with a lip more chill than stone,
>   And put it in her bosom, where it dries
> And freezes utterly unto the bone
>   Those dainties made to still an infant's cries:
> Then 'gan she work again; nor stay'd her care,
> But to throw back at times her veiling hair.
>
> That old nurse stood beside her wondering,
>   Until her heart felt pity to the core
> At sight of such a dismal labouring,
>   And so she kneeled, with her locks all hoar,
> And put her lean hands to the horrid thing:
>   Three hours they labour'd at this travail sore;
> At last they felt the kernel of the grave,
> And Isabella did not stamp and rave.

And while no two stanzas can show how this unpleasant story is tamed by art and sometimes rendered very beautiful, the couple in front of us do force upon the judgment a decisive alternative. In fact it is impossible to start reading the poem at any point without quickly having to decide whether the poem under contemplation is the work of a sick erotic fancy, or something very like such a work on the surface and very different underneath. In our stanzas the alternative voices itself as a choice between taking the kissing of the glove as a rather obscene necrophiliac key to the whole or as a link in the chain of feel which extends from the initial insistence upon temperature, through the touching action of 'put' with its verbal and physical repetition in the next stanza, to the even bolder duplication of 'felt' in its symmetrical balancing of inward feel towards the heart's 'core' and outward feel towards the grave's 'kernel'. Altogether an interesting test case. 'At last they felt the kernel of the grave' is a blazing inspiration, but it is not easy to say why. The verbal sumptuousness, the standard Keats, of 'Her silk had play'd in purple phantasies' looks small beside it. One runs one's eye back and notes the emotional ground-swell building up under the commonplace little 'felt'. The point I made a moment ago about the vital feel-situation and the dead (sexual) remainder, is illustrated by the freezing and especially the drying touch in contrast with the almost unbelievable vulgar fatuity of 'Those dainties made to still an infant's cries' – though the turn towards family and home is an omen of greatness. [. . .]

'Isabella' transmutes the beastliness of Boccaccio's story not by spiritualising it, nor by cunning selection, but by squeezing the last sensuous drop out of each phase in turn; and this is true equally of direct touch, taste, smell, and of the negative-capable projection of feel. The stanza in which Isabella dotes upon Lorenzo's severed head, foul with 'smeared loam':

> She calm'd its wild hair with a golden comb,
>   And all around each eye's sepulchral cell
> Pointed each fringed lash

presents the exhilarating spectacle of a very young poet daring to be himself. And the later one in which the decomposing head nourishes the basil plant growing above it, takes us much further again:

> And so she ever fed it with thin tears,
>   Whence thick, and green, and beautiful it grew,
> So that it smelt more balmy than its peers
>   Of basil-tufts in Florence; for it drew
> Nurture besides, and life, from human fears,
>   From the fast mouldering head there shut from view . . .

It declares life's total dependence upon death in a sudden knife-flash premonition of the greatest of all his poems, the ode 'To Autumn'. This 'nurture' of 'Isabella' points to the entirely unwitty confluence of opposites in the ode, where it is made obvious that life and death are inexplicable apart, and no more in need of explanation, together, than a fine autumn day – or a healthy plant. The characteristically bold repose upon smell leaves nothing to be explained; but it is also true that we are in the grip of a wonder of nature as we enjoy the sweetness drawn by the basil-tuft from Lorenzo's 'fast-mouldering head'.

These were the thoughts prompting my initial claim for 'Isabella', that it is often open and generous and even grand, where everything would seem to point to an oppressive narrowness. The emphasis of Keats's treatment is not, despite appearances, perverse; he conceives Isabella kissing Lorenzo's exhumed head, and combing its hair and pointing its eyelashes, not in order to show what he can achieve in the teeth of decorum, but because his gift happens to be thus. And his gift is a large one, and marvelously sane.

From **Carl Woodring, *Politics in English Romantic Poetry*,** Cambridge, Mass.: Harvard University Press, 1970, pp. 77–83

Woodring's important study of the sociohistorical significance of a literary form, Romantic poetry, which had been too often caricatured as apolitical, argues that Keats – the poet most often cited as a pure poet of the imagination

– was preoccupied with politics, and that his supposedly escapist poetry often endorsed 'progressive politics'. That said, Woodring (b. 1919, formerly American Professor of Literature at Columbia University) argues that 'political and humanitarian impulses did not elicit the full strength of Keats's genius', a claim which later historical critics such as Nicholas Roe have repudiated (**pp. 69–72**). And Woodring sees the ideological trajectory of Keats's poetry as moving from the political to the apolitical; like Jerome J. McGann after him (**pp. 57–60**), he sees Keats's last great poem, 'To Autumn', as marking a turning away from the political investments of his early work.

Keats is cited [. . .] as evidence that romantic faith – for example, in the faery power of imagination – was incompatible with all politics whatsoever. Of the major poets, Keats is thought to have evaded most successfully the impurities of political reference [. . .] Yet Keats's personal adherence to the Opposition side is not in doubt. His letters [. . .] show that Hunt and Hazlitt taught him which political views were proper for his confined station in society and his bursting genius [. . .] Hazlitt provided Keats with the living myth of the constant, fearless, heroic fighter for the democratic idea.

It is easy to wish that Keats had avoided politics in his poems [. . .] In several of the longer poems, passages of utilitarian, progressive politics and of angry humanitarianism erupt like measles [. . .] Yet politics has an integral place in Keats's canon [and it] is possible, while admitting that political and humanitarian impulses did not elicit the full strength of Keats's genius, to avoid the error of believing that the political passages interrupt his larger intentions. The first forty lines of Book III of *Endymion*, it is said, jar the reader out of the world of myth:

> There are those who lord it o'er their fellow-men
> With most prevailing tinsel [. . .]

This 'stern alarum' may be what Douglas Bush calls it, 'the badly written blast of a young liberal against the Establishment and spurious public values', but it belongs to the poem Keats set out to write [. . .]

In another passage frequently deplored, stanzas 14–18 of 'Isabella' [. . .] Keats attacks the two murderous 'ledger-men', Isabella's brothers, for their ignorant rule over an empire [. . .] extending its power of misery from Ceylonese divers to dart-filled seals lying 'on the cold ice with piteous bark'. The poet's protest has seemed extraneous to later critics, for his two Florentine 'money-bags' have a larger empire than the plot requires. [However,] Keats's Ceylonese divers oppressed by two capitalists represent a still larger public issue [. . .] In sum, Boccaccio's tale of Florentine intrigue is updated by Keats, specifically in the stanzas on the Ceylonese [. . .] to [. . .] protest [against] the growth of British Empire in India and the Indian Ocean [. . .]

Keats demonstrated the holiness of the imagination in [. . .] 'To Autumn', accepting the progression of the seasons with their anticlimax of twittering swallows and wailful choir of small gnats [. . .] Keats had a suddenly enveloping sense of the triviality of political concern and the possible triviality of all he had written.

From **Stuart M. Sperry, *Keats the Poet*,** Princeton, NJ: Princeton University Press, 1973, pp. 243–5, 258–60

Stuart M. Sperry is Professor Emeritus of English at Indiana University. His *Keats the Poet* (1973) remains a landmark volume in modern Keatsian criticism. It focuses upon Keats's preoccupation with the poetic imagination and the nature of poetry, and stresses the indeterminacy of meaning evident in his poetry. Here Sperry addresses the odes in terms of Keats's career-long preoccupation with the 'nature of the poetic process'. He then goes on to read the 'Ode to Psyche' as a metapoetical[2] work which encapsulates his wider arguments about the inconclusiveness, irony and indeterminacy of Keatsian poetry.

Ultimately the odes have most to tell us when they are taken not only together as a group but as an integral part of Keats's total achievement, as a mature reflection of the particular concerns with which he wrestled throughout his career. Very broadly they are best considered as a series of closely related and progressive meditations on the nature of the creative process, the logical outgrowth of his involvement with Negative Capability. Needless to say, the latter phrase must now be taken to encompass something more than the capability 'of being in uncertainties, Mysteries, doubts, without any irritable reaching after fact & reason' ([*Letters*,] l. 193); it now embraces a set of related premises and attitudes [. . .] his habitual distrust of 'Dogmas' and 'seeming sure points of Reasoning' (l. 282), his preference for 'sensation' and 'speculation' as opposed to thought, his ideal of the 'camelion Poet' (l. 387), and his commitment, above all, to creativity as an expression of an evolving state of consciousness [. . .] One way of approaching such a complex of related issues is through a consideration of the odes as the culmination of the ironic sense that, in its development, has been a major theme throughout this study [. . .] Within the movement of nineteenth-century European literature we call 'Romanticism' there develops a new conception of irony [. . .] Irony in its Romantic sense is related to Shelley's habitual inability to choose, his recognition, after a point, of the irrelevance of choosing, between skepticism and 'mild faith'. It is akin to the state of sensibility Byron, who at least by the time of *Don Juan* had come to some of the same conclusions, described as 'mobility'. In Keats's case we are apt to fall back on the poet's own phrase, Negative Capability, but if we had to use one of our own, we might describe it as a state of perpetual *indeterminacy*. [. . .]

Over and beyond the particular ironies of style and technique that complicate the texture of the ode's conclusion, there emerges, however, the further kind of

---

2   i.e. a poem about poetry.

irony I have attempted to define at the outset of this chapter. That irony, it may be recalled, can be thought to reside in a sense of perpetual *indeterminacy* [. . .] 'To Psyche' returns through a related set of metaphors to treat the burden of modern consciousness and the 'many doors' opening before the poet 'on all sides.' Yet the direction it suggests for further progress, for a continuation of the task of poetical investigation and discovery, is neither clear nor certain. Indeed the recognition the ode finally intimates is that for the poet of the present day there can be no escape from shadowiness and subjectivity, that the effort to push further into the region of the unknown leads only to the perception of further passages and implications, that it results in a sense of ultimate inconclusiveness that is ironic.

While the poetic garden exists for the cultivation of consciousness and the fruits of 'a working brain', the kind of 'thoughts' we find elaborated there are forever in a process of becoming, forever changing, forever 'new grown.' If the poem's earliest flowers, 'Blue, silver-white and budded Tyrian,' are richly, perhaps too richly sensuous, these are disconcertingly ephemeral and tenuous – 'buds, and bells, and stars without a name.' The progression from 'buds' to 'bells and stars', from nature to artifice, suggests comparison with those related kinds of development the logic or illogic of which was, as we have seen, at one time or another so preoccupying: the change from material substance to essence, from sensation to thought, from life to poetry. Such flowers may be of a superior breed, but at the same time they are too hybridised and delicate even to support the bare identity of a name. They bear witness to the inexhaustible inventiveness of the gardener, Fancy, who, while forever 'breeding flowers, will never breed the same.' The garden affords the promise of infinite profusion and fertility but little suggestion of order and coherence that 'growth' usually implies, those indications, as Keats had briefly pondered them in an earlier letter to Bailey, of 'a *complex Mind* – one that is imaginative and at the same time careful of its fruits' (l. 186). For any end to the process of continual proliferation is quite literally unthinkable. If the teeming garden of the ode's final stanza is Keats's metaphor for the modern poetic process, one can say the possibilities it offers for cultivation are either limitless or depressingly circumscribed, depending on the state of one's hopes and expectations as regards the functions of verse.

From **Christopher Ricks, Keats and Embarrassment**, Oxford: Oxford University Press, 1974, pp. 97, 118–19

Christopher Ricks (b. 1933) is Warren Professor of the Humanities at Boston University. His remarkable study *Keats and Embarrassment* builds upon John Bayley's passing references in 'Keats and Reality' to the importance of embarrassment in Keats's work, offering a sustained account of the importance of the concept to 'the shape of [the poet's] imagination'. If Keats's poetry is sometimes disconcerting, embarrassing, even distasteful, then it is consciously so, and exploits these qualities in a way which adds to the affective power of the verse.

It is therefore not an objection to Keats's erotic writing that it can cause a twinge of distaste, since the accommodation of distaste can be a humanly and artistically valuable thing, especially when it coexists with a frank delight [. . .]

> My river-lily bud! one human kiss!
> One sigh of real breath – one gentle squeeze,
> Warm as a dove's nest among summer trees,
> And warm with dew at ooze from living blood!
> (*Endymion*, IV, 664–7)

I think it not right of Mrs Allott[3] to annotate the last line with 'an elegant periphrasis for the Indian maid's perspiration' [. . .] 'Perspiration' itself has its faintly uneasy elegance; the line is certainly a periphrasis, but is it elegant? On the contrary, it seems to me to be (quite properly) at once forceful and odd. If I wished to be elegantly periphrastic in a lady's company, I do not think that I should speak of anything about her as 'at ooze'. 'Ooze' is one of Keats's strong necessary words precisely because it compacts sensation pleasant and unpleasant. The teasing quality of Keats's periphrasis or euphemism, unlike the decrepit genteelism 'perspiration', is its strange combination of an encompassing indirectness with a directness that is indeflectible; this is an effect not only of diction – 'ooze', or 'warm' gathering 'warm' up into itself from the previous line – but also of the advancing prepositions; 'with . . . at . . . from'. Dew from the blood is not merely elegant or romantic (the basis for the metaphor is the salt in both sweat and dew); and the liquidity of dew and blood is, as a matter of physical sensation, counterbalanced by the dry 'nest' of the previous lines, rather as the high 'summer trees' come down to earth with 'dew'. Mrs Allott dislikes 'one gentle squeeze': 'A phrase illustrating what Colvin calls ". . . the simpering familiar mood which Keats at this time had caught from or naturally shared with Leigh Hunt"'. I cannot see in what way the phrase simpers; it manifests a faint paradox, and a yearning that is simply ordinary, not at all grand, and necessarily an inducer of unease.

From Jerome J. McGann, 'Keats and the Historical Method in Literary Criticism', in *The Beauty of Inflections: Literary Investigations in Historical Method and Theory*, Oxford: Clarendon Press, 1979, pp. 51–62[4]

Whether it is being repudiated or celebrated, Jerome J. McGann's essay remains a defining moment in Keatsian studies over the last twenty-five years. It initiated a series of sociohistorical accounts of Keats which examined the politics of the poet's work. McGann (b. 1937) is the most notable exponent of New Historicist criticism active in Romantic studies. His most influential and controversial

---

3   Miriam Allott, the editor of the extensively annotated *The Poems of John Keats* (London: Longman 1970).

4   First published in *Modern Language Notes*, 94(5), 1979, pp. 988–1032.

book is *The Romantic Ideology* (1983), a volume which attacks concepts of Romantic poetry which see it as transcending time and circumstance. To McGann, Romantic poetry is 'marked by extreme forms of displacement [. . .] whereby the actual human issues with which the poetry is concerned are resituated and deflected in various ways'. His interpretations of individual poems show how the traces of this displacement are manifested, demonstrating (and condemning) Romantic acts of sociohistorical 'evasion'. There is nothing new in reading Keats in political terms; what differentiates McGann from such scholars as Woodring is his attention to what a poem attempts to silence rather than, as in previous expositions of explicitly political aspects of Romanticism, what it actually says. To this end, 'Keats and the Historical Method' traces the publication history of *Lamia, Isabella, The Eve of St. Agnes, and other Poems* (1820), which McGann sees as a 'politically reactionary book', inasmuch as it attempts to evade the turbulent political scene of contemporary England. For McGann, works of art never succeed in totally disguising their involvement in history, and his reading of 'To Autumn' attends to the traces of history within the poem, to the political turmoils which the poet cannot, in the final analysis, avoid.

'To Autumn' was first published in *Lamia, Isabella, The Eve of St. Agnes, and other Poems*, the so-called 1820 volume [. . .] [T]he character of this book – widely and, generally speaking, very favourably reviewed – is intimately related to the meaning of 'To Autumn'. To elucidate the nature of this relationship we have to see the book, and its original context, very clearly.

The publishers of the 1820 volume were Taylor and Hessey, who also published *Endymion* in 1818. It was *Endymion* (not the 1817 volume, published by Ollier) that had been the target of the hostile reviews of Keats, and the poet was not the only person who suffered in that literary whirl-wind. Consequently, when Keats approached Taylor and Hessey again, in the latter part of 1819, about publishing the new book of poems he had been planning, they were interested but wary. They had no intention of bringing out a volume that would call down again the sort of hostility and ridicule which greeted *Endymion*.

Keats's struggles with his publishers over the 1820 volume are well known. At first it seemed the poems would not be published at all, but a stroke of luck – the decision (later rescinded) by Drury Lane Theatre to stage *Otho the Great* – changed Taylor's mind about Keats's new poems. If the play were to be performed, a book of poems might just have a chance of succeeding, despite the apparently hostile predisposition of the periodical establishment.

The key fact in the pre-publication history of the 1820 poems is the insistence by Keats's publishers that the book not contain anything that would provoke the reviewers to attack (they were especially concerned about charges of indecency and political radicalism). Keats struggled with them over these issues, but he was eventually persuaded to follow their line. The two poems published in Leigh Hunt's *Indicator* did not find a place in the 1820 volume, and the reason for this is that Keats and his publishers did not want to give the reviewers any occasion for linking Keats's new work with the politically sensitive name of Leigh Hunt. For his part, Keats was also worried about the book's reception, but his concerns were slightly different. His principal interests were to show (a) the strength of his poetic technique, and (b) that he was not a 'sentimental' or 'weak-sided' poet.

The 1820 volume, in other words, was constructed with a profoundly self-conscious attitude toward that climate of literary opinion which prevailed at the time. It was designed as a book that would not provoke the critics in the ways that *Endymion* had done earlier. [. . .]

The special character of Keats's 1820 volume manifests itself very clearly if we compare it to some other books published around that time. Byron's *Don Juan* volumes – especially Cantos I–II (1819) and Cantos VI–VIII (1823) – were deliberately written to provoke discussion and conflict, and the same is true of all of Shelley's works published in 1819–20: *Rosalind and Helen*, for example, or *Prometheus Unbound*, or *Oedipus Tyrannus* (the last a work of such inflammatory character that its publication had to be suppressed). Keats's 1820 poems, however, were issued not to provoke but to allay conflict [. . .] The whole point of Keats's great and (politically) reactionary book was not to enlist poetry in the service of social and political causes – which is what Byron and Shelley were doing – but to dissolve social and political conflicts in the mediations of art and beauty.

All of these matters constitute an 'explicit' part of a poem like 'To Autumn' [. . .] Keats encountered his imaginative autumn when he fled his 'little coffin of a room at Shanklin' for the ease and tranquil beauty of Winchester, where he wrote 'To Autumn' in the middle of September. His letters from 12 August to the beginning of October – the period of his Winchester sojourn – recur to his feelings of pleasure and relief. Winchester, and his time there, are repeatedly seen as a respite from the tensions not only of his own personal affairs, but of the contemporary social scene at large. The massacre at St. Peter's Fields (Peterloo) took place four days after Keats arrived in Winchester, and he was glad to feel removed from the turmoil which followed in its wake. 'We shall have another fall of Seige-arms', he wrote to Woodhouse, but even as he followed the events of August and September in the *Examiner*'s radical reports, he found Winchester a wonderful refuge [. . .] Winchester has for Keats an old world, even a slightly archaic quality about it which he consistently refers to in his letters. 'The abbottine Winchester', he calls it in a letter to his brother. The city and its environs are magical in their ability to carry him away to a charmed world far removed from the quotidian press of his money affairs and the dangerous political tensions of his society [. . .]

Keats's autumn is the emblem of a condition freed from all weariness, fever, and fret, and his effort to describe such an autumn 'impersonally' is the sign of his own attempt to achieve such a condition himself [. . .] the poem's autumn is an historically specified fiction dialectically called into being by John Keats as an active response to, and alteration of, the events which marked the late summer and early fall of a particular year in a particular place. Keats's poem is an attempt to 'escape' the period which provides the poem with its context, and to offer its readers the same opportunity of refreshment. By this I do not mean to derogate from Keats's poem, but to suggest what is involved in so illusive a work as 'To Autumn', and in all the so-called escapist poetry which so many readers have found so characteristic of Romanticism. For the preoccupations of the Romantic style came to pass a fearful judgment upon the age which generated its various forms of artistic extremity. Already in Keats we begin to hear whispers of the motto of his great inheritor, D. G. Rossetti: '*Fiat ars, pereat mundus*'.[5] And why not? The viewless wings of poesy will carry one to the havens of intensity where pleasure and pain, life and even death, all seem to repossess some lost original value. This is the reflexive world of Romantic art, the very negation of the negation itself, wherein all events are far removed from the Terror, King Ludd, Peterloo, the Six Acts, and the recurrent financial crises of the Regency, and where humanity escapes the inconsequence of George III, the absurd Prince Regent, the contemptible Wellington. Here evil itself may appear heroic, Satanic, Byronic – not banal, like Castlereagh.[6]

From **Helen Vendler, The Odes of John Keats**, Cambridge, Mass. and London: The Belknap Press of Harvard University Press, 1983, pp. 93–5

Helen Vendler (b. 1933) is A. Kingsley Porter University Professor at Harvard University. *The Odes of John Keats* offers detailed close readings, in the New Critical manner, of the six 'great odes' ('Indolence', 'Psyche', 'Nightingale', 'Grecian Urn', 'Melancholy', 'To Autumn'), a 'group of works in which the English language finds an ultimate embodiment'. However, Vendler also maintains that the odes should be read together as a series of meditations on 'creativity [. . .] the relation of art to the order of nature, and the relation of art to human life and death'. The following extract is taken from her chapter on the 'Ode to a Nightingale'. Immediately before this passage, Vendler reads stanza 6 of the poem as marking 'the end of the aesthetic trance; just as Keats comes near to abandoning himself altogether to death or trance [. . .] he summons up the thought of himself "become a sod", and ends the embowered trance. At the moment of near acquiescence in dissolution, Keats chooses life, and thought'. She then turns to stanza 7.

The means Keats employs by which to put this choice of life to himself offers yet another instance of the trope of reiteration – this time a list of putative audiences for the bird's song. Though this list, it would seem, might be infinitely extended, since the bird has sung in all ages and to all audiences, there is in fact a structure to the list. We recall that in his decision to leave the world behind, Keats had banished human beings from his poem; at that point, consciousness had seemed the grimmest cause of sorrow. Now, at this later point, the obliteration of consciousness in death seems a worse evil. Death, even if postponed, cannot be avoided; in Keats's bitter view, each hungry generation tramples its forebears underfoot, and

---

5   'Let art prevail, though the world perish.'
6   The Tory politician Viscount Castlereagh (1769–1822), then Foreign Secretary.

Tom's fate was only, however premature, the common one. In the nightingale's song there are only notes, there is no tale of death; since the nightingale, for the purposes of the ode, *is* its song, it is exempt from death, or the consciousness of death, and goes on singing unconscious of the obliterations of time. In an attempt to repudiate the terrible vision of the nightingale eternally singing above the carnage of generations, Keats rejects his earlier flight from human presence, and reintroduces human beings to his poem, imagining himself, in his function as the nightingale's present audience, linked to a brotherhood of other listeners in other ages. At first Keats sees in the nightingale's song a democratic diffusion: the song is audible to all alike, whether emperor or rustic (culture, as Arnold said, seeks to do away with classes). Next the audience becomes any soul which, like Keats's own, stands in need of consolation, and the song, for a moment given purpose in a pathetic fallacy of providential intent, is said to find a path into the hearts of those who, like Ruth, are sick for home, standing in tears in alien stubble-fields. I recapitulate: in the first of these reiterations of audience, art is for everyone; in the second, art, it is promised will find a path into the being of those whose woe needs solace. Or – a chilling hypothesis following on these two humane ones – art is for no one. Keats takes his list of auditors to its beautiful and empty conclusion: art, in the last reiteration of audience, richly fills its own land, a land with nobody in it. The last listeners to the bird are those unpeopled magic casements, in their land forlorn of all human inhabitants, opening onto a perilous sea harboring no vessel.

If we now stop to reflect on the large formal shape of *Ode to a Nightingale*, we can say that it is one of entrance and exit, of entrancement and disillusion, one long, unbroken trajectory, beginning with a repudiation of both the human world and of Bacchic intoxication, continuing with a descent into a disembodied but intense listening in a dark bower, and ending in a reentry into the world as soon as consciousness reawakens and trance is broken, a breach initiated by the memory of earlier literary invocations of Death and symbolized by the departing flight of the nightingale. The Fancy, so constructively mentally active as the gardener in *Psyche*, is here accused as the deceitfully inhuman agent of a Spenserian faery-delusion, its charming open of casements alliterating with its cheating.

Keats attempts in the *Ode to a Nightingale* a view of the aesthetic act more complex than the one he had postulated in *Psyche*, where the act had been considered only from the point of view of the constructing artist. Now he also includes the audience and the artifact, in his trio of bird, listener and song. Art in this ode, has no conceptual or moral content. Ravishingly beautiful and entirely natural, it is a stream of invention, pure sound, in no way mimetic, on which we as listeners project our own feelings of ecstasy or grief. Art utters itself unconscious of any audience, pouring its soul abroad in pure self-expressiveness. Though its audience may be consoled by it, art is indifferent to that audience, singing as raptly to a clown as to an emperor, as beautifully to empty rooms and lands forlorn as to Ruth in tears. It is available to us only in a moment of sensual trance in which we suspend intelligence and consciousness of our suffering human lot. Its immortality ranks it among Keats's divinities, but unlike Psyche it needs no cult, being wholly self-sufficient. Between its solipsistic immortal world and our social and mortal one there can be no commerce except by the viewless wings of sensation in Poesy-Fancy, which cannot bear us long aloft.

From **Marjorie Levinson, *Keats's Life of Allegory: The Origins of a Style*,** Oxford: Basil Blackwell, 1988, pp. 5–15

In *Keats's Life of Allegory: The Origins of a Style*, the American critic Marjorie Levinson (b. 1951, Professor of English at the University of Michigan) offers a provocative New Historicist account of Keats as a 'marginally middle-class, professionally unequipped, nineteenth-century male adolescent'. Levinson's account of Keats's class status, is, it might be said, not much different from that offered by J. G. Lockhart in 1818 and, like Lockhart, Levinson sees Keats's lowly social rank as a crucial determinant on his poetry. The *petit bourgeois* youth aspires to membership of a social class to which he can never properly belong. Similarly, as a poet Keats is drawn to high culture and simultaneously resentful of his exclusion from that culture. Excluded from the canonical tradition, Keats writes a literary pastiche, or 'parody', and the poet's social resentments are figured in his 'subversive' and 'anti-literary' style.

The deep contemporary insult of Keats's poetry, and its deep appeal (and long opacity) for the modern reader, is its idealized enactment of the conflicts and solutions which defined the middle class at a certain point in its development and which still to some extent still obtain. We remember that Keats's style can delineate that station so powerfully because of his marginal, longing relation to the legitimate bourgeoisie (and its literary exemplars) of his day. In emulating the condition of the accomplished middle class (the phrase is itself an oxymoron), Keats isolated the constitutive contradictions of that class. The final fetish in Keats's poetry is precisely that stationing tension.

By the stylistic contradictions of his verse, Keats produces a writing which is aggressively *literary* and therefore not 'just literature' but, in effect, *anti*-Literature: a parody. We will see that Keats's most successful poems are those most elaborately estranged from their own materials and procedures and thus from both a readerly and a writerly subjectivity. The poetic I describe, following the lead of Keats's contemporaries, is the opposite of 'unmisgiving'. The triumph of the great poetry is not its capacious, virile, humane authenticity, but its subversion of those authoritarian values, effects which it could not in any case, and for the strongest reasons, realize. [. . .]

Keats's poetry was at once a tactical activity, or an escape route from an actual life, and a final construction: the concrete imaginary to the apparitional actual. What was, initially, a substitute *for* a grim life became for Keats a substitute life: a real life of substitute things – simulacra – which, thought they do not nourish, neither do they waste [. . .] It is crucial to see, as Bayley saw, that the deep desire in Keats's poetry is not for aesthetic things *per se* (that is, Byron's 'finery'), but for the social code inscribed in them, a code which was, to Keats, a human

transformational grammar. Indeed, all Keats's meditations on art a'
ically, plasticity), should be related to his abiding desire, to live. Th
of Keats's poetry is not its display of its cultural fetishes but its p
the system felt to organize those talismanic properties. Keats ⌣
the urns, Psyches, nightingales, Spenserianism, Miltonisms, Claudes, a.
he wanted; he was not, however, permitted possession of the social gra⌣.
inscribed in that aesthetic array, and this was just what Keats was after [. . .]

Chatterton, the poet with whom Keats felt the strongest affinities, developed a
most economical solution to this problem [in] his perfect reproduction of 'the
medieval' [. . .] Keats sidestepped Chatterton's final solution. By the self-
signifying *imperfection* of his canonical reproductions (a parodic return upon his
own derivativeness), Keats drew upon the licensing primacy of the code even as
his *representation* of that total form changed the nature of its authority. The
pronounced badness of Keats's writing figures the mythic goodness of the canon
and, by figuring, at once exalts and delimits it. Thus did Keats plot for himself a
scene of writing. By the double unnaturalness of his style, Keats projects the
authority of an *anti*-nature, stable by virtue of its continuous self-revolutionizing
and secured by its contradictions [. . .] [L]et me offer as a critical instance a
reading of 'Chapman's Homer'.

[Levinson quotes 'On First Looking into Chapman's Homer'.]

The contemporary reader might have observed [. . .] some internal contradic-
tions: not only is Homer the Golden Age, but not to 'have' Greek and not to have
encountered Homer by the age of twenty-three is to make one's claims to any
portion of the literary empire suspect [. . .] Keats effectively assumes the role of
the literary adventurer (with the commercial nuance of that word) as opposed to
the mythic explorer: Odysseus, Cortes, Balboa. More concretely, he advertises his
corrupt access to the literary system and to those social institutions which inscribe
that system systematically in the hearts and minds of young men. To read Homer
in translation and after having read Spenser, Coleridge, Cary, and whoever else is
included in Keats's travelogue is to *read* Homer badly (in a heterodox and alien-
ated way), and to subvert the system which installs Homer in a particular and
originary place. Moreover, to 'look into' Chapman's Homer is to confess – in this
case, *profess* – one's fetishistic relation to the great Original. Keats does not read
even the translation. To 'look into' a book is to absorb it idiosyncratically at best,
which is to say, with casual or conscious opportunism [. . .] To 'breathe' a text is
to take it in, take from it and let it out, somewhat the worse for wear. It is, more
critically, to miscategorize the object and in such a way as to proclaim one's
intimacy with it. Both the claim and the title of Keats's sonnet are, in a word,
vulgar [. . .]

Rather than imitate Chapman, Keats reproduces Chapman's necessarily parodic
(that is, Elizabethan) inscription of Homer. The queerness of Chapman's 'mighty
line, loud-and-bold' version is rewritten in Keats's own parodic Elizabethan*ism*,
and through the queerness of the Cortes/Balboa image. It is the self-reflexive,
fetishistic inscription of the canon – the display of bad access and misappro-
priation – that emancipates Keats's words. Keats's sonnet breaks free of Homer
and Chapman by mis-giving both [. . .]

The contained badness of 'Chapman's Homer' constitutes its goodness, which is to say its rhetorical force. The paradox, hinges, naturally, on the word 'contains'. When Keats is great, it is because he signifies his alienation from his *materia poetica*, a fact that modern criticism and textual studies have suppressed. This alienation – inevitable given Keats's education, class, and opportunities – was highly expedient [. . .] Keats's poetry, inspired by translations, engravings, reproductions, schoolroom mythologies [. . .] delivers itself through these double and triple reproductions as the 'true, the blushful Hippocrene'. That phrase describes, ironically, *precisely* a substitute truth. Again, Byron understood these things; 'You know my opinion of that *second-hand* school of poetry'.

From **Anne K. Mellor, Romanticism and Gender,** London and New York: Routledge, 1993, pp. 170–6

Anne Kostelanetz Mellor (b. 1941), Professor of English at the University of California, Los Angeles, has produced a series of influential books on issues of gender within Romantic poetry and on Romantic period poetry by women. *Romanticism and Gender* offers an account of 'Keats's ambivalent attitude toward gender'. Whilst some contemporary Keatsians have argued that the poet demonstrates misogynist tendencies, Mellor's approach, though it does not absolve Keats entirely from the charge of masculinism, is more positive. Here she sees the poet as an 'ideological cross-dresser' who was able to embrace some aspects of what she calls 'feminine Romanticism'.

The two Romanticisms that I have been distinguishing as masculine and feminine should not be identified with biological sexuality. Some romantic writers were 'ideological cross-dressers'. It was possible for a male romantic writer to embrace all or parts of feminine Romanticism, just as it was possible for a female to embrace aspects of masculine Romanticism. But these are complicated crossovers and need to be described with care. There are some senses in which a male could not enter a feminine ideology, not could a female fully identify with a masculine ideology. To adopt our current vocabulary, certain Romantic writers might have been ideological transvestites, but they were not transsexuals.

[The] male Romantic poet who has most often been characterised as 'effeminate' [is] John Keats [. . .] Keats subtly complicates the issue of gender and ideology, as others have remarked, either by occupying the position of the woman in life or in discourse, or by blurring the distinction between genders, between masculinity and femininity. Let us focus first on a few aspects of Keats' life and death, which has been so fully described by Walter Jackson Bate and others. Orphaned at the age of fourteen, the second son in a family of four children, Keats immediately took on the role of mother to his younger siblings. He corresponded faithfully with his sister Fanny, comforting and advising her. When his brother Tom fell sick of the family disease, tuberculosis, he became Tom's nurse, tending Tom until his death. Keats' first choice of profession, that of apothecary or, in modern terminology, a combination of pharmacist and lower-level general practitioner, may also be significant. While the male medical profession has long sought to cure disease, nursing the sick and the dying has traditionally been an occupation associated with women, and Keats' desire – to help others and to bear their pain and suffering – might be construed as feminine [. . .]

Keats' poetic theory is self-consciously positioned within the realm of the feminine gender. Keats' famous definitions of the 'poetical character' and of 'negative capability', as Barbara Gelpi and Adrienne Rich recently reminded us, presuppose an anti-masculine conception of identity. If we take the example of William and Dorothy Wordsworth as representative of a wider construction of gendered subjectivity in the nineteenth century, the masculine self was thought to have a strong sense of its own ego boundaries, the feminine self was not. In his descriptions both of his own sense of identity and of the appropriate consciousness of the true poet, Keats reversed these gender stereotypes:

> As to the poetical Character itself (I mean that sort of which, if I am any thing, I am a Member – that sort distinguished from the Wordsworthian or egotistical sublime, which is a thing per se and stands alone) it is not itself – it has no self – it is everything and nothing – it has no character – it enjoys light and shade; it lives in gusto, be it foul or fair, high or low, rich or poor, mean or elevated. It has as much delight in conceiving an Iago as an Imogen. What shocks the virtuous Philosopher delights the camelion poet.

Keats here resists a masculinist construction of the self as bounded, unitary, complete, and instrumental – the consciousness of self-as-agent which he (perhaps unfairly) assigned to the William Wordsworth of *The Prelude*.

In its place Keats promotes a very different concept of self, one similar to Dorothy Wordsworth's floating island self. Like the contemporary Self-in-Relation school of psychology or the French psychoanalytical school inspired by Lacan and Kristeva, Keats images the self as unbounded, fluid, decentred, inconsistent – not 'a' self at all. Keats – like the Poet he describes – 'has no Identity – he is continually in form[ing] and filling some other Body'.

A self that continually overflows itself, that melts into the Other, that *becomes* the Other, is conventionally associated with the female, and especially with the pregnant woman who experiences herself and her child as one. Such a self erases the differences between one and two, and by denying the validity of logical Aristotelian distinctions, has seemed to many rationalists to embrace irrationality and confusion. Keats advocates such 'confusion' (and appropriates such a self for the male sex) when he insists that the quality which forms 'a man of achievement especially in literature and which Shakespeare possessed so enormously' is '*Negative Capability*; that is, when man is capable of being in uncertainties, mysteries, doubts, without any irritable reaching after fact and reason.' Above all, Keats defines the true poet as empathic, a quality everywhere identified with femininity in the eighteenth century. The literature of sensibility, even as it developed the image of 'the man of feeling', appropriated to that man qualities traditionally defined as feminine: tears, heightened emotions, excessive passion or love, extreme irrationality, wasting diseases, suicidal impulses and madness [. . .]

Keats's ambivalent attitude toward gender infiltrates his poetry as well as his letters. On the one hand, Keats repeatedly assigns to the feminine gender the possession of beauty, power and knowledge, everything that the male poet yearns to possess. On the other hand, he anxiously tries to establish a space between the male poet and the female object of desire, a space where the poet can preserve a recognizable masculinity. In the 'Ode to Psyche', Keats explicitly engenders his own imagination, his soul or psyche, as feminine, following a classical convention that represent both the soul and the muse as female. At the same time, he defines his possession of that imagination as a kind of rape: his 'tuneless numbers' are 'by sweet enforcement' wrung [. . .] and his inspired chorus song will 'make a moan/ upon the midnight hours.' The poems Keats will write as a result of this ravishment of, or by, his own imagination – the poem calculatedly obscures who is ravishing whom – are figured as 'the wreath'd trellis of a working brain'. The visual images of the spatially radiating, interwoven trellis resembles that of the spiderweb, the trope of feminine production. And the poem ends with an affirmation of female sexuality, of a vaginal 'casement ope at night/To let the warm Love in!'. In this ode, Keats triumphantly and climactically occupies the positions of both the male and the female lover: he has made love to, penetrated, received, and possessed his own Fancy, his own 'shadowy thought'.

From **Daniel P. Watkins, 'History, Self, and Gender in "Ode to Psyche"'**, in Nicholas Roe (ed.), *Keats and History*, Cambridge: Cambridge University Press, 1995, pp. 96–103

Daniel P. Watkins (b. 1952, Professor of English at Duquesne University in Pittsburgh, Pennsylvania) is the author of *Keats's Poetry and the Politics of the Imagination* (1987), a volume which subjects Keats's work to Marxist critique. This later essay, 'History, Self and Gender in "Ode to Psyche"', fuses Marxian analysis with gender criticism and is a representative, if perhaps a particularly intense, example of that body of Keatsian scholarship which holds that the poet's work clearly demonstrates misogynist tendencies. The extract begins by examining the vale of soul-making passage of the journal-letter to George and Georgiana Keats written on 21 April 1819 (pp. 19–20). Watkins interprets Keats's concern with personal identity in political terms: a preoccupation with the individual psyche is 'perhaps the key ideological feature of the emergent bourgeois self in the eighteenth and early nineteenth centuries', and the 'Ode to Psyche' is part of this bourgeois project. He develops this position into a gendered account of the poem; though a surface reading of Keats's text implies 'that the poet is subordinate to the female figure', because Psyche is voiceless, 'passive, silent, ideal', the poem is actually a misogynist display of the 'determining authority' of the masculine poet. The final section deepens this anxiety about Keats's 'masculinist poetic strategy', arguing that Psyche's 'helplessness' demonstrates an underlying 'need for violence against feminine existence'.

At the centre of Keats's letter are two major concerns that suggest the intellectual position at which, following Hazlitt, he had begun to arrive in 1819: *identity* and *circumstance*. In his three-part formulation – '*Intelligence* – the *human heart* . . . and the *World*' – he not only asserts the determining role that material circumstance plays in human life ('man was formed by circumstances') but, more importantly, seeks to explain why the authority of circumstance is proper and valuable in human life: 'Do you not see how necessary a World of Pains and troubles is to school an Intelligence and make it a soul?' He knowingly distances himself from a Christian explanation that would see human life as irredeemably fallen, and capable of salvation only by professions of faith and prayers calling for the aid of God. Unlike Christianity, he says, the 'system of Salvation' that he imagines 'does not affront our reason and humanity' because it finds a way to exist meaningfully within circumstances that, in Keats's view, provide the necessary bases of human knowledge and capacity.

In this explanation of human salvation, Keats focuses on the question of identity, to show that identity is not pre-given but rather emerges from situations of conflict and difficulty. His account approaches what would now be called a materialist explanation of identity, and goes a long way toward rewriting certain assumptions about identity that had governed the vision of some poets only a generation earlier, especially Wordsworth. But the explanation that he offers is itself implicated in the very circumstances that it is meant to address, so that its materialist intention is only partly realised. That is, the explanation, while rejecting Wordsworth's view of the defining authority of the individual imagination, points toward a view of identity as the happy influence of painful circumstantial pressures in forming a spiritual material essence, and thus it is, finally, but a modified version of the Christian idealism to which Keats objects [. . .]

[The] final stanza of *Psyche* allows us to see clearly what goes largely unremarked in the letter, namely the active *construction* of identity. The poem traces, in imaginative form, the world of circumstance – with its 'enforcement' (2), surprise (8), spiritual void (36–41), and 'pleasant pain' (52) – and, at the same time, it describes the process of producing identity out of circumstance. Moreover, that identity is emphatically shown to be individual, rather than communal, with its desires, integrity, love, and hope housed entirely within the mind. It is as though circumstance is a necessary starting point for the poet, but only that; circumstance is eventually abandoned in favour of the mind's imaginings that resolve circumstantial tensions within the authority of self-identity.

This obsessive concern with individual identity and possibility is, perhaps, the key ideological feature of the emergent bourgeois self in the eighteenth and early nineteenth centuries. A visibly changeful world generates tremendous liberating energies, which, though they transform society, leave people without full control of, or access to, that world. What people are left with, instead, is their own privatised self-identity, which they mistake for freedom. Within the frame of such transformation, human desire and hope are real, but mistaken, claiming freedom under the very conditions of its denial. In Psyche, the ideological movement of the poem is very much in this direction; the poem's expression is full of goodness, while its political unconscious carries within it the very contradictions, inconsistencies, and injustices that the poet believes have been overcome [. . .]

Psyche enters Keats's poem [. . .] as the symbolic projection of the masculine poet's dreaming ego [. . .] While the poem purports to be about Psyche, offering a laudatory description of her, it actually focuses on the male poet's imagination. Throughout, Psyche is passive, silent, ideal, while the poet is active, vocal, and imaginatively industrious. The apparent idealisation of Psyche becomes in fact the idealisation of the poet himself.

This strategy discloses the process of masculine subject construction under the pressure of an emergent bourgeois world; it is a process that energises the autonomous self through the paradoxical denial of self – and it is a process that can exist only within particular (bourgeois) frames of reference. The poem gives the impression throughout that the poet is subordinate to the female figure he would worship: he is apologetic (1–4), proceeds almost as if against his will (1–4), and seems committed, in the face of all obstacles (36–7, 40–1), to praising Psyche as 'loveliest' of the Olympians. Each gesture and manoeuvre, however, calls attention to the poet himself, often in quite explicit ways. In the initial diffident expressions, for instance, it is clear that the poet, for all his timidity, is sufficient bold to address the goddess – 'And pardon that thy secrets should be sung/Even into thine own soft-conched ear' (3–4) – even as he apologises for doing so. Read literally, these lines state the poet's relation to his subject, establishing him as a benevolent, though nonetheless controlling, presence, who alone gives voice to (and shapes the value of) her 'secrets' – which of course, insofar as he controls them, are not her secrets at all, but signs of his determining authority [. . .]

Gender in the poem has another, more disturbing aspect as well. The masculine identity articulated on the surface structure arises from a much deeper pornographic, and Sadeian, logic, which itself emerged with capitalism and carries with it a need for violence against feminine existence. Admittedly, this is a strong expression of one kind of operation in the poem, but it nevertheless describes an important dimension of the relation between the poet and Psyche, and gender and society. For at the heart of Sadeian logic is not physical violence, but rather the absolute domination of femininity by masculinity, and the definition of pleasure *as domination* [. . .] The poet's vision is not a liberating myth, an alternative to the poet's original recognition of Psyche as lovely though 'faded', for her situation does not change significantly from the classical past to the Keatsian present. Rather, she has in effect been shifted from one sort of helplessness to another; in the modern world she is made to serve the poet's desire for transcendence, even as the poet claims to be liberating her from a past that never properly acknowledged her beauty.

It is important to call the logic of this masculinist poetic strategy *Sadeian*, because the word suggests the severity of the poem's portrayal of gender and helps to link various social and cultural energies of the age within a single historical and cultural framework. The logic of the poem is not entirely under the control of Keats the poet; it is, rather, the logic of an age, and Keats's Romantic vision is constrained by that logic even as he invests it with his own particular shaping desire. While he attempts to break free of a modern age that no longer knows 'happy pieties', 'antique vows', and the 'fond believing lyre', and to offer a vision of hope and possibility, he remains situated within the historical moment of an emergent industrial capitalism, his imagination implicated in the broad and deep controls that it would transcend. Those controls are both bourgeois and patriarchal.

From **Nicholas Roe,** *John Keats and the Culture of Dissent*, Oxford: Oxford University Press, 1997, pp. 197–201

The work of Nicholas Roe, Professor of English at the University of St Andrews, attends to the political and historical significance of Romantic poetry. *John Keats and the Culture of Dissent* views Keats's poems as socially revealing documents, but also attends to the poet's artistry, fusing close readings with nuanced political enquiry. Roe is adept in teasing out the sociohistorical resonance of poetry which is not explicitly political in its content. Whereas McGann dismisses Keats's 1820 volume as a 'reactionary' and 'escapist' book, Roe sees it as deeply engaged with liberal politics. For him, even the 'Ode to a Nightingale', which is rarely read as a politically suggestive poem, subtly engages with sociopolitical issues. Roe argues that it draws on two existing politically charged strands within Keats's work, his outlaw lyrics[7] and his 'pharmacopolitical'[8] poetry: 'To a Nightingale' 'imaginatively assimilat[es] Keats's medical training with the political interests of his outlaw lyrics.' Roe begins by citing a passage from 'Tintern Abbey' which deals with London and which 'contributes to Wordsworth's recognition of the city as a life-consuming environment now fully associated with a particular psychological state'.

> how oft,
> In darkness, and amid the many shapes
> Of joyless day-light; when the fretful stir
> Unprofitable, and the fever of the world,
> Have hung upon the beatings of my heart,
> Howe oft, in spirit, have I turned to thee,
> O sylvan Wye! (51–7)

The city's random and turbulent activity is a debilitating burden, eased only when displaced by the heart's recourse to the memory of scenes formerly known and loved. As is well known, Keats echoed these lines from 'Tintern Abbey' in 'Ode to a Nightingale', evoking a comparable state of oppression in which he turns to the consolation of the nightingale's song:

---

7   In 1818, Keats had written 'Robin Hood. To a Friend' for J. H. Reynolds. Roe sees the poem's commemoration of a 'greenwoods' outlaw as a celebration of 'the origin and continuity of radical opposition'.
8   Roe argues that 'the politics of medicine in the revolutionary period after 1789' was an important influence on Keats's poetry.

> That I might drink, and leave the world unseen,
>   And with thee fade away into the forest dim:
>
> Fade far away, dissolve, and quite forget
>   What thou among the leaves hast never known,
> The weariness, the fever, and the fret
>   Here, where men sit and hear each other groan;
> Where palsy shakes a few, sad, last gray hairs,
>   Where youth grows pale, and spectre-thin, and dies;
>   Where but to think is to be full of sorrow
>   And leaden-eyed despairs . . . (19–28)

Often cited as Keats's memory of his brother Tom's death from tuberculosis, these lines undoubtedly also respond to the powerful sense of physical distemper conveyed in 'Tintern Abbey', where the city's 'fretful stir' and 'the fever of the world' had combined to 'h[a]ng upon the beatings of [the] heart'. And in this respect 'Ode to a Nightingale' shows Keats's distinctive transformation of the Wordsworthian and Miltonic figures of city and country [. . .]

Whereas Wordsworth and Coleridge had developed the 'populous city' into the symbolic environment of alienated spiritual and mental life, 'Ode to a Nightingale' dwells upon the realities of bodily contamination arising from the cramped and unhealthy conditions of city life, as a burden affecting all humankind:

> The weariness, the fever, and the fret
>   Here, where men sit and hear each other groan;
> Where palsy shakes a few, sad, last gray hairs,
>   Where youth grows pale, and spectre-thin, and dies . . . (23–6)

Here Keats modifies the symbolic associations of the city by drawing language and imagery from his medical training, presenting 'the fever, and the fret' as typical of the wasting of all humankind. At the same time, the poem moves beyond the personal circumstances of illness and bereavement: 'men' are both old and young, some 'shaken' by palsy, other 'growing' pale. The eye of the physician discriminates one affliction coming to its last 'acute' stage, and another of lingering 'chronic' decline. In response to these effigies of pain, the imagination of the poet creates a sylvan retreat or hospice, 'some melodious plot/Of beechen green . . . far away . . . among the leaves' (8–9, 21–2), where dying seems to hold no mortal agony. [. . .] The magic greenwood which [. . .] had represented pastoral and political liberties in Keats's and Reynolds's Robin Hood poems, is transformed in 'Ode to a Nightingale' into the verdurous dwelling of reverie, the 'embalmed darkness' of vision. So internalised, the woodland home of freedom and justice is recognised as the resort of self-forgetfulness or 'negative capability' – where the poet may become outlaw to his own identity and 'half in love with easeful Death' (52). The desire to pass beyond earthly existence,

To cease upon the midnight with no pain,
    While thou art pouring forth thy soul abroad
        In such an ecstasy! (56–8)

– would of course transgress the melancholy laws of mortality, and it is this realization which revives that aspect of the poet's consciousness still 'half in love' with selfhood:

Still wouldst thou sing, and I have ears in vain –
    To thy high requiem become a sod. (59–60)

The recognition leads in stanza vii of the ode to a curious echo of half-memory of the earlier lament for Robin Hood:

No! those days are gone away,
And their hours are old and gray,
And their minutes buried all,
Under the down-trodden pall
Of the leaves of many years . . . ('Robin Hood', 1–5)

Much as the outlaw life of Sherwood had served to highlight the harsh realities of the present, the 'immortal Bird' – which sings beyond the boundaries of human life – brings an intimation of the unescapable facts of existence: 'hungry generations' down-trodden by the passage of many years; the divisions of life between 'emperor' and 'clown', ruler and subject; and the misery of another, unwilling outlaw, the exiled Ruth 'in tears amid the alien corn'. At the close of 'Ode to a Nightingale', vision unravels to reveal a world forlorn as that in 'Robin Hood'; like that earlier lyric, Keats's ode bids farewell to romance as a 'deceiving elf':

Adieu! adieu! thy plaintive anthem fades
    Past the near meadows, over the still stream,
        Up the hill-side; and now 'tis buried deep
            In the next valley-glades . . . (75–8)

Both Sherwood Forest, where Robin Hood lies in 'his turfed grave', and the 'valley-glades' of the Ode are sites of romantic internment; they remind of 'music fled' and the confused possibility (vision or dream?) of an ideal existence that has already passed 'over the still stream', or bourne, into the otherwhere beyond.

'Ode to a Nightingale' is, in effect, a subtle elaboration of the greenwood poems written by Keats and Reynolds early in 1818. Imaginatively assimilating Keats's medical training with the political interests of his outlaw lyrics, the 'Ode' is definitely the creation of a 'pharmacopolitical poet' – but it is also, of course much more [. . .] The 'Ode' intensifies those circumstantial concerns to reveal how tragedy dwells inside romance: to aspire to a perfected existence – through the use of medicine, by means of political revolution, or in achieving unity with 'divine immortal essence' – is to know oneself already forlorn. As fevered creatures existing amid 'uncertainties, Mysteries, doubts' (*Letters*, i. 193), the only course open for humankind may be to live in and through negative capability, aware that our welfare depends upon the interdependence – or 'interassimulation' (*Letters*, ii. 208) – of self, humankind, and the natural world.

From **Susan J. Wolfson, 'Keats and Gender Criticism'**, in Robert M. Ryan and Ronald A. Sharp (eds), *The Persistence of Poetry: Bicentennial Essays on Keats*, Amherst, Mass.: University of Massachusetts Press, 1998, pp. 88–97

Susan Wolfson (b. 1948), Professor of English at Princeton University, is the author of a series of books on Romantic poetry, including *The Questioning Presence: Wordsworth, Keats, and the Interrogative Mode in Romantic Poetry* (1988). Wolfson's work on Keats, in such essays as 'Feminizing Keats' (1990), has often focused upon questions of gender and cultural reception, and these issues inform 'Keats and Gender Criticism', which offers a useful historical account of gendered readings of Keats. Wolfson's survey addresses both the enthusiastic partisans of a feminised Keats and those who condemn him as a 'patrilinear' or misogynist figure. For Wolfson, Keats's position is more complex and ambiguous than these polarised views would suggest: the poet's 'overall syntax of gender is more zig-zag than linear, and the total story more indeterminate than definitive'.

Both as a writer and as a subject of writing, Keats vexes the question of gender, especially when it is negotiated at unstable boundaries between masculine and feminine. This essay concerns the relation between Keats as the agent of thinking (not always critically) about gender, and the situation of Keats in gender criticism [. . .]

From his debut, Keats attracted, even courted, judgments in the language of gender. To review the outline. The favourable reviews of his work, mostly from friends, gave an inadvertently feminizing emphasis to his stylistic beauties, and/or celebrated a budding masculine power of intellect, evident, say, in the sonnet on Chapman's Homer and the scrappy assault upon Augustan poetics in *Sleep and Poetry*. More divided notices spoke of promising talent, but also of unripe judgment. The hostile judgments, motivated by political and class antipathy, mobilized Keats's youth to ridicule unmanly, adolescent affectation. This last Keats – inept, puerile, pretentious – was the infamous abject hero of the anti-Cockney reviews of the 1817 *Poems* and *Endymion*. The obituaries – unwittingly, Shelley's *Adonais* and, wittily, Byron's soon-to-be-famous stanza in *Don Juan* ('John Keats . . . killed off by one critique'; 'Poor fellow! . . . snuffed out by an Article') – whipped this abjection alternatively into pathos or farce, with the result that by midcentury, Keats was culturally installed as a sensitive and vulnerable boy, a creature of too-feminine delicacy.

The first biographers (Leigh Hunt, Richard Monckton Milnes, Sidney Colvin) tried to resurrect Keats-the-man, but seemed to protest too much, belaboring his boyhood pugnacity, his terrier courage, his drubbing a butcher, and the manliness (sometimes called precocious) of the sonnet on Chapman's Homer and the Preface to *Endymion*. Or, on another tack, they advocated more liberal borders of the 'manly', to include gentleness, tenderness, and sensitivity. Oscar Wilde complicated things further when his rhapsodic romance of martyred Keats amplified the homoerotic aura of the Keats circle. The question of gender was still demanding spin control from twentieth-century editors and biographers, including Amy Lowell, Douglas Bush, Walter Jackson Bate, Lionel Trilling, and Aileen Ward. Jack Stillinger's (in)famous essay, 'The Hoodwinking of Madeline', then produced a seismic shift in the trials of Keats's manliness, not just entering the defense, but prosecuting the alliance of Porphyro (at least) with aggressive, even Satanic seducers and summoning the salaciously male-tuned passages of 'The Eve of St. Agnes' that Keats's publishers demanded he revise, to his annoyance ('He says he does not want ladies to read his poetry; that he writes for men,' reported Richard Woodhouse, the publishers' advisor). Meanwhile, Christopher Ricks was reviewing the nineteenth-century diagnosis of 'effeminate' Keats – that regressive sensuous imagination, those habitual swoons – with an eye to revaluation. Ricks wanted to praise a poet unembarrassed by such embarrassments, and so able to indulge audacious expression of them: this was a decidedly mature, if not conventionally manly, performance.

Then, in the 1970s, Keats was embraced by feminist criticism. His limited education, economic insecurity, and class status – the 'Cockney' targets of Regency disdain – seemed akin to the marginality of women, while his poetics of 'Negative Capability' and 'no self'/'no identity' were recruited for a 'feminist' poetics and ego ideal, an enabling alternative to the strong ego boundaries and egotism taken to characterize 'masculine' practices. Within a decade, however, this adoption was contested by another turn of reading that restored Keats to the patriarchy, not only marking his commitment to male heroes, 'brother Poets' ('To George Felton Matthew'), and to fame in the patrilinear canon, also pointing to the sexism, sometimes misogyny, informing his figures of women and the feminine.

These various descriptions, a virtual polymorphism[9] of Keats's gender, are the epiphenomenon[10] of the provocation, and problem, of its referent. More than any other male poet of the Romantic era, Keats writes from a confluence of poetic genius, penetrating critical insight, and adolescent uncertainty. In this entanglement of adolescence and genius, and in its nexus of intellectual, psychological, and social pressures, Keats shows divided, often contradictory investments – by turns, speculative, anxious, risky – in a variety of masculinities and their proximity to a 'feminine' differential. About women, he is (also by turns) adoring, sympathetic, defensive, and hostile, especially about their status as readers, writers, and arbiters of his personal and professional self-definition. His overall syntax of gender is more zigzag than linear, and the total story more indeterminate than definitive. [. . .]

9   The occurrence of something in many forms.
10 Secondary manifestation, by-product.

How has Keats managed to inform and fill so many different, even contradictory perspectives? Although I've just used his language for his self-effacing 'camelion' poetics, this is a misleading key insofar as it suggest a deliberate strategy, aesthetically controlled. A more accurate measure would be Keats's sense, in the same letter, of the correlation of his aesthetic preference with, and emergence from, a related existential sensation:

> When I am in a room with People, if I ever am free from speculating on creations of my own brain, then not myself goes home to myself: but the identity of everyone in the room begins so to press upon me that, I am, in a very little time, an[ni]hilated . . . among Men; . . . I know not whether I make myself wholly understood.

At the end of his twenty-third year, Keats recognizes his social identity as still unsettled, still not fully legible, still susceptible of varying impressions and self-readings in the contradictory pressures of self-definition [. . .] Keats's amused, aggrieved confessions mark an intelligently ironic, nervously alert, ideological irresolution, generated by a provisional, unauthorized sensation of distance, dislocation, and sometimes critical alienation from the cultural stage of manhood and the sorts of performances it requires. The pleomorphic[11] array of gender forms and the contradictions between them are part of Keats's historical meaning, both as these varying positions reflect ideological divisions in his own age and as they are transmitted through his captivating example.

From **Jeffrey N. Cox, Poetry and Politics in the Cockney School: Keats, Shelley, Hunt and their Circle**, Cambridge: Cambridge University Press, 1998, 185–6

Jeffrey N. Cox (b. 1953) is Professor of Comparative Literature at the University of Colorado, Boulder. His *Poetry and Politics in the Cockney School* situates Keats in the context of his membership of Hunt's radical coterie, and argues that the *Lamia* volume of 1820 has deep investments in liberal politics (a reading of the book which, like Roe's, differs significantly from the 'reactionary' account offered by McGann). The 'Ode on a Grecian Urn' is seen as part of the Hunt circle's attempt to reclaim classical poetry from conservative poets, notably Wordsworth, and sees Keats aligning himself with the 'Cockney School' as 'a poet of a radical eroticism'.

The *Blackwood's* Cockney School attack on Keats praised Wordsworth as 'the most classical of living English poets'. If Wordsworth – who dismissed Keats's 'Hymn to Pan' as a 'pretty piece of paganism' [. . .] and who, most important, in

---

11 Having more than one form.

The Excursion explained Greek myth as a shadowy adumbration of Christian transcendentalism – if Wordsworth is the 'most classical' of writers, then Hunt, Keats, and Shelley clearly are not. But against the cold classicism of the author of *Laodamia* (1815), the Hunt circle sought a paganism ever warm, ever panting, and forever young. 'Ode on a Grecian Urn' is part of a Cockney project of wresting the control of the definition of the classical from the conservative defenders of a deadening, urnlike tradition.

Keats's poetry at the time was considered scandalous – and to do it justice, we must rediscover the scandal of a poem such as the 'Ode on a Grecian Urn'. The great scandal of Catullus' love poetry was that in his affair with the older, married Lesbia he adopted the 'feminized' position of longing and loss, rejecting the demands of the supposedly heroic and certainly civic, public and warlike Roman ethos in doing so. When we are reminded by Marjorie Levinson of the sexual language in the contemporary criticism of Keats – where his verse is called 'unclean,' 'profligate,' 'disgusting' – and when we are taught by Susan Wolfson to see again the nineteenth century's 'feminised Keats', we find, I think a similar concern: that Keats, who should be a productive member of society as an apothecary – 'back to the shop Mr John,' advises Z. – has instead joined Hunt and Shelley in imagining a life of democratised love and luxury; that Keats, in his friend Benjamin Bailey's phrase, had adopted 'that abominable principle of Shelley's – that Sensual Love is the principle of things'. In a society that had been mobilized for war for two decades and that continued to imagine much of its culture as a celebration of military heroism and conquests, Keats joined with the Hunt circle to offer his pretty pieces of paganism in an attempt 'to put a mite of help to the liberal side' (to C. W. Dilke, 22 September 1819). Keats aligns himself with Shelley, Byron and Hunt – and with their precursor Catullus – as a poet of a radical eroticism.

3

Key Poems

Key Poems

On First Looking into Chapman's Homer

'On First Looking into Chapman's Homer' was composed one morning in October 1816. The previous evening, Keats's friend Charles Cowden Clarke had read him portions of George Chapman's *The Whole Works of Homer* (1614). Returning home, in Cowden Clarke's phrase, 'at day-spring', his imagination at its most febrile, Keats had completed the first draft of the sonnet 'by ten o'clock'.[1] It was first published in the *Examiner* for 1 December 1816 (in Leigh Hunt's essay on the 'Young Poets', pp. 33–4), and was reprinted in Keats's 1817 *Poems*.[2] Critical opinion about the sonnet can be loosely grouped into the biographical, the literary and the sociopolitical. From Hunt onwards, critics and biographers (such as Bate, Walsh and Gittings) have read the poem as veiled autobiography, betokening Keats's exhilarated sense of poetic possibility, that he, too, might achieve great things in the poetic 'realms of gold'. Other critics (Sperry, Levinson and others) have examined the poem in terms of its literary resonance; in particular its attention, or lack of it, to its nominal subject, Chapman's translation of Homer. In recent years, there has also been an attention, exemplified in the work of Roe and Newey, to the political and historical resonance of the poem. There are also a number of useful studies of the sources of the poem (Murry, Evans, Roe again), which examine its allusions to Homeric epic, to historical narrative and to astronomical writing.

The first significant blossoming of Keats's talent, few critics have demurred at Leigh Hunt's 1827 declaration that the poem 'completely announced the new poet taking possession'.[3] Walter Jackson Bate, for example, declares that here Keats's previous poetic explorations were 'suddenly transmuted into actual

---

1 Charles and Mary Cowden Clarke, *Recollections of Writers*, introduced by Robert Gittings, Fontwell, Sussex: Centaur Press, 1969, p. 130.
2 The source text used here.
3 Leigh Hunt, *Lord Byron and Some of his Contemporaries; with Recollections of the Author's Life, and of his Visit to Italy*, London: H. Colburn, 1828, p. 248.

discovery',[4] whilst William Walsh sees Keats moving from the anxiety mani-fested in his previous work as to 'whether or not [he] could become a poet' to the triumphant production of a poem of 'power and perfection'.[5] To a certain extent, such declarations are prompted by the nature of the poem itself. A poem about poetry, the image of the Spanish soldier and adventurer Cortez and his men staring at the Pacific becomes a metaphor for Keats's feeling that he, too, was on the brink of significant discoveries, albeit poetical rather than geographical ones. 'Keats himself,' writes Robert Gittings, 'stands on the edge of discovery, like the Spanish explorer and the astronomer Herschel.'[6]

Despite the poem's title, Keats seems little interested here in commenting on the nature of Chapman's work, only in recording his impressions on hearing it.[7] Stuart Sperry writes that Keats's poem does not 'attempt to render a clear impression of the work [it] pretend[s] to celebrate. Any sense of Chapman's translation . . . is rapidly subsumed within the feeling of the sublime . . . the sudden shock and wonder that the highest art inspires.'[8] However, it should be noted, against Sperry, that Gittings traces what he sees as direct echoes of Chapman's poetry in Keats's work.[9] Marjorie Levinson agrees with Sperry rather than Gittings, pointing out that 'Keats does not *read* even the translation', merely 'looks into it', part of his 'opportunistic' assault upon the literary tradition which by comment consent originates in Homer: Keats 'subvert[s] the system which installs Homer in a particular and originary place'. For Levinson, Keats 'assumes the role of the literary adventurer (with the commercial nuance of that word) as opposed to the mythic explorer: Odysseus, Cortes' (see **pp. 62–4**). Other critics have, unlike Levinson, identified Keats with Cortez. To Nicholas Roe, the imperialistic adventuring of Cortez, who conquered Mexico for the Spanish and was more warrior than explorer, underpins Keats's poem, demonstrating the poet's own grand ambitions: 'Imagination and imperial power coincide in the appropriation of wonderful new worlds.'[10] Roe points out that 'Keats's sonnet omits the tragic human cost of Spanish activities in the new world'. Vincent Newey also offers an historically charged handling of the poem.[11] Newey sees Cortez as a symbol of imperialist society, writing of the 'concern in Keats's sonnet with conquest and command – both of course called to mind by the very name of Cortez, and by his *over-seeing* of the

4 Walter Jackson Bate, *John Keats*, London: Chatto & Windus, 1963, p. 85.
5 William Walsh, *Introduction to Keats*, London: Methuen, 1981, pp. 23–4.
6 Robert Gittings, *John Keats*, London: Heinemann, 1968, p. 131.
7 And Marjorie Levinson asks a pertinent question: 'What happened to Homer?' (Marjorie Levinson, *Keats's Life of Allegory: The Origins of a Style*, Oxford: Blackwell, 1980, p. 14).
8 Stuart M. Sperry, *Keats the Poet*, Princeton, NJ: Princeton University Press, 1973, p. 74.
9 Gittings, *John Keats* pp. 128–30.
10 Nicholas Roe, *John Keats and the Culture of Dissent*, Oxford: Oxford University Press, 1997, p. 58.
11 Nicholas Roe (ed.), *Keats and History*, Cambridge: Cambridge University Press, 1995, pp. 183–90. See also John Kandl's 'Private Lyrics in the Public Sphere: Leigh Hunt and the Construction of a Public "John Keats"', *Keats–Shelley Journal*, 44, 1995, p. 90, which argues that the sonnet offers a 'challenge to prevailing ideas of order in Regency England'.

productive landscape before and beneath him'.[12] And he takes issue with Levinson's account of the poem's subversiveness: 'Keats's text is a private dream of self-elevation, but it nevertheless reproduces and endorses the values of the status quo ... His desire for advancement and the possession of space enacts at the individual level the core impulses of a competitive and expansionist – incipiently imperialist society.'[13]

The composition of the poem is discussed in detail by Walter Jackson Bate in *John Keats*.[14] John Middleton Murry's *Keats and Shakespeare*[15] and B. Ifor Evans's 'Keats's Approach to the Chapman Sonnet'[16] offer detailed discussion of the poem's antecedents. Daniel P. Watkins in *Keats's Poetry and the Politics of the Imagination*[17] and Nicholas Roe in *John Keats and the Culture of Dissent*[18] focus in particular upon the sonnet's engagement with William Robertson's *History of America* (1777).

Much have I travelled in the realms of gold,[19]   1
    And many goodly states and kingdoms seen;
    Round many western islands have I been
Which bards in fealty[20] to Apollo[21] hold.
Oft of one wide expanse had I been told
    That deep-browed Homer ruled as his demesne;[22]
    Yet did I never breathe its pure serene
Till I heard Chapman speak out loud and bold.
Then felt I like some watcher of the skies[23]
    When a new planet swims into his ken;[24]   10

---

12 Roe, *Keats and History*, pp. 184–5.
13 *Ibid.*, p. 184.
14 Bate, *John Keats*, pp. 84–9.
15 John Middleton Murry, *Keats and Shakespeare: A Study of Keats' Poetic Life from 1816 to 1820*, London: Oxford University Press, Humphrey Milward, 1925, pp. 15–33.
16 *Essays and Studies by Members of the English Association*, XVI, Oxford: Clarendon Press, 1931, pp. 26–52.
17 Daniel P. Watkins, *Keats's Poetry and the Politics of the Imagination*, Rutherford, NJ: Fairleigh Dickinson University Press, pp. 26–31.
18 Roe, *John Keats*, pp. 57–8.
19 i.e the realms of the imagination (or, more specifically, and according to Leigh Hunt, of poetry). John Barnard writes that the reference is 'probably also to the gold leaf embossing on the covers and spines of books' (ed., *John Keats: The Complete Poems*, Harmondsworth: Penguin, 1973). Keats writes in 'Isabella', ll. 92–3: 'Too many doleful stories do we see,/Whose matter in bright gold were best be read.'
20 The obligation of fidelity due from a vassal to his master in feudal times.
21 The Greek sun-god, who was also the patron deity of poetry.
22 His domain or territory.
23 i.e. an astronomer. Miriam Allott (ed., *Keats: The Complete Poems*, 1970) argues that Keats had the specific example of Herschel's 1781 discovery of Uranus in mind (as described in John Bonnycastle's *An Introduction to Astronomy* (1803), which Keats owned). However, Roe, *John Keats*, maintains that the image is more general and reflects Keats's memory of his excited discovery of astronomy at Enfield School.
24 Knowledge.

Or like stout Cortez[25] when with eagle eyes
He stared at the Pacific—and all his men
Looked at each other with a wild surmise—
Silent, upon a peak in Darien.[26]

From *Endymion*

A mythological romance in four books, *Endymion* was first published in 1818.[1] It tells the story of the shepherd-prince Endymion of Latmos, who falls in love with Cynthia, the moon, and pursues her to the earth's depths. There he encounters a woman of flesh and blood, Phoebe, and gives up his quest for the ideal (in the shape of the goddess). However, Phoebe is finally revealed as none other than Cynthia herself and Endymion is borne away to love and eternal life. From its first appearance *Endymion* has always been Keats's most controversial poem. It was savagely reviewed and has had few unqualified admirers since its first publication. Indeed, Keats himself described it as a 'feverish attempt, rather than a deed accomplished' and Leigh Hunt declared that it 'partook of the faults of youth, though the best ones'. Despite Hunt's reservations about *Endymion*, the poem has always been seen as Keats's most Huntian poem, and certainly much of the antipathy to the poem was attributable to the fact that it was caught in the crossfire between the Hunt circle and their ultra-Tory enemies at the *Quarterly* and *Blackwood's*. Both journals attacked Keats on both political and poetical grounds (in Lockhart's words, Keats belonged to 'the Cockney School of Politics, as well as the Cockney School of Poetry'). Croker's review in the *Quarterly* declared Keats 'a copyist of Mr. Hunt' and *Endymion* 'uncouth ... unintelligible, ... tiresome and absurd' (p. 34), whilst J. G. Lockhart's notice in *Blackwood's* lamented 'the calm, settled, imperturbable drivelling idiocy of *Endymion*' (pp. 34–6). (For J. H. Reynold's 1818 defence of Keats and *Endymion* from Croker's onslaught, see pp. 37–8.) More recent criticism, though it has no quarrels with Keats's politics, tends to share the view that Hunt was a bad poetic influence upon *Endymion* and that the poem was mediocre by the standards of Keats's later work. If few critics went so far as Thomas De Quincey, who declared the poem 'vile,' before the revisionary and usefully corrective 1962 reading by Bayley, which is extracted on pp. 49–50 ('I prefer the more immediate and emotional manner of *Endymion* to that of *Hyperion* . . .

---

25 The poet Tennyson pointed out in 1861 that 'History requires [Vasco Nunez de] Balboa' rather than Cortez. It was Balboa (1475–1519) who, in 1513, was the first European to see the Pacific, from a Darien mountain. Cortez (1485–1547) conquered Mexico for Spain several years later, entering Mexico City in 1519.
26 Now Panama.

---

1 In *Endymion: A Poetic Romance*, London: Taylor and Hessey, 1818, the source of the present text.

Hunt is a wholly benign influence on Keats's poetic make-up'[2]), the best that was often said of *Endymion* was that it was an important part of Keats's poetic apprenticeship, clearing the way for the triumphs of late 1818 onwards. Even now, John Barnard's 1987 assessment of *Endymion* is still consensual: though the poem is an 'adolescent failure . . . its 4,000 lines of poetry [were] essential to [Keats's] development as a poet'.[3] Though Barnard finds Bayley's reassessment of the quality of *Endymion* 'over-stated', he takes the poem seriously, seeing it as 'a Romantic quest-poem portraying the poet's search for true imaginative powers'. For Barnard, the poem is close to allegory: 'Endymion is the alienated modern poet bearing the cost of consciousness.' This reading is part of a long tradition of symbolic accounts of the narrative; many critics have interpreted it in allegorical terms, notably in a sense that the poem represents the quest for beauty, imagination or the ideal. The poet Robert Bridges, for example, writing in 1896, sees Endymion as 'Man' and the moon as 'Poetry, or the Ideality of desired objects, "the principle of Beauty in all things"'.[4]

Even its detractors admit that *Endymion* has moments of poetic grandeur,[5] and the poem rewards extraction. The following passages are taken from Book I of the poem: the first the poem's opening, and the second the famous 'Hymn to Pan'.[6]

From Book I

A thing of beauty is a joy for ever:	1
Its loveliness increases; it will never	
Pass into nothingness; but still will keep	
A bower quiet for us, and a sleep	
Full of sweet dreams, and health, and quiet breathing.	
Therefore, on every morrow, are we wreathing	
A flowery band to bind us to the earth,	
Spite of despondence, of the inhuman dearth	
Of noble natures, of the gloomy days,	
Of all the unhealthy and o'er-darkened ways	10
Made for our searching: yes, in spite of all,	
Some shape of beauty moves away the pall	
From our dark spirits. Such the sun, the moon,	
Trees old and young, sprouting a shady boon	
For simple sheep; and such are daffodils	

2   John Bayley, 'Keats and Reality', in *Proceedings of the British Academy*, XLVIII, London: Oxford University Press, 1962, p. 118.
3   John Barnard, *John Keats*, Cambridge: Cambridge University Press, 1987, p. 35.
4   See Clarice Godfrey's 'Endymion' (in Kenneth Muir, ed., *Keats: A Reassessment*, 1958, pp. 20–39) for a discussion of this and other allegorical interpretations of the poem.
5   Croker himself declared that Keats had 'gleams of genius'.
6   Which the poet Wordsworth labelled 'a Very pretty piece of paganism'.

With the green world they live in; and clear rills
That for themselves a cooling covert make
'Gainst the hot season; the mid forest brake,
Rich with a sprinkling of fair musk-rose blooms:
And such too is the grandeur of the dooms   20
We have imagined for the mighty dead;
All lovely tales that we have heard or read:
An endless fountain of immortal drink,
Pouring unto us from the heaven's brink.

Nor do we merely feel these essences
For one short hour; no, even as the trees
That whisper round a temple become soon
Dear as the temple's self, so does the moon,
The passion poesy, glories infinite,
Haunt us till they become a cheering light   30
Unto our souls, and bound to us so fast,
That, whether there be shine, or gloom o'ercast,
They alway must be with us, or we die.

"Hymn to Pan"

"O thou, whose mighty palace roof doth hang
From jagged trunks, and overshadoweth
Eternal whispers, glooms, the birth, life, death
Of unseen flowers in heavy peacefulness;
Who lov'st to see the hamadryads[7] dress
Their ruffled locks where meeting hazels darken;
And through whole solemn hours dost sit, and hearken
The dreary melody of bedded reeds—
In desolate places, where dank moisture breeds   240
The pipy hemlock[8] to strange overgrowth;
Bethinking thee, how melancholy loth
Thou wast to lose fair Syrinx[9]—do thou now,
By thy love's milky brow!
By all the trembling mazes that she ran,
Hear us, great Pan!

O thou, for whose soul-soothing quiet, turtles[10]
Passion their voices cooingly 'mong myrtles,
What time thou wanderest at eventide

---

7 Wood-nymphs.
8 The poisonous hemlock has hollow stems.
9 Pan pursued Syrinx, who was transformed into a reed.
10 Turtle-doves.

Through sunny meadows, that outskirt the side   250
Of thine enmossed realms: O thou, to whom
Broad leaved fig trees even now foredoom
Their ripen'd fruitage; yellow-girted bees
Their golden honeycombs; our village leas
Their fairest blossom'd beans and poppied corn;
The chuckling[11] linnet its five young unborn,
To sing for thee; low creeping strawberries
Their summer coolness; pent up butterflies[12]
Their freckled wings; yea, the fresh budding year
All its completions—be quickly near,   260
By every wind that nods the mountain pine,
O forester divine!

Thou, to whom every fawn and satyr flies
For willing service; whether to surprise
The squatted hare while in half sleeping fit;
Or upward ragged precipices flit
To save poor lambkins from the eagle's maw;
Or by mysterious enticement draw
Bewildered shepherds to their path again;
Or to tread breathless round the frothy main,   270
And gather up all fancifullest shells
For thee to tumble into naiads'[13] cells,
And, being hidden, laugh at their out-peeping;
Or to delight thee with fantastic leaping,
The while they pelt each other on the crown
With silvery oak apples, and fir cones brown—
By all the echoes that about thee ring,
Hear us, O satyr king!

O Hearkener to the loud clapping shears,
While ever and anon to his shorn peers   280
A ram goes bleating: Winder[14] of the horn,
When snouted wild-boars routing tender corn
Anger our huntsman: Breather round our farms,
To keep off mildews, and all weather harms:
Strange ministrant of undescribed sounds,
That come a swooning over hollow grounds,
And wither drearily on barren moors:
Dread opener of the mysterious doors

---

11 i.e. clucking.
12 i.e. chrysalises.
13 Water-nymphs.
14 Blower.

Leading to universal knowledge—see,
Great son of Dryope,[15]   290
The many that are come to pay their vows
With leaves about their brows!

Be still the unimaginable lodge
For solitary thinkings; such as dodge
Conception to the very bourne of heaven,
Then leave the naked brain: be still the leaven,
That spreading in this dull and clodded earth
Gives it a touch ethereal—a new birth:
Be still a symbol of immensity;   300
A firmament reflected in a sea;
An element filling the space between;
An unknown—but no more: we humbly screen
With uplift hands our foreheads, lowly bending,
And giving out a shout most heaven rending,
Conjure thee to receive our humble paean,[16]
Upon thy Mount Lycean!"[17]

From 'Isabella; or, The Pot of Basil. A Story from Boccaccio'

Keats's narrative poem 'Isabella; or, The Pot of Basil', written in the spring of
1818, is based on a gruesome tale from Giovanni Boccaccio's fourteenth-
century collection The Decameron. It was originally intended for an abortive
volume of verse translations from Boccaccio which Keats and his friend J. H.
Reynolds projected and later abandoned.[1] In Keats's account, Isabella, sister to
two avaricious Florentine merchants who intend to marry her off to some rich
nobleman, falls in love with their hireling Lorenzo. The brothers discover the
romance, murder Lorenzo and bury him in a forest. However, Lorenzo's ghost
appears to his beloved, who unearths his body, cuts off his head and places it in a
garden pot. Topping the pot with basil, she nourishes the ghastly relic with her
tears. The brothers, suspicious of Isabella's obsession with the pot of basil,
discover her secret and flee into exile. Isabella pines away without her basil pot,
pathetically declining into near-madness and death. This macabre tale, which
reflects to some extent the contemporary vogue for grotesquery evident in the
Gothic novel and the supernatural ballads of S. T. Coleridge, remained

---

15 Pan's mother, according to Homer.
16 Hymn of praise.
17 The Arcadian mountain sacred to Pan.

---

1 Keats had heard Hazlitt declare in February 1818 that 'I should think that a translation of some of
the other serious tales in Boccaccio [. . .] as that of Isabella [. . .] could not fail to succeed'.

unpublished until 1820 (in *Lamia, Isabella, The Eve of St. Agnes, and other Poems*[2]).
Given the chorus of jeers which had greeted *Endymion* in some quarters, Keats
had reservations about publishing the poem, writing to Richard Woodhouse on
21 September 1819 about his concerns that the poem was 'mawkish' and might
be 'smokeable' (i.e. easily mocked): 'I shall persist in not publishing The Pot of
Basil – It is too smokeable . . . There is too much inexperience of li[f]e, and
simplicity of knowledge in it . . . I intend to use more finesse with the Public. It is
possible to write fine things which cannot be laugh'd at in any way. Isabella is
what I should call were I a reviewer "A weak-sided Poem" with an amusing
sober-sadness about it.'

Keats's ambivalence about his poem is reflected in the divided nature of
critical opinion about it. In his review of the 1820 collection, Charles Lamb rated
it 'the best thing in the volume', ranking it above the odes and 'The Eve of St.
Agnes'. The 'simplicity' which troubled Keats appealed to Lamb, who writes (of
stanzas 46–8) that 'there is nothing more awfully simple in diction, more nakedly
grand and moving in sentiment, in Dante, in Chaucer, or in Spenser'. Lamb's
friend John Scott of the *London Magazine*, though he disliked the satirical attack
on mercantilism in Keats's treatment of Isabella's grasping brothers (in stanzas
14–16) also valued the poem's sentimentality, praising the 'musical tenderness'
of Keats's 'delicious tale'. Another nineteenth-century commentator, the poet
Swinburne, was less positive, labelling 'Isabella' 'feeble and awkward in narrative',
and much twentieth-century criticism has agreed with him. Ian Jack, for instance,
dislikes the poem's 'elaborate rhetoric of pathos'; 'Isabella' 'now appears
distasteful in theme and in parts poorly written'.[3] For Walter Jackson Bate,
Keats was 'only marking time' in 'Isabella',[4] whilst M. R. Ridley offers a
withering, almost line-by-line[5] assault in *Keats's Craftsmanship*: 'Isabella' 'is surely
a poor poem that can only be read with pleasure if it is also read with
inattention'. To Ridley, the poem's significance lies in its status as a part of
Keats's poetical apprenticeship, a staging post between the (even more flawed)
Endymion to the triumph of 'The Eve of St. Agnes': 'It is a poem of transition . . .
In *Isabella* the course is known, the control is being learned.'[6] Miriam Allott's
important 1958 essay on Keats's narrative poems makes a similar point. Allott
repudiates F. W. Bateson's argument in *English Poetry* (1950) that '*Endymion*
(finished November 1817) is adolescent, "Isabella" (finished April 1818) is

---

2   The source of the current text.
3   Ian Jack, *English Literature 1815–1832*, Oxford: Clarendon Press, 1963, p. 111.
4   Walter Jackson Bate, *John Keats*, London: Chatto & Windus, 1963.
5   An example: ' "And poesied with hers in dewy rhyme", which, apart from conveying a sensation
    of somewhat tasteless lusciousness, seems to convey as little meaning as is possible for seven
    English words arranged in a grammatical clause' (M. R. Ridley, *Keats's Craftmanship: A Study
    in Poetic Development*, Oxford: Clarendon Press, 1933, p. 28). Christopher Ricks offers a
    fine defence of the line (*Keats and Embarrassment*, Oxford: Oxford University Press, 1974,
    pp. 97–100).
6   Ridley, *Keats's Craftmanship*, p. 56.

adult'; for her, 'Isabella' is 'in some respects an advance of *Endymion*', but it is only a 'varying success'.[7]

Recent criticism has been more willing to take the poem on its own merits. Some is negative, sharing William Walsh's feeling that the poem is 'not much more than a feeble nineteenth-century fantasy'[8] or Jack Stillinger's that it is Keats's 'last poetic failure'. Other critics have been more enthusiastic. Louise Z. Smith argues that the poem is not escapist romance and that it manifests a 'material sublime' in which medievalist romance is tempered by 'elements of human suffering'. Keats does not offer 'a perfect world, but . . . reveal[s] hope and beauty in an imperfect world'.[9] Inspired by John Bayley's revaluation of 'Isabella' in 'Keats and Reality' (**pp. 49–50**), John Jones's *John Keats's Dream of Truth* offers a detailed discussion of sexuality in 'Isabella' and a defence of the poem as demonstrating a life-affirming and 'marvelously sane' vision (**pp. 51–3**). John Barnard is less optimistic about the tone of the later sections of 'Isabella', and foregrounds their oppressive atmosphere: 'claustrophobic physical and mental violence is all, its effect sharpened by the contrast between the tender idyll of the poem's first part and the suffering of the final movement.'[10] Barnard also reads the poem in sociohistoricist terms; the political axe-grinding found in Keats's satire on Isabella's 'money-bags' brothers (the stanzas which so offended John Scott) marks 'an attack upon capitalist wealth'. The brothers are 'commercial imperialists', and Keats's poem is predicated upon 'an opposition between commercialism and love'. For further discussion of the politics of 'Isabella', see the extract on **pp. 53–5** from Carl Woodring's *Politics in English Romantic Poetry*.[11] Kelvin Everest expands on this division in his account of the sexual politics of 'Isabella' and the way in which the poem articulates one mode 'of oppression suffered by women', an oppression in which Lorenzo is subtly complicit:

> Lorenzo and Isabella both subordinate their mutual sexual feeling to a code of sexual behaviour and courtship. This code sentimentalises and disguises the motivating desire of the relationship and subdues it to forms which express the commodified status of the woman in sexual relations. Lorenzo plays the coy courtly lover, and Isabella too willingly goes along with the role of demure and passive object. But these roles in sexual conduct are in fact in the service of larger economic

7 ' "Isabella", "The Eve of St. Agnes" and "Lamia" ', in Kenneth Muir (ed.), *John Keats: A Reassessment*, Liverpool: Liverpool University Press, 1958, p. 52.
8 William Walsh, *Introduction to Keats*, London: Methuen, 1981, p. 115.
9 Louise Z. Smith, 'The Material Sublime: Keats and *Isabella*', *Studies in Romanticism*, 13, 1974, p. 301.
10 John Barnard, *John Keats*, Cambridge: Cambridge University Press, 1988, p. 78.
11 See also Martin Aske's 'Keats, the Critics, and the Politics of Envy', in Nicholas Roe (ed.), *Keats and History*, Cambridge: Cambridge University Press, 1995, pp. 55–9.

interests, where making and sealing of marital alliances is closely bound up with financial and property deals. The brothers' motive in their murder is indeed specifically economic.[12]

I.

Fair Isabel, poor simple Isabel!   1
   Lorenzo, a young palmer[13] in Love's eye!
They could not in the self-same mansion dwell
   Without some stir of heart, some malady;[14]
They could not sit at meals but feel how well
   It soothed each to be the other by;
They could not, sure, beneath the same roof sleep
But to each other dream, and nightly weep.

II.

With every morn their love grew tenderer,
   With every eve deeper and tenderer still;   10
He might not in house, field, or garden stir,
   But her full shape would all his seeing fill;
And his continual voice was pleasanter
   To her, than noise of trees or hidden rill;[15]
Her lute-string gave an echo of his name,
She spoilt her half-done broidery[16] with the same.

III.

He knew whose gentle hand was at the latch,
   Before the door had given her to his eyes;
And from her chamber-window he would catch
   Her beauty farther than the falcon spies;   20
And constant as her vespers[17] would he watch,
   Because her face was turn'd to the same skies;
And with sick longing all the night outwear,
To hear her morning-step upon the stair.

IV.

A whole long month of May in this sad plight
   Made their cheeks paler by the break of June:
"To-morrow will I bow to my delight,

12 In Roe, *Keats and History*, p. 123.
13 A pilgrim.
14 Love-sickness.
15 Stream.
16 Embroidery.
17 Evening prayers.

To-morrow will I ask my lady's boon."[18]—
"O may I never see another night,
    Lorenzo, if thy lips breathe not love's tune."—   30
So spake they to their pillows; but, alas,
Honeyless days and days did he let pass;

V.

Until sweet Isabella's untouch'd cheek
    Fell sick within the rose's just domain,[19]
Fell thin as a young mother's, who doth seek
    By every lull to cool her infant's pain:
"How ill she is," said he, "I may not speak,
    And yet I will, and tell my love all plain:
If looks speak love-laws, I will drink her tears,
And at the least 'twill startle off her cares."   40

VI.

So said he one fair morning, and all day
    His heart beat awfully against his side;
And to his heart he inwardly did pray
    For power to speak; but still the ruddy tide
Stifled his voice, and puls'd[20] resolve away—
    Fever'd his high conceit of such a bride,
Yet brought him to the meekness of a child:
Alas! when passion is both meek and wild!

VII.

So once more he had wak'd and anguished
    A dreary night of love and misery,   50
If Isabel's quick eye had not been wed
    To every symbol on his forehead high;[21]
She saw it waxing very pale and dead,
    And straight all flush'd; so, lisped tenderly,
"Lorenzo!"—here she ceas'd her timid quest,
But in her tone and look he read the rest.

VIII.

"O Isabella, I can half perceive
    That I may speak my grief into thine ear;
If thou didst ever any thing believe,
    Believe how I love thee, believe how near   60

18 Gift, favour.
19 i.e. Isabella's formerly rosy cheeks pale.
20 Drove. The pulsing of the 'ruddy tide' of Lorenzo's heart renders him incapable of verbal
    expression.
21 i.e. Isabella reads Lorenzo's emotion on his face.

My soul is to its doom: I would not grieve
    Thy hand by unwelcome pressing, would not fear
Thine eyes by gazing; but I cannot live
Another night, and not my passion shrive.[22]

IX.
"Love! thou art leading me from wintry cold,
    Lady! thou leadest me to summer clime,
And I must taste the blossoms that unfold
    In its ripe warmth this gracious morning time."
So said, his erewhile[23] timid lips grew bold,
    And poesied with hers in dewy rhyme:[24]   70
Great bliss was with them, and great happiness
Grew, like a lusty flower in June's caress.

[. . .]

XIV.
With her two brothers this fair lady dwelt,
    Enriched from ancestral merchandize,
And for them many a weary hand did swelt[25]
    In torched mines and noisy factories,
And many once proud-quiver'd loins did melt
    In blood from stinging whip;—with hollow eyes   110
Many all day in dazzling river stood,
To take the rich-ored driftings of the flood.[26]

XV.
For them the Ceylon diver held his breath,[27]
    And went all naked to the hungry shark;
For them his ears gush'd blood; for them in death
    The seal on the cold ice with piteous bark
Lay full of darts; for them alone did seethe
    A thousand men in troubles wide and dark:
Half-ignorant, they turn'd an easy wheel,
That set sharp racks[28] at work, to pinch and peel.   120

XVI.
Why were they proud? Because their marble founts[29]
    Gush'd with more pride than do a wretch's tears?—

22 Confess.
23 Formerly.
24 Either 'they speak of their love in the metaphors of love poetry' or, more likely, 'they kiss' (their
    lips pairing like a poetic couplet).
25 Swelter.
26 i.e. pan for gold.
27 i.e. to dive for pearls.
28 Medieval instruments of torture.
29 Fountains.

Why were they proud? Because fair orange-mounts[30]
    Were of more soft ascent than lazar stairs?[31]—
Why were they proud? Because red-lin'd[32] accounts
    Were richer than the songs of Grecian years?—
Why were they proud? again we ask aloud,
Why in the name of Glory were they proud? [. . .]

The brothers kill Lorenzo. His ghost appears to Isabella, tells her of his fate and where his body lies. Isabella and her nurse dig up the corpse.

XLVII.
Soon she turn'd up a soiled glove, whereon
    Her silk had play'd in purple phantasies,   370
She kiss'd it with a lip more chill than stone,
    And put it in her bosom, where it dries
And freezes utterly unto the bone
    Those dainties made to still an infant's cries:[33]
Then 'gan she work again; nor stay'd her care,
But to throw back at times her veiling hair.

XLVIII.
That old nurse stood beside her wondering,
    Until her heart felt pity to the core
At sight of such a dismal labouring,
    And so she kneeled, with her locks all hoar,[34]   380
And put her lean hands to the horrid thing:
    Three hours they labour'd at this travail[35] sore;
At last they felt the kernel of the grave,
And Isabella did not stamp and rave.

XLIX.
Ah! wherefore all this wormy circumstance?
    Why linger at the yawning tomb so long?
O for the gentleness of old Romance,
    The simple plaining[36] of a minstrel's song!
Fair reader, at the old tale take a glance,
    For here, in truth, it doth not well belong   390

---

30 i.e. the sides of mountains planted with orange groves.
31 i.e. the stairs in 'lazar houses' for the poor and sick.
32 i.e. balance sheets circled or marked in red ink.
33 Her breasts. A Spenserian periphrasis.
34 White or grey with age.
35 Task.
36 Lamentation.

To speak:—O turn thee to the very tale,
And taste the music of that vision pale.

L.

With duller steel than the Persèan sword[37]
    They cut away no formless monster's head,
But one, whose gentleness did well accord
    With death, as life. The ancient harps have said,
Love never dies, but lives, immortal Lord:
    If Love impersonate was ever dead,
Pale Isabella kiss'd it, and low moan'd.
'Twas love; cold,—dead indeed, but not dethroned.   400

LI.

In anxious secrecy they took it home,
    And then the prize was all for Isabel:
She calm'd its wild hair with a golden comb,
    And all around each eye's sepulchral cell
Pointed each fringed lash; the smeared loam[38]
    With tears, as chilly as a dripping well,
She drench'd away:—and still she comb'd, and kept
Sighing all day—and still she kiss'd, and wept.

LII.

Then in a silken scarf,—sweet with the dews
    Of precious flowers pluck'd in Araby,   410
And divine liquids come with odorous ooze
    Through the cold serpent-pipe[39] refreshfully,—
She wrapp'd it up; and for its tomb did choose
    A garden-pot, wherein she laid it by,
And cover'd it with mould, and o'er it set
Sweet Basil,[40] which her tears kept ever wet.

LIII.

And she forgot the stars, the moon, and sun,
    And she forgot the blue above the trees,
And she forgot the dells where waters run,
    And she forgot the chilly autumn breeze;   420
She had no knowledge when the day was done,
    And the new morn she saw not: but in peace
Hung over her sweet Basil evermore,
And moisten'd it with tears unto the core.

---

37 Perseus slew the fearsome Gorgon Medusa and cut off her head.
38 Dirt.
39 A sexually charged poeticism for the winding tube of perfume which 'oozes' the divine liquids.
40 Basil is a culinary herb.

LIV.
And so she ever fed it with thin tears,
  Whence thick, and green, and beautiful it grew,
So that it smelt more balmy than its peers
  Of Basil-tufts in Florence; for it drew
Nurture besides, and life, from human fears,
  From the fast mouldering head there shut from view: 430
So that the jewel, safely casketed,
Came forth, and in perfumed leafits[41] spread.

LV.
O Melancholy, linger here awhile!
  O Music, Music, breathe despondingly!
O Echo, Echo, from some sombre isle,
  Unknown, Lethean,[42] sigh to us—O sigh!
Spirits in grief, lift up your heads, and smile;
  Lift up your heads, sweet Spirits, heavily,
And make a pale light in your cypress glooms,
Tinting with silver wan your marble tombs.   440

LVI.
Moan hither, all ye syllables of woe,
  From the deep throat of sad Melpomene![43]
Through bronzed lyre in tragic order go,
  And touch the strings into a mystery;
Sound mournfully upon the winds and low;
  For simple Isabel is soon to be
Among the dead: She withers, like a palm
Cut by an Indian for its juicy balm.

LVII.
O leave the palm to wither by itself;
  Let not quick Winter chill its dying hour!—   450
It may not be—those Baälites of pelf,[44]
  Her brethren, noted the continual shower
From her dead eyes; and many a curious elf,
  Among her kindred, wonder'd that such dower
Of youth and beauty should be thrown aside
By one mark'd out to be a Noble's bride.

41 Young leaves.
42 The waters of the Hadean river Lethe induced oblivion.
43 The Muse of tragedy.
44 In the Old Testament, Baal is a false god. Thus Isabella's brothers are worshippers of money ('pelf').

LVIII.

And, furthermore, her brethren wonder'd much
   Why she sat drooping by the Basil green,
And why it flourish'd, as by magic touch;
   Greatly they wonder'd what the thing might mean: 460
They could not surely give belief, that such
   A very nothing would have power to wean
Her from her own fair youth, and pleasures gay,
And even remembrance of her love's delay.

LIX.

Therefore they watch'd a time when they might sift
   This hidden whim; and long they watch'd in vain;
For seldom did she go to chapel-shrift,[45]
   And seldom felt she any hunger-pain;
And when she left, she hurried back, as swift
   As bird on wing to breast its eggs again;   470
And, patient as a hen-bird, sat her there
Beside her Basil, weeping through her hair.

LX.

Yet they contriv'd to steal the Basil-pot,
   And to examine it in secret place:
The thing was vile with green and livid spot,
   And yet they knew it was Lorenzo's face:
The guerdon[46] of their murder they had got,
   And so left Florence in a moment's space,
Never to turn again.—Away they went,
With blood upon their heads, to banishment.   480

LXI.

O Melancholy, turn thine eyes away!
   O Music, Music, breathe despondingly!
O Echo, Echo, on some other day,
   From isles Lethean, sigh to us—O sigh!
Spirits of grief, sing not your "Well-a-way!"
   For Isabel, sweet Isabel, will die;
Will die a death too lone and incomplete,
Now they have ta'en away her Basil sweet.

LXII.

Piteous she look'd on dead and senseless things,
   Asking for her lost Basil amorously;   490

45 Confession.
46 Reward, 'just deserts'.

And with melodious chuckle in the strings
  Of her lorn voice, she oftentimes would cry
After the Pilgrim in his wanderings,
  To ask him where her Basil was; and why
'Twas hid from her: "For cruel 'tis," said she,
"To steal my Basil-pot away from me."

LXIII.
And so she pined, and so she died forlorn,
  Imploring for her Basil to the last.
No heart was there in Florence but did mourn
  In pity of her love, so overcast.   500
And a sad ditty of this story born
  From mouth to mouth through all the country pass'd:
Still is the burthen[47] sung—"O cruelty,
To steal my Basil-pot away from me!"

From *Hyperion. A Fragment*

Keats's unfinished epic was begun in the autumn of 1818 and abandoned in
April 1819. It was first published in its fragmentary state in *Lamia, Isabella, The
Eve of St. Agnes, and other Poems* (1820).[1] Heavily indebted to Milton in both its
manner (mythical epic) and metre (Miltonic blank verse), the poem is a kind of
classical recasting of *Paradise Lost*, with the conflict between Saturn, leader of
the Titans, and Jove, leader of the Olympians, mirroring that between Satan and
God. In this version of the Fall, Saturn has been overthrown by Jove, and Books
I and II see him lamenting the loss of his kingdom and debating with his fellow
Titans as to how they can regain their supremacy. Their principal hope lies in
the figure of the sun god Hyperion, who remains unfallen (though if the poem
had been completed, it would have shown Hyperion's final defeat at the hands
of Apollo[2]). Book III introduces Apollo, who expresses his torment and agony to
the Titan goddess Mnemosyne, who has joined the Olympians. At the moment
of Apollo's deification, the fragment breaks off.

Writing in 1845, the critic George Gilfillan argued that *Hyperion* is 'the
greatest of poetical Torsos', and the poem has received much critical attention.
H. W. Garrod, in a passage from his 1926 volume *Keats* (**pp. 45–6**), argues that

---

47 Refrain.

1 The source of the present text.
2 Keats's friend Richard Woodhouse writes that 'The poem, if completed, would have treated of the
dethronement of Hyperion, the former God of the Sun, by Apollo, – and incidentally those of
Oceanus by Neptune, of Saturn by Jupiter etc., and of the war of the Giants for Saturn's reestab-
lishment – with other events, of which we have but very dark hints in the mythological poets of
Greece and Rome. In fact the incidents would have been pure creations of the Poet's brain.'

the unfinished poem remains an 'indeterminate allegory', open to a number of different interpretations and that Keats's need to stabilise the poem's significance caused him to abandon it, leaving it a suggestive fragment which refuses to yield up a single clear meaning. Harold Bloom's view is very different; for him, the poem is, in a sense, finished and Keats would have damaged his poem to take it further: 'Hyperion is already a complete poem once Apollo has realized himself, and the poet in Keats seemed to have recognized this by refusing to go on. Whatever the planned length, nothing could be added to the fragment without some redundancy ... Human tragedy has claimed the Titans who are doomed to mortality by no fault of their own [and] the birth of an artist beyond tragedy has been enacted in the transformation of Apollo, whose growing pains are his only human element, and whose completion is an apotheosis of poetry itself.'[3] John Jones, on the other hand, sees the poem's fragmentary status as a mark of failure: Hyperion 'sets out to interpret the world's pain, and the venture fails'. Unlike the odes, the poem is too 'hyper-Miltonic' and 'abstract' to confront the 'agonies of human hearts': 'His failure is two-sided. The "first in beauty should be first in might" thesis [II. 229] could never be adequate to human suffering. Second, the poet who resorts to a mythological story to demonstrate this thesis can hardly pretend to be jostling "in the world".'[4]

According to his 23 January 1818 letter to B. R. Haydon, Keats planned Hyperion as a poem which would replace the 'sentimental cast' of Endymion with 'a more naked and Grecian manner'. Shelley's admiration for Keats's 'genius' was almost entirely based on his enthusiasm for Hyperion (which he considered 'second to nothing that was ever produced by a writer of the same years', p. 41), and many poets and critics have preferred the spare grandeur of Hyperion to the more fevered atmospherics of Endymion (to John Clare it was Keats's 'best' poem and to Byron his 'one diamond'). Indeed, Thomas De Quincey confessed his 'incredulity' at the fact that the same poet could produce two such dissimilar poems: Hyperion 'presents the majesty, the austere beauty, and the simplicity of Grecian temples', but Endymion 'belongs essentially to the vilest collections of wax-work filigree, or gilt gingerbread'.[5] Bayley's 'Keats and Reality' (extracted on pp. 49–50) offers a salutary riposte to De Quincey in its argument that Hyperion was a deviation from the poet's true talents: Keats's work is laboured and over-deliberate when it strives for 'correctness', and Bayley prefers the 'sensual' Keats of 'Isabella' or Endymion to the 'safe, depersonalised Keats of Hyperion'.

3   Harold Bloom, The Visionary Company: A Reading of English Romantic Poetry, Ithaca, NY: Cornell University Press (1st edn 1961), rev. edn 1971, p. 398.
4   John Jones, John Keats's Dream of Truth, London: Chatto & Windus, 1969, pp. 89–90.
5   The Collected Writings of Thomas De Quincey, ed. David Masson, 14 vols, Edinburgh: Adam and Charles Black, 1889–90, vol. xi, p. 389.

Much twentieth-century criticism of *Hyperion* has been preoccupied with Keats's debt to Milton in the poem. To Stuart Sperry, '*Hyperion* displays the most remarkable assimilation of *Paradise Lost* of any poem in English after Milton'.[6] Marjorie Levinson, in her paradoxical manner, argues that the poem was discontinued because Keats had become Milton, dismissing 'the standard account of *Hyperion*'s abandonment (that is, Keats's rejection of its derivativeness) . . . There is nothing derivative, nothing "Miltonic" about *Hyperion*, and that is precisely its problem: it *is* Milton.'[7] Keats had written to Haydon on 23 January 1818 that *Hyperion* would deal with 'the march of passion and endeavour', and for John Barnard, the poem fuses Keats's poetic preoccupation with Milton with his personal philosophy, set out in his letter to J. H. Reynolds of 3 May 1818 (pp. 16–17), of the 'grand march of intellect' evident throughout history: 'Keats transmutes Milton's Christian epic into a modern myth of the necessity of change and progress.'[8] For Barnard, 'Keats's theme [is] of the "march of passion and suffering" – that is, of human progress in which Apollo's disinterested suffering makes him into a symbolic representative of the dreamer-poet, a new and higher force born out of the pain of the "vale of soul-making"'.[9]

There are discussions of *Hyperion* in Walter Jackson Bate's *John Keats*,[10] Douglas Bush's *John Keats*,[11] Robert Gittings's *John Keats*[12] and Lucy Newlyn's *Paradise Lost and the Romantic Reader*.[13] Kenneth Muir's 'The Meaning of Hyperion'[14] remains of value, especially in its stress on the political resonance of *Hyperion*. The poem's sources in Greek myth and visual arts are discussed in Ian Jack's *Keats and the Mirror of Art*.[15]

Book I

Deep in the shady sadness of a vale   1
Far sunken from the healthy breath of morn,
Far from the fiery noon, and eve's one star,
Sat gray-hair'd Saturn,[16] quiet as a stone,
Still as the silence round about his lair;
Forest on forest hung about his head
Like cloud on cloud. No stir of air was there,

---

6 Stuart M. Sperry, *Keats the Poet*, Princeton, NJ: Princeton University Press, 1973, p. 165.
7 Marjorie Levinson, *Keats's Life of Allegory: The Origins of a Style*, Oxford: Blackwell, 1988, p. 193.
8 John Barnard, *John Keats*, Cambridge: Cambridge University Press, 1987, p. 129.
9 John Barnard (ed.), *John Keats: The Complete Poems*, Harmondsworth: Penguin, 1973, p. 610.
10 Walter Jackson Bate, *John Keats*, London: Chatto & Windus, 1963, pp. 413–17.
11 Douglas Bush, *John Keats: His Life and Writings*, New York: Macmillan, 1966, pp. 95–108.
12 Robert Gittings, *John Keats*, London: Heinemann, 1968, pp. 363–77.
13 Lucy Newlyn, *Paradise Lost and the Romantic Reader*, Oxford: Clarendon Press, pp. 250–4.
14 In Kenneth Muir (ed.), *Keats: A Reassessment*, Liverpool University Press, 1958, pp. 103–23.
15 Ian Jack, *Keats and the Mirror of Art*, Oxford: Oxford University Press, 1967, pp. 161–75.
16 The Roman term for the pre-Olympian god Cronus, leader of the Titans. Saturn was brother to Hyperion and father to Jove (Jupiter).

Not so much life as on a summer's day
Robs not one light seed from the feather'd grass,
But where the dead leaf fell, there did it rest.   10
A stream went voiceless by, still deadened more
By reason of his fallen divinity
Spreading a shade: the Naiad[17] 'mid her reeds
Press'd her cold finger closer to her lips.

Along the margin-sand large foot-marks went,
No further than to where his feet had stray'd,
And slept there since. Upon the sodden ground
His old right hand lay nerveless, listless, dead,
Unsceptred; and his realmless eyes were closed;
While his bow'd head seem'd list'ning to the Earth,   20
His ancient mother,[18] for some comfort yet.

It seem'd no force could wake him from his place;
But there came one,[19] who with a kindred hand
Touch'd his wide shoulders, after bending low
With reverence, though to one who knew it not.
She was a Goddess of the infant world;
By her in stature the tall Amazon
Had stood a pigmy's height: she would have ta'en
Achilles by the hair and bent his neck;
Or with a finger stay'd Ixion's wheel.[20]   30
Her face was large as that of Memphian sphinx,[21]
Pedestal'd haply in a palace court,
When sages look'd to Egypt for their lore.
But oh! how unlike marble was that face:
How beautiful, if sorrow had not made
Sorrow more beautiful than Beauty's self.
There was a listening fear in her regard,
As if calamity had but begun;
As if the vanward[22] clouds of evil days
Had spent their malice, and the sullen rear   40
Was with its stored thunder labouring up.
One hand she press'd upon that aching spot
Where beats the human heart, as if just there,
Though an immortal, she felt cruel pain:
The other upon Saturn's bended neck

17 Water-nymph.
18 Tellus, the goddess of the earth, was the mother of Saturn.
19 Thea, wife (and sister) of Hyperion.
20 Jupiter punished Ixion, king of the Lapiths, by binding him to an ever-revolving wheel of fire.
21 Memphis was an ancient Egyptian city. The sphinx was usually represented as having the body of a
    lion and the head of a pharaoh.
22 Positioned at the front. Vanward clouds promise thunder.

She laid, and to the level of his ear
Leaning with parted lips, some words she spake
In solemn tenour and deep organ tone:
Some mourning words, which in our feeble tongue
Would come in these like accents; O how frail   50
To that large utterance of the early Gods!
"Saturn, look up!—though wherefore, poor old King?
I have no comfort for thee, no not one:
I cannot say, 'O wherefore sleepest thou?'
For heaven is parted from thee, and the earth
Knows thee not, thus afflicted, for a God;
And ocean too, with all its solemn noise,
Has from thy sceptre pass'd; and all the air
Is emptied of thine hoary[23] majesty.
Thy thunder, conscious of the new command,   60
Rumbles reluctant o'er our fallen house;
And thy sharp lightning in unpractised hands
Scorches and burns our once serene domain.
O aching time! O moments big as years!
All as ye pass swell out the monstrous truth,
And press it so upon our weary griefs
That unbelief has not a space to breathe.
Saturn, sleep on:—O thoughtless, why did I
Thus violate thy slumbrous solitude?
Why should I ope thy melancholy eyes?   70
Saturn, sleep on! while at thy feet I weep."

As when, upon a tranced summer-night,
Those green-rob'd senators of mighty woods,
Tall oaks, branch-charmed by the earnest stars,
Dream, and so dream all night without a stir,
Save from one gradual solitary gust
Which comes upon the silence, and dies off,
As if the ebbing air had but one wave;
So came these words and went; the while in tears
She touch'd her fair large forehead to the ground,   80
Just where her falling hair might be outspread
A soft and silken mat for Saturn's feet.
One moon, with alteration slow, had shed
Her silver seasons four upon the night,
And still these two were postured motionless,
Like natural sculpture in cathedral cavern;[24]

---

23 Grey- or white-haired. Here used as synonymous with 'ancient'.
24 Like the contours of huge rocks.

The frozen God still couchant[25] on the earth,
And the sad Goddess weeping at his feet:
Until at length old Saturn lifted up
His faded eyes, and saw his kingdom gone,   90
And all the gloom and sorrow of the place,
And that fair kneeling Goddess; and then spake,
As with a palsied[26] tongue, and while his beard
Shook horrid[27] with such aspen-malady:[28]
"O tender spouse of gold[29] Hyperion,
Thea, I feel thee ere I see thy face;
Look up, and let me see our doom in it;
Look up, and tell me if this feeble shape
Is Saturn's; tell me, if thou hear'st the voice
Of Saturn; tell me, if this wrinkling brow,   100
Naked and bare of its great diadem,[30]
Peers like the front of Saturn. Who had power
To make me desolate? whence came the strength?
How was it nurtur'd to such bursting forth,
While Fate seem'd strangled in my nervous grasp?
But it is so; and I am smother'd up,
And buried from all godlike exercise
Of influence benign on planets pale,
Of admonitions to the winds and seas,
Of peaceful sway above man's harvesting,   110
And all those acts which Deity supreme
Doth ease its heart of love in.—I am gone
Away from my own bosom: I have left
My strong identity, my real self,
Somewhere between the throne, and where I sit
Here on this spot of earth. Search, Thea, search!
Open thine eyes eterne,[31] and sphere them round
Upon all space: space starr'd, and lorn[32] of light;
Space region'd with life-air; and barren void;
Spaces of fire, and all the yawn of hell.—   120
Search, Thea, search! and tell me, if thou seest
A certain shape or shadow, making way
With wings or chariot fierce to repossess
A heaven he lost erewhile: it must—it must

---

25 Lying.
26 Trembling.
27 Rough or bristling.
28 The leaves of the aspen are proverbially renowned for trembling.
29 A reference to Hyperion's association with the sun.
30 Crown.
31 A poetical form of 'eternal'.
32 Bereft.

Be of ripe progress—Saturn must be King.
Yes, there must be a golden victory;
There must be Gods thrown down, and trumpets blown
Of triumph calm, and hymns of festival
Upon the gold clouds metropolitan,[33]
Voices of soft proclaim, and silver stir   130
Of strings in hollow shells; and there shall be
Beautiful things made new, for the surprise
Of the sky-children; I will give command:
Thea! Thea! Thea! where is Saturn?"

This passion lifted him upon his feet,
And made his hands to struggle in the air,
His Druid locks[34] to shake and ooze with sweat,
His eyes to fever out, his voice to cease.
He stood, and heard not Thea's sobbing deep;
A little time, and then again he snatch'd   140
Utterance thus.—"But cannot I create?
Cannot I form? Cannot I fashion forth
Another world, another universe,
To overbear and crumble this to nought?
Where is another chaos?[35] Where?"—That word
Found way unto Olympus,[36] and made quake
The rebel three.[37]— Thea was startled up,
And in her bearing was a sort of hope,
As thus she quick-voic'd spake, yet full of awe.
"This cheers our fallen house: come to our friends,   150
O Saturn! come away, and give them heart;
I know the covert,[38] for thence came I hither."
Thus brief; then with beseeching eyes she went
With backward footing through the shade a space:
He follow'd, and she turn'd to lead the way
Through aged boughs, that yielded like the mist
Which eagles cleave upmounting from their nest.

Meanwhile in other realms big tears were shed,
More sorrow like to this, and such like woe,
Too huge for mortal tongue or pen of scribe: 160
The Titans fierce, self-hid, or prison-bound,
Groan'd for the old allegiance once more,

---

33 The clouds here serving as the city of the gods.
34 Druids' hair is generally portrayed as being wild and knotted.
35 In Greek myth, Chaos was the formless void from which the universe evolved.
36 Mount Olympus, seat of Jupiter and his cohorts.
37 Jupiter, Neptune and Pluto, the rebellious sons of Saturn.
38 Hiding-place.

And listen'd in sharp pain for Saturn's voice.
But one of the whole mammoth-brood[39] still kept
His sov'reignty, and rule, and majesty;—
Blazing Hyperion on his orbed fire[40]
Still sat, still snuff'd the incense, teeming up
From man to the sun's God; yet unsecure:
For as among us mortals omens drear
Fright and perplex, so also shuddered he—   170
Not at dog's howl, or gloom-bird's[41] hated screech,
Or the familiar visiting of one
Upon the first toll of his passing-bell,[42]
Or prophesyings of the midnight lamp;
But horrors, portion'd to a giant nerve,
Oft made Hyperion ache. His palace bright
Bastion'd with pyramids of glowing gold,
And touch'd with shade of bronzed obelisks,[43]
Glar'd a blood-red through all its thousand courts,
Arches, and domes, and fiery galleries;   180
And all its curtains of Aurorian clouds[44]
Flush'd angerly: while sometimes eagle's wings,
Unseen before by Gods or wondering men,
Darken'd the place; and neighing steeds were heard,
Not heard before by Gods or wondering men.
Also, when he would taste the spicy wreaths
Of incense, breath'd aloft from sacred hills,
Instead of sweets, his ample palate took
Savour of poisonous brass and metal sick:
And so, when harbour'd in the sleepy west,   190
After the full completion of fair day,—
For rest divine upon exalted couch
And slumber in the arms of melody,
He pac'd away the pleasant hours of ease
With stride colossal, on from hall to hall;
While far within each aisle and deep recess,
His winged minions in close clusters stood,
Amaz'd and full of fear; like anxious men
Who on wide plains gather in panting troops,
When earthquakes jar their battlements and towers.[45]   200

---

39 A metaphorical glance at the Titans' enormity.
40 The sun. Hyperion was sometimes identified as the god of the sun.
41 The owl.
42 Death-knell.
43 A tapering stone pillar. Cleopatra's Needle is a famous example.
44 i.e. clouds illuminated by the roseate hue of the dawn.
45 ll. 196–200 echo 'Milton's description of the fallen angels in Pandemonium, *Paradise Lost* I,
767–71' (Barnard, *John Keats: The Complete Poems*, p. 612).

Even now, while Saturn, rous'd from icy trance,
Went step for step with Thea through the woods,
Hyperion, leaving twilight in the rear,
Came slope upon the threshold of the west;
Then, as was wont, his palace-door flew ope
In smoothest silence, save what solemn tubes,[46]
Blown by the serious Zephyrs,[47] gave of sweet
And wandering sounds, slow-breathed melodies;
And like a rose in vermeil[48] tint and shape,
In fragrance soft, and coolness to the eye,   210
That inlet to severe magnificence
Stood full blown, for the God to enter in.

He enter'd, but he enter'd full of wrath;
His flaming robes stream'd out beyond his heels,
And gave a roar, as if of earthly fire,
That scar'd away the meek ethereal Hours[49]
And made their dove-wings tremble. On he flared,
From stately nave to nave, from vault to vault,
Through bowers of fragrant and enwreathed light,
And diamond-paved lustrous long arcades,   220
Until he reach'd the great main cupola;[50]
There standing fierce beneath, he stampt his foot,
And from the basements deep to the high towers
Jarr'd his own golden region; and before
The quavering thunder thereupon had ceas'd,
His voice leapt out, despite of[51] godlike curb,
To this result: "O dreams of day and night!
O monstrous forms! O effigies of pain!
O spectres busy in a cold, cold gloom!
O lank-eared Phantoms of black-weeded pools!   230
Why do I know ye? why have I seen ye? why
Is my eternal essence thus distraught
To see and to behold these horrors new?
Saturn is fallen, am I too to fall?
Am I to leave this haven of my rest,
This cradle of my glory, this soft clime,
This calm luxuriance of blissful light,
These crystalline pavilions, and pure fanes,[52]

---

46 As in the tubes of an organ.
47 Personifications of the winds.
48 Bright red.
49 The rosy-bosomed divinities of the seasons.
50 A domed roof.
51 i.e. in spite of.
52 Temples.

Of all my lucent[53] empire? It is left
Deserted, void, nor any haunt of mine.   240
The blaze, the splendor, and the symmetry,
I cannot see—but darkness, death and darkness.
Even here, into my centre of repose,
The shady visions come to domineer,
Insult, and blind, and stifle up my pomp.—
Fall!—No, by Tellus[54] and her briny robes![55]
Over the fiery frontier of my realms
I will advance a terrible right arm
Shall scare that infant thunderer, rebel Jove,
And bid old Saturn take his throne again."—   250
He spake, and ceas'd, the while a heavier threat
Held struggle with his throat but came not forth;
For as in theatres of crowded men
Hubbub increases more they call out "Hush!"
So at Hyperion's words the Phantoms pale[56]
Bestirr'd themselves, thrice horrible and cold;
And from the mirror'd level where he stood
A mist arose, as from a scummy marsh.
At this, through all his bulk an agony
Crept gradual, from the feet unto the crown,   260
Like a lithe serpent vast and muscular
Making slow way, with head and neck convuls'd
From over-strained might. Releas'd, he fled
To the eastern gates, and full six dewy hours
Before the dawn in season due should blush,
He breath'd fierce breath against the sleepy portals,[57]
Clear'd them of heavy vapours, burst them wide
Suddenly on the ocean's chilly streams,
The planet orb of fire, whereon he rode
Each day from east to west the heavens through,   270
Spun round in sable[58] curtaining of clouds;
Not therefore veiled quite, blindfold, and hid,
But ever and anon the glancing spheres,
Circles, and arcs, and broad-belting colure,[59]
Glow'd through, and wrought upon the muffling dark

---

53 Lustrous, shining.
54 The goddess of the earth and mother of the Titans.
55 i.e. the seas.
56 This passage owes something to Milton's portrayal of Satan's entrance into Eden in *Paradise Lost*, IX, 180–90.
57 Gates.
58 Black.
59 The colures are the longitudinal circles which intersect at the poles. Keats is also alluding to Satan's journey in *Paradise Lost* ('From pole to pole, traversing each colure' (IX, 66)).

Sweet-shaped lightnings from the nadir deep
Up to the zenith,—hieroglyphics old,[60]
Which sages and keen-eyed astrologers
Then living on the earth, with labouring thought
Won from the gaze of many centuries: 280
Now lost, save what we find on remnants huge
Of stone, or marble swart;[61] their import gone,
Their wisdom long since fled.—Two wings this orb
Possess'd for glory, two fair argent[62] wings,
Ever exalted at the God's approach:
And now, from forth the gloom their plumes immense
Rose, one by one, till all outspreaded were;
While still the dazzling globe maintain'd eclipse,
Awaiting for Hyperion's command.
Fain would he have commanded, fain took throne   290
And bid the day begin, if but for change.
He might not:—No, though a primeval God:
The sacred seasons might not be disturb'd.
Therefore the operations of the dawn
Stay'd in their birth, even as here 'tis told.
Those silver wings expanded sisterly,
Eager to sail their orb; the porches wide
Open'd upon the dusk demesnes[63] of night;
And the bright Titan, phrenzied with new woes,
Unus'd to bend, by hard compulsion bent   300
His spirit to the sorrow of the time;
And all along a dismal rack of clouds,
Upon the boundaries of day and night,
He stretch'd himself in grief and radiance faint.
There as he lay, the Heaven with its stars
Look'd down on him with pity, and the voice
Of Coelus,[64] from the universal space,
Thus whisper'd low and solemn in his ear.
"O brightest of my children dear, earth-born
And sky-engendered, Son of Mysteries   310
All unrevealed even to the powers
Which met at thy creating; at whose joys
And palpitations sweet, and pleasures soft,
I, Coelus, wonder, how they came and whence;
And at the fruits thereof what shapes they be,

---

60 i.e. zodiacal signs.
61 Swarthy, i.e. black marble.
62 Silver.
63 Regions.
64 God of the heavens and father to Hyperion, Saturn and the Titans.

Distinct, and visible; symbols divine,
Manifestations of that beauteous life
Diffus'd unseen throughout eternal space:
Of these new-form'd art thou, oh brightest child!
Of these, thy brethren and the Goddesses!   320
There is sad feud among ye, and rebellion
Of son against his sire. I saw him fall,
I saw my first-born[65] tumbled from his throne!
To me his arms were spread, to me his voice
Found way from forth the thunders round his head!
Pale wox[66] I, and in vapours hid my face.
Art thou, too, near such doom? vague fear there is:
For I have seen my sons most unlike Gods.
Divine ye were created, and divine
In sad demeanour, solemn, undisturb'd,   330
Unruffled, like high Gods, ye liv'd and ruled:
Now I behold in you fear, hope, and wrath;
Actions of rage and passion; even as
I see them, on the mortal world beneath,
In men who die.—This is the grief, O Son!
Sad sign of ruin, sudden dismay, and fall!
Yet do thou strive; as thou art capable,
As thou canst move about, an evident God;[67]
And canst oppose to each malignant hour
Ethereal presence:—I am but a voice;   340
My life is but the life of winds and tides,
No more than winds and tides can I avail:—
But thou canst.—Be thou therefore in the van
Of circumstance; yea, seize the arrow's barb
Before the tense string murmur.—To the earth!
For there thou wilt find Saturn, and his woes.
Meantime I will keep watch on thy bright sun,
And of thy seasons be a careful nurse."—
Ere half this region-whisper had come down,
Hyperion arose, and on the stars   350
Lifted his curved lids, and kept them wide
Until it ceas'd; and still he kept them wide:
And still they were the same bright, patient stars.
Then with a slow incline of his broad breast,
Like to a diver in the pearly seas,
Forward he stoop'd over the airy shore,
And plung'd all noiseless into the deep night.

65 Saturn.
66 Waxed.
67 i.e. Saturn has, unlike the god of the skies, a material form.

Book II

Just at the self-same beat of Time's wide wings   1
Hyperion slid into the rustled air,
And Saturn gain'd with Thea that sad place
Where Cybele[68] and the bruised Titans mourn'd.
It was a den where no insulting light
Could glimmer on their tears; where their own groans
They felt, but heard not, for the solid roar
Of thunderous waterfalls and torrents hoarse,
Pouring a constant bulk, uncertain where.
Crag jutting forth to crag, and rocks that seem'd   10
Ever as if just rising from a sleep,
Forehead to forehead held their monstrous horns;
And thus in thousand hugest phantasies
Made a fit roofing to this nest of woe.
Instead of thrones, hard flint they sat upon,
Couches of rugged stone, and slaty ridge
Stubborn'd with iron. [. . .]

Keats lists the fallen Titans.

Creüs[69] was one; his ponderous iron mace
Lay by him, and a shatter'd rib of rock
Told of his rage, ere he thus sank and pined.
Iäpetus[70] another; in his grasp,
A serpent's plashy[71] neck; its barbed tongue
Squeez'd from the gorge, and all its uncurl'd length
Dead; and because the creature could not spit
Its poison in the eyes of conquering Jove.
Next Cottus:[72] prone he lay, chin uppermost,
As though in pain; for still upon the flint   50
He ground severe his skull, with open mouth
And eyes at horrid working. Nearest him
Asia, born of most enormous Caf,[73]
Who cost her mother Tellus keener pangs,
Though feminine, than any of her sons:

---

68 A nature deity, mother goddess of Asia. She is sometimes (though not in this context) identified as
   Ops, the wife of Saturn.
69 One of the sons of Uranus.
70 The father of the rebel Titans Atlas and Prometheus.
71 'Marked as if splashed with colour', according to the *Oxford English Dictionary*. Keats's use of the
   word is the sole example of the sense cited in the dictionary.
72 A son of Uranus.
73 Keats seems to have invented this personage.

More thought than woe was in her dusky face,
For she was prophesying of her glory;[74]
And in her wide imagination stood
Palm-shaded temples, and high rival fanes,
By Oxus[75] or in Ganges' sacred isles.   60
Even as Hope upon her anchor leans,[76]
So leant she, not so fair, upon a tusk
Shed from the broadest of her elephants.
Above her, on a crag's uneasy shelve,
Upon his elbow rais'd, all prostrate else,
Shadow'd Enceladus;[77] once tame and mild
As grazing ox unworried in the meads;
Now tiger-passion'd, lion-thoughted, wroth,
He meditated, plotted, and even now[78]
Was hurling mountains in that second war,[79]   70
Not long delay'd, that scar'd the younger Gods[80]
To hide themselves in forms of beast and bird.
Not far hence Atlas;[81] and beside him prone
Phorcus,[82] the sire of Gorgons. Neighbour'd close
Oceanus,[83] and Tethys,[84] in whose lap
Sobb'd Clymene[85] among her tangled hair.
In midst of all lay Themis,[86] at the feet
Of Ops[87] the queen all clouded round from sight;
No shape distinguishable, more than when
Thick night confounds the pine-tops with the clouds: 80
And many else whose names may not be told.
For when the Muse's wings are air-ward spread,
Who shall delay her flight? And she must chaunt
Of Saturn, and his guide, who now had climb'd
With damp and slippery footing from a depth
More horrid still. Above a sombre cliff

---

74 Asia anticipates being the object of worship in future millennia.
75 An Asian river.
76 Iconographic representations of Hope and the anchor derive from the Christian symbolism of St
   Paul: 'what hope we have as an anchor of the soul' (Hebrews 6:19).
77 Keats frequently drew on John Lemprière's *Bibliotheca Classica* (1788). Lemprière writes that
   Enceladus was 'A son of Titan and Terra, [and was] the most powerful of all the giants who
   conspired against Jupiter'.
78 i.e. in his imagination.
79 Keats may have intended to deal with this second war in a later book of his poem.
80 i.e. the Olympians.
81 Atlas, the son of Iapetus and Clymene, was punished for his part in the Titan rebellion by being
   made to hold up the heavens with his head and hands.
82 A sea-deity.
83 The Titan Oceanus was the husband of Tethys and father of the water-nymphs.
84 The wife of Oceanus.
85 The mother of Atlas.
86 The Titan Themis was the goddess of order.
87 The fertility goddess who is often described as the wife of Saturn.

Their heads appear'd, and up their stature grew
Till on the level height their steps found ease:
Then Thea spread abroad her trembling arms
Upon the precincts of this nest of pain,   90
And sidelong fix'd her eye on Saturn's face:
There saw she direst strife; the supreme God
At war with all the frailty of grief,
Of rage, of fear, anxiety, revenge,
Remorse, spleen, hope, but most of all despair.
Against these plagues he strove in vain; for Fate
Had pour'd a mortal oil upon his head,
A disanointing[88] poison: so that Thea,
Affrighted, kept her still, and let him pass
First onwards in, among the fallen tribe.   100
As with us mortal men, the laden heart
Is persecuted more, and fever'd more,
When it is nighing to the mournful house
Where other hearts are sick of the same bruise;[89]
So Saturn, as he walk'd into the midst,
Felt faint, and would have sunk among the rest,
But that he met Enceladus's eye,
Whose mightiness, and awe of him, at once
Came like an inspiration; and he shouted,
"Titans, behold your God!" at which some groan'd;   110
Some started on their feet; some also shouted;
Some wept, some wail'd, all bow'd with reverence;
And Ops, uplifting her black folded veil,
Show'd her pale cheeks, and all her forehead wan,
Her eye-brows thin and jet, and hollow eyes.
There is a roaring in the bleak-grown pines
When Winter lifts his voice; there is a noise
Among immortals when a God gives sign,
With hushing finger, how he means to load
His tongue with the full weight of utterless[90] thought,   120
With thunder, and with music, and with pomp:
Such noise is like the roar of bleak-grown pines;
Which, when it ceases in this mountain'd world,
No other sound succeeds; but ceasing here,
Among these fallen, Saturn's voice therefrom
Grew up like organ, that begins anew
Its strain, when other harmonies, stopt short,

---

88 The Olympian revolt has had the effect of negating the anointing, or consecration, of Saturn as a
    deity.
89 Human woes are exacerbated by our fellow-feeling with other sufferers.
90 Unutterable (i.e. beyond the expressive powers of the human imagination).

Leave the dinn'd[91] air vibrating silverly.[92]
Thus grew it up—"Not in my own sad breast,
Which is its own great judge and searcher out,   130
Can I find reason why ye should be thus:
Not in the legends of the first of days,
Studied from that old spirit-leaved book[93]
Which starry Uranus[94] with finger bright
Sav'd from the shores of darkness, when the waves
Low-ebb'd still hid it up in shallow gloom;—
And the which book ye know I ever kept
For my firm-based footstool:—Ah, infirm!
Not there, nor in sign, symbol, or portent
Of element, earth, water, air, and fire,—   140
At war, at peace, or inter-quarreling
One against one, or two, or three, or all
Each several one against the other three,
As fire with air loud warring when rain-floods
Drown both, and press them both against earth's face,
Where, finding sulphur, a quadruple wrath
Unhinges the poor world;—not in that strife,
Wherefrom I take strange lore, and read it deep,
Can I find reason why ye should be thus:
No, no-where can unriddle, though I search,   150
And pore on Nature's universal scroll
Even to swooning, why ye, Divinities,
The first-born of all shap'd and palpable Gods,
Should cower beneath what, in comparison,
Is untremendous might. Yet ye are here,
O'erwhelm'd, and spurn'd, and batter'd, ye are here!
O Titans, shall I say 'Arise!'?"—Ye groan;
Shall I say 'Crouch!'?—Ye groan. What can I then?
O Heaven wide! O unseen parent dear!
What can I? Tell me, all ye brethren Gods,   160
How we can war, how engine our great wrath![95]
O speak your counsel now, for Saturn's ear
Is all a-hunger'd.[96] Thou, Oceanus,
Ponderest high and deep; and in thy face
I see, astonied,[97] that severe content
Which comes of thought and musing: give us help!"

---

91 Noisy.
92 i.e. with a silvery sound.
93 i.e. in the myths of creation.
94 i.e. Coelus, father of Saturn.
95 i.e. 'How can we focus our anger as the engine of our counterattack upon the Olympians?'
96 i.e. avid to hear.
97 Astonished.

So ended Saturn; and the God of the Sea,
Sophist and sage, from no Athenian grove,
But cogitation in his watery shades,
Arose, with locks not oozy, and began,   170
In murmurs, which his first-endeavouring tongue
Caught infant-like from the far-foamed sands.
"O ye, whom wrath consumes! who, passion-stung,
Writhe at defeat, and nurse your agonies!
Shut up your senses, stifle up your ears,
My voice is not a bellows unto ire."[98]
Yet listen, ye who will, whilst I bring proof
How ye, perforce, must be content to stoop:
And in the proof much comfort will I give,
If ye will take that comfort in its truth.   180
We fall by course of Nature's law, not force
Of thunder, or of Jove. Great Saturn, thou
Hast sifted well the atom-universe;[99]
But for this reason, that thou art the King,
And only blind from sheer supremacy,
One avenue was shaded from thine eyes,
Through which I wandered to eternal truth.
And first, as thou wast not the first of powers,
So art thou not the last; it cannot be:
Thou art not the beginning nor the end.[100]   190
From chaos and parental darkness came[101]
Light, the first fruits of that intestine broil,[102]
That sullen ferment, which for wondrous ends
Was ripening in itself. The ripe hour came,
And with it light, and light, engendering
Upon its own producer,[103] forthwith touch'd
The whole enormous matter into life.
Upon that very hour, our parentage,
The Heavens and the Earth, were manifest:
Then thou first-born, and we the giant-race,   200
Found ourselves ruling new and beauteous realms.

---

98 Iron.
99 i.e. the whole universe, indivisible (in the 1810s) as the single atom.
100 An echo of Revelation 1:8: 'I am Alpha and Omega, the beginning and the end, saith the Lord.'
101 Oceanus' quietest account of creation and the ongoing development of the world reflects Keats's own sense that human history followed a model of progress. Compare his notion of the 'grand march of intellect' in the May 1818 letter to J. H. Reynolds (pp. 16–17). In the month in which he began *Hyperion*, September 1818, Keats writes to George and Georgiana Keats that 'All civil[is]ed countries become gradually more enlighten'd and there should be a continual change for the better'.
102 Internal conflict, i.e. civil war.
103 Light incestuously engenders the world upon darkness ('its own producer').

Now comes the pain of truth, to whom 'tis pain;[104]
O folly! for to bear all naked truths,
And to envisage circumstance, all calm,
That is the top of sovereignty. Mark well!
As Heaven and Earth are fairer, fairer far
Than Chaos and blank Darkness, though once chiefs;
And as we show beyond[105] that Heaven and Earth
In form and shape compact and beautiful,
In will, in action free, companionship,   210
And thousand other signs of purer life;
So on our heels a fresh perfection treads,[106]
A power more strong in beauty, born of us
And fated to excel us, as we pass
In glory that old Darkness: nor are we
Thereby more conquer'd, than by us the rule
Of shapeless Chaos. Say, doth the dull soil
Quarrel with the proud forests it hath fed,
And feedeth still, more comely than itself?
Can it deny the chiefdom[107] of green groves?   220
Or shall the tree be envious of the dove
Because it cooeth, and hath snowy wings
To wander wherewithal and find its joys?
We are such forest-trees, and our fair boughs
Have bred forth, not pale solitary doves,
But eagles golden-feather'd, who do tower
Above us in their beauty, and must reign
In right thereof; for 'tis the eternal law
That first in beauty should be first in might:
Yea, by that law, another race may drive   230
Our conquerors to mourn as we do now.
Have ye beheld the young God of the Seas,[108]
My dispossessor? Have ye seen his face?
Have ye beheld his chariot, foam'd along
By noble winged creatures he hath made?
I saw him on the calmed waters scud,[109]
With such a glow of beauty in his eyes,
That it enforc'd me to bid sad farewell
To all my empire: farewell sad I took,
And hither came, to see how dolorous fate   240
Had wrought upon ye; and how I might best

104 For those to whom the knowledge is painful.
105 i.e. demonstrate beyond doubt.
106 i.e. the Olympians.
107 i.e. the superiority.
108 Neptune.
109 Sailing.

Give consolation in this woe extreme.
Receive the truth, and let it be your balm."[110] [. . .]

Clymene speaks, and then the wrathful Enceladus.

"Now ye are flames,[111] I'll tell you how to burn,
And purge the ether[112] of our enemies;
How to feed fierce the crooked stings of fire,[113]
And singe away the swollen clouds of Jove,   330
Stifling that puny essence in its tent.
O let him feel the evil he hath done;
For though I scorn Oceanus's lore,
Much pain have I for more than loss of realms:
The days of peace and slumberous calm are fled;
Those days, all innocent of scathing war,
When all the fair Existences of heaven
Came open-eyed to guess what we would speak:—
That was before our brows were taught to frown,
Before our lips knew else but solemn sounds;   340
That was before we knew the winged thing,
Victory,[114] might be lost, or might be won.
And be ye mindful that Hyperion,
Our brightest brother, still is undisgraced—
Hyperion, lo! his radiance is here!"

All eyes were on Enceladus's face,
And they beheld, while still Hyperion's name
Flew from his lips up to the vaulted rocks,[115]
A pallid gleam across his features stern:
Not savage, for he saw full many a God   350
Wroth as himself. He look'd upon them all,
And in each face he saw a gleam of light,
But splendider in Saturn's, whose hoar locks
Shone like the bubbling foam about a keel
When the prow sweeps into a midnight cove.
In pale and silver silence they remain'd,
Till suddenly a splendour, like the morn,

110 Consolation.
111 i.e. inflamed with wrath.
112 i.e. rid the air.
113 i.e. Jove's lightning bolts.
114 According to Lemprière, 'the goddess of Victory . . . was represented with wings'.
115 The rocks give the impression of a vaulted roof above the Titans.

Pervaded all the beetling[116] gloomy steeps,
All the sad spaces of oblivion,
And every gulf, and every chasm old,   360
And every height, and every sullen depth,
Voiceless, or hoarse with loud tormented streams:
And all the everlasting cataracts,
And all the headlong torrents far and near,
Mantled before in darkness and huge shade,
Now saw the light and made it terrible.
It was Hyperion:—a granite peak
His bright feet touch'd, and there he stay'd to view
The misery his brilliance had betray'd
To the most hateful seeing of itself.   370
Golden his hair of short Numidian curl,[117]
Regal his shape majestic, a vast shade
In midst of his own brightness, like the bulk
Of Memnon's[118] image at the set of sun
To one who travels from the dusking East:
Sighs, too, as mournful as that Memnon's harp
He utter'd, while his hands contemplative
He press'd together, and in silence stood.
Despondence seiz'd again the fallen Gods
At sight of the dejected King of Day,   380
And many hid their faces from the light:
But fierce Enceladus sent forth his eyes
Among the brotherhood; and, at their glare,
Uprose Iäpetus, and Creüs too,
And Phorcus, sea-born, and together strode
To where he towered on his eminence.[119]
There those four shouted forth old Saturn's name;
Hyperion from the peak loud answered, "Saturn!"
Saturn sat near the Mother of the Gods,
In whose face was no joy, though all the Gods   390
Gave from their hollow throats the name of "Saturn!"

Book III

Thus in alternate uproar and sad peace,   1
Amazed were those Titans utterly.

---

116 Overhanging, projecting.
117 Numidia was an ancient African country. Hyperion's hair is tightly curled, like that, to Keats, of
   an African.
118 The Greeks called the statue of Amenophis III at Thebes that of Memnon, the Ethiopian or
   oriental prince who was slain by Achilles in the Trojan War. It was supposed to make a mournful
   sound each evening at dusk.
119 Mountain.

O leave them, Muse! O leave them to their woes;
For thou art weak to sing such tumults dire:
A solitary sorrow best befits
Thy lips, and antheming a lonely grief.
Leave them, O Muse! for thou anon wilt find
Many a fallen old divinity[120]
Wandering in vain about bewildered shores.

[. . .]

Apollo is once more the golden theme!
Where was he, when the Giant of the Sun[121]
Stood bright, amid the sorrow of his peers?   30
Together had he left his mother fair[122]
And his twin-sister[123] sleeping in their bower,
And in the morning twilight wandered forth
Beside the osiers of a rivulet,[124]
Full ankle-deep in lilies of the vale.
The nightingale had ceas'd, and a few stars
Were lingering in the heavens, while the thrush
Began calm-throated. Throughout all the isle
There was no covert,[125] no retired cave
Unhaunted by the murmurous noise of waves,   40
Though scarcely heard in many a green recess.
He listen'd, and he wept, and his bright tears
Went trickling down the golden bow he held.
Thus with half-shut suffused[126] eyes he stood,
While from beneath some cumbrous boughs hard by
With solemn step an awful goddess came,[127]
And there was purport in her looks for him,
Which he with eager guess began to read
Perplex'd, the while melodiously he said:
"How cam'st thou over the unfooted sea?   50
Or hath that antique mien[128] and robed form
Mov'd in these vales invisible till now?
Sure I have heard those vestments[129] sweeping o'er
The fallen leaves, when I have sat alone

---

120 God.
121 Hyperion.
122 Latona.
123 Diana.
124 i.e. the weavings of a stream.
125 Hiding-place.
126 Tearful.
127 This is the Titan Mnemosyne, the mother of the Muses by Jupiter.
128 Demeanour.
129 Clothes.

In cool mid-forest. Surely I have traced
The rustle of those ample skirts about
These grassy solitudes, and seen the flowers
Lift up their heads, as still the whisper pass'd.
Goddess! I have beheld those eyes before,
And their eternal calm, and all that face,   60
Or I have dream'd."—"Yes," said the supreme shape,
"Thou hast dream'd of me; and awaking up
Didst find a lyre all golden by thy side,
Whose strings touch'd by thy fingers, all the vast
Unwearied ear of the whole universe
Listen'd in pain and pleasure at the birth
Of such new tuneful wonder. Is't not strange
That thou shouldst weep, so gifted? Tell me, youth,
What sorrow thou canst feel; for I am sad
When thou dost shed a tear: explain thy griefs   70
To one who in this lonely isle hath been
The watcher of thy sleep and hours of life,
From the young day when first thy infant hand
Pluck'd witless the weak flowers, till thine arm
Could bend that bow heroic to all times.
Show thy heart's secret to an ancient Power
Who hath forsaken old and sacred thrones[130]
For prophecies of thee, and for the sake
Of loveliness new born."—Apollo then,
With sudden scrutiny and gloomless eyes,[131]   ·80
Thus answer'd, while his white melodious throat
Throbb'd with the syllables.—"Mnemosyne!
Thy name is on my tongue, I know not how;
Why should I tell thee what thou so well seest?
Why should I strive to show what from thy lips
Would come no mystery? For me, dark, dark,
And painful vile oblivion seals my eyes:
I strive to search wherefore I am so sad,
Until a melancholy numbs my limbs;
And then upon the grass I sit, and moan,   90
Like one who once had wings. – O why should I
Feel curs'd and thwarted, when the liegeless air[132]
Yields to my step aspirant? Why should I
Spurn the green turf as hateful to my feet?
Goddess benign, point forth some unknown thing:
Are there not other regions than this isle?

---

130 Mnemosyne has abandoned her allegiance to the Titans and aligned herself to Apollo and the
    Olympians.
131 i.e. Apollo's gloom is momentarily lifted on hearing Mnemosyne.
132 The air has no master.

What are the stars? There is the sun, the sun!
And the most patient brilliance of the moon!
And stars by thousands! Point me out the way
To any one particular beauteous star,   100
And I will flit into it with my lyre,
And make its silvery splendour pant with bliss.
I have heard the cloudy thunder. Where is power?
Whose hand, whose essence, what divinity
Makes this alarum[133] in the elements,
While I here idle listen on the shores
In fearless yet in aching[134] ignorance?
O tell me, lonely Goddess, by thy harp,
That waileth every morn and eventide,
Tell me why thus I rave, about these groves!   110
Mute thou remainest—Mute! yet I can read
A wondrous lesson in thy silent face:
Knowledge enormous makes a God of me.[135]
Names, deeds, gray legends, dire events, rebellions,
Majesties, sovran[136] voices, agonies,
Creations and destroyings, all at once
Pour into the wide hollows of my brain,
And deify me, as if some blithe wine
Or bright elixir peerless I had drunk,
And so become immortal."—Thus the God,   120
While his enkindled eyes, with level glance—
Beneath his white soft temples, stedfast kept
Trembling with light upon Mnemosyne.
Soon wild commotions shook him, and made flush
All the immortal fairness of his limbs;
Most like the struggle at the gate of death;
Or liker still to one who should take leave
Of pale immortal death, and with a pang
As hot as death's is chill, with fierce convulse[137]
Die into life: so young Apollo anguish'd: 130
His very hair, his golden tresses famed
Kept undulation round his eager neck.
During the pain Mnemosyne upheld
Her arms as one who prophesied.—At length
Apollo shriek'd;—and lo! from all his limbs
Celestial[138] [. . .]

---

133 Turmoil.
134 Longing.
135 Apollo's knowledge of suffering and pain has served to deify him.
136 Sovereign.
137 Convulsion.
138 The fragment breaks off at this point.

The Eve of St. Agnes

'The Eve of St. Agnes' was composed between 18 January and 2 February 1819, revised in September 1819 and first published in 1820.[1] It is the most read and anthologised of Keats's narrative poems. A tale of young love played out against a backdrop of family rivalry and ill-concealed undertones of violence, its atmosphere is heavily indebted to Shakespeare's *Romeo and Juliet*, though it also owes something to the medieval settings of the narrative poems of Sir Walter Scott (notably *The Lay of the Last Minstrel* (1805)) and S. T. Coleridge (most particularly the recently published 'Christabel'). The poem also, perhaps, reflects Keats's personal life; Miriam Allott writes that 'its romantic celebration of erotic fantasy was almost certainly inspired by the early stages of Keats's association with Fanny Brawne'.[2] As Keats writes to Benjamin Bailey in August 1819, his 'tale' was based 'on a popular superstition'; folklore has it that on St Agnes' Eve, assuming that they perform certain rituals (fast and, when in bed, remain silent and immobile) maidens would see their future husbands in their dreams. The protagonists of the romance, Madeline and Porphyro, come from hostile families. Porphyro steals into the castle where Madeline is surrounded by her belligerent kinsmen and, with the help of the aged Angela, contrives to steal into her room. Madeline performs the ceremonies of Agnes' Eve and retires. Her reveries of ethereal, idealised love are interrupted by a physical, erotic reality; she is awoken – and deflowered – by Porphyro. The lovers escape the house and make off 'into the storm'.

Most critics see 'The Eve of St. Agnes' as Keats's first fully achieved romance and as a far more accomplished narrative poem than its predecessor, 'Isabella'. '[I]t is not far short of perfection,' writes M. R. Ridley: 'Keats has at last entered triumphantly into his kingdom.'[3] From its first publication, 'The Eve of St. Agnes' has had its idolaters, many of whom were content to luxuriate in its atmospherics. 'Can the beautiful go beyond this?' asked Leigh Hunt in 1835; 'We never saw it.' Nineteenth-century critics often saw the poem, with Hunt, as enchanting fantasy. W. M. Rossetti writes of the 'spell' of the poem, and revels in its lack of external resonance: 'it means next to nothing, but means that little so exquisitely.' Some modern critics have concurred; as late as 1959 Douglas Bush described the poem as 'no more than a romantic tapestry of colour'.[4] Character analysis, thematic overview, historical significance: all are dismissed in favour of rhapsodic pleasure in the poem's 'incidental and innumerable beauties

---

1   In *Lamia, Isabella, The Eve of St. Agnes, and other Poems*, the source of the present text.
2   Miriam Allott (ed.), *The Poems of John Keats*, London: Longman, 1970, p. 451.
3   M. R. Ridley, *Keats' Craftmanship: A Study in Poetic Development*, Oxford: Clarendon Press, 1933, p. 96.
4   Douglas Bush (ed.), *John Keats: Selected Poems and Letters*, Boston, Mass.: Houghton Mifflin, 1959, p. xvi.

of descriptive phrase and rhythm'.[5] In reaction to readings of the poem which see it as 'a series of pretty pictures',[6] Earl R. Wasserman argued for the essential seriousness of 'The Eve of St. Agnes', constructing an elaborate reading of the poem as a profound allegory of the soul's ascent. Porphyro's progress through the castle and up into Madeline's bedroom symbolises a pilgrimage to 'heaven's bourne' and the sexual union of the lovers represents 'a mystic blending of mortality and immortality'. At the end of the poem, Porphyro and Madeline are 'No longer [. . .] human actors [. . .] but the selfless spirit of man forever captured in the dimensionless mystery beyond our mortal vision'.[7] Jack Stillinger replied to Wasserman in his influential essay, 'The Hoodwinking of Madeline' (1961),[8] which rejected both the rhapsodic eulogies of the 'Eve' and what he saw as the over-extended metaphorical readings of 'metaphysical' critics such as Wasserman. Stillinger's provocative reading sees the poem as an anti-romance. Porphyro is a 'peeping Tom' who achieves his desires through deviousness, and the sexual encounter between Porphyro and Madeline, echoing as it does Lovelace's rape of the unconscious Clarissa in Richardson's novel of that name, is sordid and close to violation. Though this account was a useful corrective to Wasserman's dimensionless mysteries, it prompted Stuart Sperry to argue in 1973 that both discussions were 'one-sided' and 'seem to reduce the poem to the value of a simple thesis'. To Sperry, the 'union of the two lovers in no way resembles rape or even a seduction of the ordinary kind'. Instead, when Madeleine 'awakes, or half-awakes from her dream (for the point is left deliberately ambiguous), she recognises Porphyro, after a moment of painful confusion, not just as a mortal lover, but also as a part of her dream, a part of her vision and her desire, and she accepts him as her lover. There is an accommodation, one that is neither easy nor untroubled, between imagination and reality.'[9]

The Wasserman–Stillinger–Sperry debate prompted an upsurge in critical attention to the meaning and significance of 'The Eve of St. Agnes'. The poem is no longer seen as a rich but essentially meaningless 'romantic tapestry', but as a work capable of generating a multiplicity of interpretations (as Jack Stillinger has demonstrated in his amusing and insightful list of 'fifty-nine interpretations' of the 'Eve'[10] published over the last thirty years). Much of this work, following Stillinger, focuses upon the poem's sexual politics. John Kerrigan and James Twitchell have developed the notion of Porphyro as rapist. The former reads 'The Eve of St. Agnes' against Shakespeare's *The Rape of Lucrece* rather than *Romeo and Juliet* (the seduction of Madeleine is 'suggestive of deception, substi-

---

5   *Ibid.*, p. 333.
6   The term is Jack Stillinger's.
7   Earl R. Wasserman, *The Finer Tone: Keats' Major Poems*, Baltimore, Md.: Johns Hopkins University Press, 1953, p. 125.
8   Jack Stillinger, 'The Hoodwinking of Madeline: Scepticism in "The Eve of St Agnes"', *Studies in Philology*, 58, 1961, pp. 533–55.
9   Stuart M. Sperry, *Keats the Poet*, Princeton, NJ: Princeton University Press, 1973, pp. 204–5.
10   Jack Stillinger, *Reading The Eve of St. Agnes: The Multiples of Complex Literary Transaction*, New York and Oxford: Oxford University Press, 1999, pp. 39–78.

tution, and sexual threat[11] in the manner of Shakespeare's poem); the latter fulminates against Porphyro as 'a villain of the first order, not an imaginary Adam in Madeleine's Edenic dream, but rather [. . .] the Satan of the piece [. . .] drawn from the myth of the vampire'.[12] Other critics have discussed Madeline as a victim of her oppressive family or, indeed, of her lover. Daniel P. Watkins, for example, declares that she represents 'woman as the Other, as the silent and passive object of masculine power [. . .] she is the site where masculine identity is stamped; she is, in short, without identity except insofar as she receives identity from that which controls her'. Returning to allegorical interpretation, Watkins also offers the most sustained sociopolitical account of the poem, arguing that it is 'an allegory of the inner workings of feudalism at the moment of its collapse'.[13] Against Watkins's view of Madeline as a passive victim, she has been seen as both a willing participant in her own seduction (by Heidi Thomson)[14] and as a *femme fatale* in the manner of the Belle Dame Sans Merci (by Mary Arseneau).[15] And Marjorie Levinson, who sees Porphyro's sexual voyeurism as Keats's, and 'The Eve of St. Agnes' as a 'masturbatory ritual', argues that Madeline herself engages in 'masturbatory dreaming'. And we as readers are also complicit: 'Voyeurs ourselves, we watch another voyeur (Keats), watching another (Porphyro), watching a woman who broods voluptuously upon herself.'[16]

1

St. Agnes' Eve—Ah, bitter chill it was!   1
The owl, for all his feathers, was a-cold;
The hare limp'd trembling through the frozen grass,
And silent was the flock in woolly fold:[17]
Numb were the Beadsman's[18] fingers, while he told[19]
His rosary, and while his frosted breath,
Like pious incense from a censer[20] old,
Seem'd taking flight for heaven, without a death,[21]
Past the sweet Virgin's picture, while his prayer he saith.

11 John Kerrigan, 'Keats and Lucrece', *Shakespeare Survey*, 41, 1989, p. 112.
12 James Twitchell, *The Living Dead: A Study of the Vampire in Romantic Literature*, Durham, NC: Duke University Press, 1981, p. 94.
13 Daniel P. Watkins, *Keats's Poetry and the Politics of the Imagination*, Rutherford, NJ: Fairleigh Dickinson University Press, 1989, p. 65.
14 Heidi Thomson, 'Eavesdropping on "The Eve of St. Agnes": Madeline's Sensual Ear and Porphyro's Ancient Ditty', *Journal of English and Germanic Philology*, 97, 1988, pp. 337–51.
15 Mary Arseneau, 'Madeline, Mermaids, and Medusas in "The Eve of St. Agnes"', *Papers on Language and Literature*, 13, 1997, pp. 227–4. Stillinger dryly labels Thomson and Arseneau's work as 'The ' "Let's-hear-it-for-Madeline" countermovement' (*Reading The Eve of St. Agnes*, p. 44).
16 Marjorie Levinson, *Keats's Life of Allegory: The Origins of a Style*, Oxford: Basil Blackwell, 1988, p. 112.
17 A poetical periphrasis for sheep.
18 Medieval beadsmen were paid to pray for the souls of their benefactors.
19 Counted.
20 A vessel in which incense was burnt.
21 i.e. the beadsman's chilled breath rises to heaven like the souls of the dead.

2

His prayer he saith, this patient, holy man;   10
Then takes his lamp, and riseth from his knees,
And back returneth, meagre,[22] barefoot, wan,
Along the chapel aisle by slow degrees:
The sculptur'd dead, on each side, seem to freeze,
Emprison'd in black, purgatorial rails:
Knights, ladies, praying in dumb orat'ries,[23]
He passeth by; and his weak spirit fails
To think how they may ache in icy hoods and mails.

3

Northward he turneth through a little door,
And scarce three steps, ere Music's golden tongue   20
Flatter'd to tears[24] this aged man and poor;
But no – already had his deathbell rung;
The joys of all his life were said and sung:
His was harsh penance on St. Agnes' Eve:
Another way he went, and soon among
Rough ashes sat he for his soul's reprieve,[25]
And all night kept awake, for sinners' sake to grieve.

4

That ancient Beadsman heard the prelude[26] soft;
And so it chanc'd, for many a door was wide,
From hurry to and fro. Soon, up aloft,   30
The silver, snarling[27] trumpets 'gan to chide:
The level chambers, ready with their pride,
Were glowing to receive a thousand guests:
The carved angels, ever eager-eyed,
Star'd, where upon their heads the cornice rests,[28]
With hair blown back, and wings put cross-wise on their breasts.

---

22 Thin.
23 Silent chapels. This passage may have been inspired by the effigies in Chichester Cathedral, which Keats visited in January 1819.
24 'The poor old man was moved, by the sweet music, to think that so sweet a thing was intended for his comfort, as well as others' (Leigh Hunt, *Imagination and Fancy; or Selections from the Best English Poets, Illustrative of those First Requisites of their Art; with markings of the best passages, critical notices of the writers, and an essay in answer to the question 'What is Poetry'*, London: Smith, Elder & Co., 1844, p. 333).
25 Redemption, i.e. reprieve from Hell.
26 Introductory music.
27 The word suggests both the noise of the trumpets and the violent tendencies of Madeline's kinsmen.
28 The top of the frieze on which the angels are depicted.

5

At length burst in the argent[29] revelry,
With plume, tiara, and all rich array,
Numerous as shadows haunting faerily[30]
The brain, new stuff'd, in youth, with triumphs gay   40
Of old romance. These let us wish away,
And turn, sole-thoughted, to one lady there,
Whose heart had brooded, all that wintry day,
On love, and wing'd St. Agnes' saintly care,
As she had heard old dames full many times declare.

6

They told her how, upon St. Agnes' Eve,
Young virgins might have visions of delight,
And soft adorings from their loves receive
Upon the honey'd middle of the night,
If ceremonies due they did aright;   50
As, supperless to bed they must retire,
And couch supine their beauties, lily white;
Nor look behind, nor sideways, but require
Of Heaven with upward eyes[31] for all that they desire.[32]

7

Full of this whim was thoughtful Madeline:
The music, yearning like a God in pain,
She scarcely heard: her maiden eyes divine,
Fix'd on the floor, saw many a sweeping train[33]
Pass by—she heeded not at all: in vain
Came many a tiptoe, amorous cavalier,   60
And back retir'd; not cool'd by high disdain,
But she saw not: her heart was otherwhere:
She sigh'd for Agnes' dreams, the sweetest of the year.

---

29 Silver.
30 Enchantedly.
31 Madeline must lie on her back, looking directly above her.
32 Keats's revised draft included an additional stanza at this point. It is worth citing inasmuch as it clarifies the poet's version of the St Agnes' Eve superstition:

> 'Twas said her future lord would there appear
> Offering, a sacrifice (all in the dream),
> Delicious food, even to her lips brought near,
> Viands, and wine, and fruit, and sugared cream,
> To touch her palate with the fine extreme
> Of relish; then soft music heard, and then
> More pleasures followed in a dizzy stream,
> Palpable almost, there to wake again
> Warm in the virgin morn, no weeping Magdalen.

33 'I do not use *train* for *concourse of passers by* but for *Skirts* sweeping along the floor' (Keats to John Taylor, c. 11 June 1820).

8

She danc'd along with vague, regardless eyes,
Anxious her lips, her breathing quick and short:
The hallow'd hour was near at hand: she sighs
Amid the timbrels,[34] and the throng'd resort
Of whisperers in anger, or in sport;
'Mid looks of love, defiance, hate, and scorn,
Hoodwink'd with faery fancy; all amort,[35]   70
Save to St. Agnes and her lambs unshorn,[36]
And all the bliss to be before to-morrow morn.

9

So, purposing each moment to retire,
She linger'd still. Meantime, across the moors,
Had come young Porphyro, with heart on fire
For Madeline. Beside the portal doors,
Buttress'd from moonlight,[37] stands he, and implores
All saints to give him sight of Madeline,
But for one moment in the tedious hours,
That he might gaze and worship all unseen;   80
Perchance speak, kneel, touch, kiss—in sooth[38] such things have been.

10

He ventures in: let no buzz'd whisper tell:
All eyes be muffled, or a hundred swords
Will storm his heart, Love's fev'rous citadel:
For him, those chambers held barbarian hordes,
Hyena foemen, and hot-blooded lords,
Whose very dogs would execrations howl
Against his lineage: not one breast affords
Him any mercy, in that mansion foul,
Save one old beldame,[39] weak in body and in soul.   90

11

Ah, happy chance! the aged creature came,
Shuffling along with ivory-headed wand,[40]
To where he stood, hid from the torch's flame,
Behind a broad half-pillar, far beyond

---

34 A hand-held percussion instrument similar to a tambourine.
35 Spiritless, uninterested.
36 The Roman basilica of St Agnes celebrates the feast of its titular saint by the blessing of two 'lambs
    unshorn'. The Latin word 'agnus' means lamb.
37 i.e. shaded by a buttress.
38 Truth.
39 Aged woman.
40 Walking stick.

The sound of merriment and chorus bland:[41]
He startled her; but soon she knew his face,
And grasp'd his fingers in her palsied hand,
Saying, "Mercy, Porphyro! hie thee from this place;
They are all here to-night, the whole blood-thirsty race!

12

Get hence! get hence! there's dwarfish Hildebrand;   100
He had a fever late, and in the fit
He cursed thee and thine, both house and land:
Then there's that old Lord Maurice, not a whit
More tame for his gray hairs—Alas me! flit!
Flit like a ghost away."—"Ah, Gossip[42] dear,
We're safe enough; here in this arm-chair sit,
And tell me how"—"Good Saints! not here, not here;
Follow me, child, or else these stones will be thy bier."

13

He follow'd through a lowly arched way,
Brushing the cobwebs with his lofty plume,   110
And as she mutter'd "Well-a—well-a-day!"
He found him in a little moonlight room,
Pale, lattic'd, chill, and silent as a tomb.
"Now tell me where is Madeline," said he,
"O tell me, Angela, by the holy loom
Which none but secret sisterhood[43] may see,
When they St. Agnes' wool are weaving piously."

14

"St. Agnes! Ah! it is St. Agnes' Eve—
Yet men will murder upon holy days:
Thou must hold water in a witch's sieve,   120
And be liege-lord of all the Elves and Fays,[44]
To venture so: it fills me with amaze
To see thee, Porphyro!—St. Agnes' Eve!
God's help! my lady fair the conjuror plays[45]
This very night: good angels her deceive![46]
But let me laugh awhile, I've mickle[47] time to grieve."

---

41 Gentle or soothing.
42 An archaic term for a (female) friend.
43 Presumably the nuns who weave the wool of the sheep used in the feast of St Agnes.
44 Fairies.
45 i.e. Madeline is attempting to 'conjure' up images of her future love.
46 i.e. send her pleasing delusions in her dreams.
47 Plenty of.

15

    Feebly she laugheth in the languid moon,
    While Porphyro upon her face doth look,
    Like puzzled urchin on an aged crone
    Who keepeth clos'd a wond'rous riddle-book,   130
    As spectacled she sits in chimney nook.
    But soon his eyes grew brilliant, when she told
    His lady's purpose; and he scarce could brook[48]
    Tears, at the thought of those enchantments cold,[49]
And Madeline asleep in lap of legends old.

16

    Sudden a thought came like a full-blown rose,
    Flushing his brow, and in his pained heart
    Made purple riot:[50] then doth he propose
    A stratagem, that makes the beldame start:
    "A cruel man and impious thou art: 140
    Sweet lady, let her pray, and sleep, and dream
    Alone with her good angels, far apart
    From wicked men like thee. Go, go!—I deem
Thou canst not surely be the same that thou didst seem."

17

    "I will not harm her, by all saints I swear,"
    Quoth Porphyro: "O may I ne'er find grace
    When my weak voice shall whisper its last prayer,
    If one of her soft ringlets I displace,
    Or look with ruffian passion in her face:
    Good Angela, believe me by these tears;   150
    Or I will, even in a moment's space,
    Awake, with horrid shout, my foemen's ears,
And beard[51] them, though they be more fang'd than wolves and bears."

18

    "Ah! why wilt thou affright a feeble soul?
    A poor, weak, palsy-stricken, churchyard thing,
    Whose passing-bell[52] may ere the midnight toll;
    Whose prayers for thee, each morn and evening,
    Were never miss'd."—Thus plaining,[53] doth she bring
    A gentler speech from burning Porphyro;

48 Restrain.
49 Madeline will only see 'cold' visions rather than a warm human being.
50 i.e. made his heart beat furiously.
51 Defy.
52 Death-bell.
53 Complaining, lamenting.

So woful, and of such deep sorrowing,   160
That Angela gives promise she will do
Whatever he shall wish, betide her weal[54] or woe.

19

Which was, to lead him, in close secrecy,
Even to Madeline's chamber, and there hide
Him in a closet, of such privacy
That he might see her beauty unespy'd,
And win perhaps that night a peerless bride,
While legion'd faeries pac'd the coverlet,[55]
And pale enchantment[56] held her sleepy-ey'd.
Never on such a night have lovers met,   170
Since Merlin paid his Demon all the monstrous debt.[57]

20

"It shall be as thou wishest," said the Dame:
"All cates[58] and dainties shall be stored there
Quickly on this feast-night: by the tambour frame[59]
Her own lute thou wilt see: no time to spare,
For I am slow and feeble, and scarce dare
On such a catering trust my dizzy head.
Wait here, my child, with patience; kneel in prayer
The while: Ah! thou must needs the lady wed,
Or may I never leave my grave among the dead."   180

21

So saying, she hobbled off with busy fear.
The lover's endless minutes slowly pass'd;
The dame return'd, and whisper'd in his ear
To follow her; with aged eyes aghast
From fright of dim espial.[60] Safe at last,
Through many a dusky gallery, they gain
The maiden's chamber, silken, hush'd, and chaste;
Where Porphyro took covert,[61] pleas'd amain.
His poor guide hurried back with agues in her brain.

---

54 Happiness.
55 Her bed's counterpane.
56 The visions are pale when compared to physical love.
57 Despite much effort, commentators have been unable to trace this reference. It is possible that
Keats invented the notion of the 'monstrous debt' to facilitate his rhyme.
58 Delicacies.
59 Embroidery frame.
60 i.e. from fear of being discovered in the gloomy light.
61 Hid.

22

Her falt'ring hand upon the balustrade,[62]   190
Old Angela was feeling for the stair,
When Madeline, St. Agnes' charmed maid,[63]
Rose, like a mission'd spirit, unaware:
With silver taper's light, and pious care,
She turn'd, and down the aged gossip led
To a safe level matting. Now prepare,
Young Porphyro, for gazing on that bed;
She comes, she comes again, like ring-dove[64] fray'd[65] and fled.

23

Out went the taper as she hurried in;
Its little smoke, in pallid moonshine, died: 200
She clos'd the door, she panted, all akin
To spirits of the air, and visions wide:
No uttered syllable, or, woe betide![66]
But to her heart, her heart was voluble,[67]
Paining with eloquence her balmy[68] side;
As though a tongueless nightingale should swell
Her throat in vain, and die, heart-stifled, in her dell.

24

A casement[69] high and triple-arch'd there was,
All garlanded with carven imag'ries[70]
Of fruits, and flowers, and bunches of knot-grass,   210
And diamonded with panes of quaint device,
Innumerable of stains and splendid dyes,
As are the tiger-moth's deep-damask'd[71] wings;
And in the midst, 'mong thousand heraldries,
And twilight saints, and dim emblazonings,
A shielded scutcheon[72] blush'd with blood of queens and kings.

25

Full on this casement shone the wintry moon,
And threw warm gules[73] on Madeline's fair breast,

62 Banister.
63 Virgin.
64 Wood pigeon.
65 Frightened.
66 i.e. 'or the charm will not work'.
67 Speaking, i.e., in a metaphorical sense, beating quickly.
68 Fragrant.
69 Window.
70 Pictures.
71 Intricately woven.
72 Coat of arms.
73 Reds.

As down she knelt for heaven's grace and boon;[74]
Rose-bloom fell on her hands, together prest,   220
And on her silver cross soft amethyst,
And on her hair a glory,[75] like a saint:
She seem'd a splendid angel, newly drest,
Save wings, for heaven:—Porphyro grew faint:
She knelt, so pure a thing, so free from mortal taint.

26

Anon his heart revives: her vespers[76] done,
Of all its wreathed pearls her hair she frees;
Unclasps her warmed jewels one by one;
Loosens her fragrant boddice; by degrees
Her rich attire creeps rustling to her knees: 230
Half-hidden, like a mermaid in sea-weed,
Pensive awhile she dreams awake, and sees,
In fancy, fair St. Agnes in her bed,
But dares not look behind, or all the charm is fled.

27

Soon, trembling in her soft and chilly nest,
In sort of wakeful swoon, perplex'd she lay,
Until the poppied warmth of sleep oppress'd
Her soothed limbs, and soul fatigued away;
Flown, like a thought, until the morrow-day;
Blissfully haven'd both from joy and pain;   240
Clasp'd like a missal where swart Paynims pray;[77]
Blinded alike from sunshine and from rain,
As though a rose should shut, and be a bud again.

28

Stol'n to this paradise, and so entranced,
Porphyro gaz'd upon her empty dress,
And listen'd to her breathing, if it chanced
To wake into a slumberous tenderness;[78]
Which when he heard, that minute did he bless,
And breath'd himself: then from the closet crept,
Noiseless as fear in a wide wilderness,   250
And over the hush'd carpet, silent, stept,
And 'tween the curtains peep'd, where, lo!—how fast she slept.

---

74 Blessing.
75 Halo.
76 Prayers.
77 Clasped like a prayer book in a land of swarthy pagans.
78 Porphyro is waiting for Madeline to fall asleep.

29

Then by the bed-side, where the faded moon
Made a dim, silver twilight, soft he set
A table, and, half anguish'd, threw thereon
A cloth of woven crimson, gold, and jet:—
O for some drowsy Morphean amulet![79]
The boisterous, midnight, festive clarion,[80]
The kettle-drum, and far-heard clarinet,
Affray his ears, though but in dying tone:—   260
The hall door shuts again, and all the noise is gone.

30

And still she slept an azure-lidded sleep,
In blanched linen, smooth, and lavender'd,
While he forth from the closet brought a heap
Of candied apple, quince, and plum, and gourd;[81]
With jellies soother[82] than the creamy curd,
And lucent syrops,[83] tinct[84] with cinnamon;
Manna[85] and dates, in argosy[86] transferr'd
From Fez;[87] and spiced dainties, every one,   270
From silken Samarcand[88] to cedar'd Lebanon.

31

These delicates he heap'd with glowing hand
On golden dishes and in baskets bright
Of wreathed silver: sumptuous they stand
In the retired quiet of the night,
Filling the chilly room with perfume light.—
"And now, my love, my seraph fair, awake!
Thou art my heaven, and I thine eremite:[89]
Open thine eyes, for meek St. Agnes' sake,
Or I shall drowse beside thee, so my soul doth ache."

32

Thus whispering, his warm, unnerved[90] arm   280
Sank in her pillow. Shaded was her dream

---

79 i.e. sleeping pill. Morpheus was the god of sleep.
80 Trumpet.
81 Melon.
82 Smoother, softer.
83 Syrups.
84 Flavoured.
85 A sweet secretion from a plant, as in Persian manna.
86 Merchant vessel.
87 In Morocco.
88 The Persian city famous for its silk.
89 Hermit.
90 i.e. tentative, nervous.

By the dusk curtains:—'twas a midnight charm
Impossible to melt as iced stream:
The lustrous salvers[91] in the moonlight gleam;
Broad golden fringe[92] upon the carpet lies:
It seemed he never, never, could redeem
From such a stedfast spell his lady's eyes;
So mus'd awhile, entoil'd in woofed[93] phantasies.

33

Awakening up, he took her hollow lute,—
Tumultuous,—and, in chords that tenderest be,   290
He play'd an ancient ditty, long since mute,
In Provence call'd, "La belle dame sans mercy":[94]
Close to her ear touching the melody;—
Wherewith disturb'd, she utter'd a soft moan:
He ceas'd—she panted quick—and suddenly
Her blue affrayed[95] eyes wide open shone:
Upon his knees he sank, pale as smooth-sculptured stone.

34

Her eyes were open, but she still beheld,
Now wide awake, the vision of her sleep:
There was a painful change, that nigh expell'd   300
The blisses of her dream so pure and deep
At which fair Madeline began to weep,
And moan forth witless words with many a sigh;
While still her gaze on Porphyro would keep;
Who knelt, with joined hands and piteous eye,
Fearing to move or speak, she look'd so dreamingly.

35

"Ah, Porphyro!" said she, "but even now
Thy voice was at sweet tremble in mine ear,
Made tuneable with every sweetest vow;
And those sad eyes were spiritual[96] and clear: 310
How chang'd thou art! how pallid, chill, and drear!
Give me that voice again, my Porphyro,
Those looks immortal, those complainings[97] dear!

---

91 Trays.
92 Of the cloth on which Porphyro's dainties are set.
93 Woven.
94 The title of an English translation of a 1424 poem by the fifteenth-century poet Alain Chartier, and, of course, Keats's 1819 poem.
95 Startled.
96 Ethereal, other-worldly.
97 Love lamentations.

Oh leave me not in this eternal woe,
For if thy diest, my Love, I know not where to go.”

36

Beyond a mortal man impassion'd far
At these voluptuous accents, he arose
Ethereal, flush'd, and like a throbbing star
Seen mid the sapphire heaven's deep repose;
Into her dream he melted, as the rose   320
Blendeth its odour with the violet—
Solution sweet:[98] meantime the frost-wind blows
Like Love's alarum[99] pattering the sharp sleet
Against the window-panes; St. Agnes' moon hath set.

37

'Tis dark: quick pattereth the flaw-blown[100] sleet:
“This is no dream, my bride, my Madeline!”
'Tis dark: the iced gusts still rave and beat:
“No dream, alas! alas! and woe is mine!
Porphyro will leave me here to fade and pine.—
Cruel! what traitor could thee hither bring?   330
I curse not, for my heart is lost in thine,
Though thou forsakest a deceived thing;—
A dove forlorn and lost with sick unpruned[101] wing.”

38

“My Madeline! sweet dreamer! lovely bride!
Say, may I be for aye thy vassal blest?

98 Keats revised ll. 314–22 in 1819 in a manner which makes the sexual nature of the encounter clear:

See, while she speaks, his arms encroaching slow,
Have zoned her, heart to heart – loud, loud the dark winds blow!

For on the midnight came a tempest fell;
More sooth, for that his quick rejoinder flows
Into her burning ear – and still the spell
Unbroken guards her in serene repose.
With her wild dream he mingled, as a rose
Marryeth its odour to a violet.
Still, still she dreams; louder the frost-wind blows [. . .]

Woodhouse strongly objected to the revision, which did not appear in 1820: 'as it is now altered [Porphyro] acts all the acts of a bona fide husband [. . .] it will render the poem unfit for ladies [. . .] He says he does not want ladies to read his poetry, that he writes for men [. . .] that he should despise a man who would be such a eunuch in sentiment as to leave a maid, with that character about her, in such a situation; and should despise himself to write about it, etc., etc., etc. – and all this sort of Keats-like rodomontade' [rodomontade is extravagant boasting or ranting].
99 Alarm bell.
100 A Keatsian neologism which means that the sleet has blown up suddenly (a 'flaw' is a sudden rush or onset).
101 i.e. unpreened.

Thy beauty's shield, heart-shap'd and vermeil[102] dyed?
Ah, silver shrine, here will I take my rest
After so many hours of toil and quest,
A famish'd pilgrim,—sav'd by miracle.
Though I have found, I will not rob thy nest   340
Saving of thy sweet self; if thou think'st well
To trust, fair Madeline, to no rude infidel.

39

"Hark! 'tis an elfin-storm from faery land,
Of haggard seeming,[103] but a boon indeed:[104]
Arise—arise! the morning is at hand;—
The bloated wassaillers[105] will never heed:—
Let us away, my love, with happy speed;
There are no ears to hear, or eyes to see,—
Drown'd all in Rhenish[106] and the sleepy mead:[107]
Awake! arise! my love, and fearless be,   350
For o'er the southern moors I have a home for thee."

40

She hurried at his words, beset with fears,
For there were sleeping dragons[108] all around,
At glaring watch, perhaps, with ready spears—
Down the wide stairs a darkling[109] way they found.—
In all the house was heard no human sound.
A chain-droop'd lamp was flickering by each door;
The arras,[110] rich with horseman, hawk, and hound,
Flutter'd in the besieging wind's uproar;
And the long carpets rose along the gusty floor.   360

41

They glide, like phantoms, into the wide hall;
Like phantoms, to the iron porch, they glide;
Where lay the Porter, in uneasy sprawl,
With a huge empty flaggon by his side:
The wakeful bloodhound rose, and shook his hide,
But his sagacious eye an inmate owns:

---

102 Bright red.
103 Wild appearance.
104 i.e the storm seems threatening but is a boon inasmuch as it will provide cover for the lovers'
    escape.
105 Revellers.
106 Rhine wine.
107 Liquor made from fermented honey and water.
108 Dragoons.
109 Obscure.
110 Tapestry.

By one, and one, the bolts full easy slide:—
The chains lie silent on the footworn stones;—
The key turns, and the door upon its hinges groans.

42

And they are gone: aye, ages long ago   370
These lovers fled away into the storm.
That night the Baron dreamt of many a woe,
And all his warrior-guests, with shade and form
Of witch, and demon, and large coffin-worm,
Were long be-nightmar'd. Angela the old
Died palsy-twitch'd, with meagre face deform;
The Beadsman, after thousand aves told,
For aye unsought for slept among his ashes cold.

La Belle Dame Sans Merci: A Ballad

This ballad was probably composed on 21 April 1819.[1] A first draft of the poem was transcribed in Keats's journal-letter to George and Georgiana Keats of 14 February to 3 May 1819 and a revised version[2] appeared in Leigh Hunt's the *Indicator* in 1820, with the original remaining unpublished until 1848, when it was included in Richard Monckton Milne's *The Life, Letters and Literary Remains of John Keats*.[3] Keats's title derives from 'La belle dame sans mercy', an English translation[4] of a 1424 poem by the French poet Alain Chartier. His thematic territory is also similar to that found in Chartier's narrative of doomed *amour*, in which a man dies for the love of a pitiless beauty. That said, the often destructive nature of desire is a common theme of medieval balladry, and Keats was probably also drawing upon his knowledge of the various collections of ancient ballads which had wide currency in the Romantic period such as Bishop Percy's *Reliques of Ancient English Poetry* (1765) and Sir Walter Scott's *Border Minstrelsy* (1802–3). Keats was also influenced by more recent balladry: Robert Burns's *Poems, chiefly in the Scottish Dialect* (1786) and, most particularly, Wordsworth and Coleridge's *Lyrical Ballads* (1798 and 1800).

'La Belle Dame Sans Merci', the tale of a knight enthralled by an elfin woman, is generally considered to be one of Keats's finest achievements. This richly enigmatic and tragic story touched a nerve with many in the nineteenth

---

1   Though Jack Stillinger has suggested that 28 April is also a possible date of composition (*The Text of Keats's Poems*, Cambridge, Mass.: Harvard University Press, 1974, p. 232).
2   Though Jerome J. McGann (in 'Keats and the Historical Method in Literary Criticism', in *The Beauty of Inflections: Literary Investigations in Historical Method and Theory*, Oxford: Clarendon Press, 1985) defends the first published version, most editors consider this version inferior and the text below follows that of 1848.
3   The source of the present text.
4   This has been attributed to Chaucer, but is more probably by Sir Richard Ros.

century. The poet Coventry Patmore, reviewing the *Literary Remains*,[5] saw the poem as 'among the most mark-worthy of the productions of Keats [...] passionate, sensuous, and, above all, truly musical'. The Pre-Raphaelites were even more enthusiastic: William Morris declared that 'it was the germ from which all the poetry of his group had sprung' and W. M. Rossetti considered it 'the cream of Keats's poetry [...] the highest point of romantic imagination' More recent Keatsian criticism has also been much preoccupied by 'La Belle Dame Sans Merci'. This is possibly because, like many of the ballads which influenced it, be they medieval or Coleridgean, the poem refuses to rationalise or explain the events which it describes. Who is this mysterious Belle Dame, and is her treatment of her suitors deliberately merciless? And what precisely is the nature of the trauma experienced by the knight-at-arms? Is his banishment callous punishment or his own fault? Such unresolved questions have provided critics with the opportunity to display their interpretative skills and the poem became a kind of scholarly adventure playground during the twentieth century. To quote Stuart Sperry: 'Over the years it has been read (with an eye to the poet's growing involvement with Fanny Brawne) as a study in the wasting power of sexual attraction and love, as an intimation of the toils of disease and early death, and as an expression of the poet's infatuation with and enslavement by his own muse.'[6] For Robert Graves, the faery's child herself symbolises all three issues ('the Belle Dame represented Love, Death by Consumption [...] and Poetry at once'[7]) and the Belle Dame has been at the centre of many readings of the poem. J. Middleton Murry sees her as a displaced, symbolic portrayal of Fanny Brawne,[8] Earl Wasserman a version of the Queen of Elfland from the medieval ballad 'Thomas the Rhymer',[9] Mario Praz the type of Coleridge's 'Dark Ladie',[10] Robert Gittings 'the "false Florimel" of the *Faerie Queene*',[11] M. L. D'Avanzo the 'elfin, poetic imagination',[12] K. M. Wilson, on the

5 Coventry Patmore, in *North British Review*, X (November), 1848, pp. 69–96.
6 Stuart M. Sperry, *Keats the Poet*, Princeton, NJ: Princeton University Press, 1973, p. 231. And Sperry goes on to offer his own take on the poem: 'To these one would want to add another kind of fatality – Keats's ever-present concern with the nature of poetic fame [...] a theme now assuming its own ironic significance from its inseparability from love and death' (pp. 231–2).
7 Robert Graves, *The White Goddess*, London: Faber and Faber, 1948, p. 378.
8 'La Belle Dame is Fanny Brawne; she is also the beauty of life itself which is claiming, through Fanny, Keats for its sacrifice and victim' (John Middleton Murry, *Keats and Shakespeare*, London: Oxford University Press, Humphrey Milward, 1925, p. 124).
9 Earl R. Wasserman, *The Finer Tone: Keats' Major Poems*, Baltimore, Md.: Johns Hopkins University Press, 1953, p. 69. In the ballad Tom meets the 'queen of fair Elfland', who takes him on her milk-white steed, feeds him fairy food and eventually takes him to her own country (for seven years 'True Thomas on earth was never seen'). To Wasserman, 'the relations of this narrative to a story of a knight-at-arms carried by a fairy's child to an elfin grot are too obvious to underscore'.
10 'It is obvious that Keats took his inspiration from this for his *Belle Dame Sans Merci*' (*The Romantic Agony*, 2nd edn, London: Geoffrey Cumberlege, Oxford University Press, 1951, p. 274).
11 Robert Gittings, *John Keats: The Living Year, 21 September 1818 to 21 September 1819*, London: Heinemann, 1954, p. 118.
12 Mario L. D'Avanzo, *Keats' Metaphors for the Poetic Imagination*, Durham, NC: Duke University Press, 1967, p. 194.

other hand, the 'Demon Poesy',[13] John Barnard a version of Morgan le Fay,[14] John Jones the incarnation of Eve[15] and Marjorie Levinson an 'empowering Otherness'.[16] The ungiving way in which the poem refuses to surrender a single meaning has not meant that the poem lacks symbolic commentary. Indeed, Harold Bloom is one of the few critics to refuse the challenge of identifying the Belle Dame: the knight-at-arms 'is in thrall forever. To whom? We cannot tell, for we have only the knight's evidence, and he may be self-deceived. He does not know her language, nor do we.'[17]

For the possible literary sources and influences of the poem, in Chartier, Spenser, Dante and Burton's *The Anatomy of Melancholy*, see the discussions in C. L. Finney's *The Evolution of Keats's Poetry*,[18] Robert Gittings's *John Keats: The Living Year*[19] and Walter Jackson Bate's *John Keats*.[20] For historicist and feminist accounts of the poem, see Theresa Kelley's 'Poetics and the Politics of Reception: Keats's "La Belle Dame Sans Merci"',[21] Marjorie Levinson's *Keats's Life of Allegory*,[22] Karen Swann's 'Harassing the Muse'[23] (which reads the poem as 'a scene of harassment'[24]) and John Barnard's 'Keats's Belle Dame and the Sexual Politics of Leigh Hunt's *Indicator*'.[25]

1

Oh, what can ail thee, knight-at-arms,   1
    Alone and palely loitering;
The sedge[26] has withered from the lake,
    And no birds sing.

2

Oh, what can ail thee, knight-at-arms,
    So haggard and so woe-begone?

---

13 Cited in John Barnard (ed.), *John Keats: The Complete Poems*, Harmondsworth: Penguin, 1973, p. 638.
14 John Barnard, *John Keats*, Cambridge: Cambridge University Press, 1987, p. 92.
15 John Jones, *John Keats's Dream of Truth*, London: Chatto & Windus, 1969, p. 176.
16 Marjorie Levinson, *Keats's Life of Allegory: The Origins of a Style*, Oxford: Blackwell, 1988, p. 48.
17 Harold Bloom, *The Visionary Company*, Ithaca, NY: Cornell University Press (1st edn 1961), rev. edn 1971, p. 387.
18 C. L. Finney, *The Evolution of Keats's Poetry*, 1936, pp. 593–9.
19 Gittings, *John Keats*, pp. 115–18.
20 Walter Jackson Bate, *John Keats*, London: Chatto & Windus, 1963, p. 478.
21 In *English Literary History*, 1987, pp. 333–62.
22 Levinson, *Keats's Life of Allegory*, Bloomington, Ind.: Indiana University Press, pp. 45–95.
23 In Anne K. Mellor's *Romanticism and Feminism*, 1988, pp. 81–92.
24 'It remains for the feminist critic to defend the lady [. . .] a feminist critic listening to the knight's tale picks up threads of another story: the hint of physical compulsion ("I made a garland"), the suggestion of interpretive violence ("And sure in language strange she said – /I love thee true"); this critic might wonder if certain signs – moans, sighs, tears – don't indicate resistance more than love or duplicity.'
25 In *Romanticism*, I, 1994–5.
26 Sedge-like plants.

The squirrel's granary is full,
 And the harvest's done.

3
I see a lily on thy brow,
 With anguish moist and fever dew;   10
And on thy cheek a fading rose
 Fast withereth too.

4
I met a lady in the meads[27]
 Full beautiful, a faery's child;
Her hair was long, her foot was light,
 And her eyes were wild.[28]

5
I made a garland for her head,
 And bracelets too, and fragrant zone;[29]
She look'd at me as she did love,
 And made sweet moan.   20

6
I set her on my pacing steed,
 And nothing else saw all day long;
For sidelong would she bend, and sing
 A faery's song.

7
She found me roots of relish sweet,
 And honey wild, and manna dew;
And sure in language strange she said,
 "I love thee true".

8
She took me to her elfin grot,[30]
 And there she gaz'd and sighed full sore   30
And there I shut her wild wild eyes—
 With kisses four.

9
And there she lulled me asleep,
 And there I dreamed, ah, woe betide,

---

27 Poeticism for 'meadows'.
28 An echo of Wordsworth's 'The Mad Mother', l. 1 ('her eyes are wild, her head is bare').
29 Girdle.
30 Grotto.

The latest[31] dream I ever dream'd
    On the cold hill side.

10

I saw pale kings, and princes too,
    Pale warriors, death-pale were they all;
They cry'd—"La Belle Dame Sans Merci
    Thee hath in thrall!"   40

11

I saw their starved lips in the gloom[32]
    With horrid warning gaped wide,
And I awoke, and found me here
    On the cold hill's side.

12

And this is why I sojourn here
    Alone and palely loitering,
Though the sedge is withered from the lake,
    And no birds sing.

To Sleep

'To Sleep' was probably written in April 1819. It was transcribed on 30 April in Keats's journal-letter to George and Georgiana Keats of 14 February to 3 May 1819 as an example of 'two or three' sonnets which the poet had 'lately written'. However, it remained unpublished until 1838, when it appeared in the *Plymouth and Devonport Weekly Journal* on 11 October.

Critical discussion of the poem has tended to foreground its formal and metrical innovativeness rather than its undoubted beauty. Along with 'How fever'd is the man' and 'If by dull rhymes', it sees Keats experimenting with stanzaic structure in a way which allowed the poet to develop a new form of English ode in the great poems which followed in May 1819. Keats had previously worked in both of the principal sonnet forms, the Petrarchan[1] and Shakespearian.[2] By January 1818, he had written over forty sonnets, all of which are Petrarchan (including 'On First Looking into Chapman's Homer',

---

31 Final.
32 Twilight.

---

1 A sonnet, named after the fourteenth-century Italian poet Petrarch, which is divided into an eight-line octave and a six-line sestet. The octave rhymes *abbaabba* and the sestet most commonly *cdecde*.
2 A sonnet, named after its most notable practitioner, which consists of three quatrains and a couplet rhymed *ababcdcdefefgg*.

pp. 79–82). Thereafter, the vast majority are Shakespearian.[3] However, by the spring of 1819, Keats had become dissatisfied with both patterns, writing to his brother and sister-in-law that he had been 'endeavouring to discover a better sonnet stanza than we have. The legitimate [i.e. Petrarchan] does not suit the language over-well from the pouncing rhymes – the other kind [the Shakespearian] appears too elegiac – and the couplet at the end of it has seldom a pleasing effect'. 'To Sleep' is one of Keats's 'experimental sonnets'. It begins with two Shakespearian quatrains (*abab*), but concludes with a sestet (*bcefef*), thereby avoiding what was, to Keats's mind, the over-discrete and sometimes clumsy final couplet of the Shakespearian sonnet. From this it is a short step to the basic metrical frame of the odes which Keats wrote in the following weeks ('Nightingale', 'Grecian Urn', 'Melancholy' and 'Indolence'), ten-line stanzas which begin with a Shakespearian quatrain (*abab*) and end with a Petrarchan sestet (*cdecde*).[4]

That said, 'To Sleep' does more than simply point the way forward to the prosodological structure of the odes. It is included in the same letter as the 'Ode to Psyche', and, according to Ian Jack, the 'syntax, diction, and imagery' of the poem 'could hardly be distinguished from those of the Odes'.[5] Certainly its central thematic concerns, escape and the attractions of oblivion, fore-shadow some of the preoccupations of the odes, though it has been argued that the sonnet lacks the complexities and ambiguities of the longer poems. If the 'Ode to a Nightingale' is ambivalent about the motif of escape, to Stuart M. Sperry 'To Sleep' is more straightforward, 'celebrat[ing] the luxury of mere obliviousness, the relief of escaping from the multiplying sorrows of the day-time world and the probings of conscience "that still lords/Its strength for darkness, burrowing like a mole"'.[6] On the other hand, Morris Dickstein dis-agrees: the sonnet, he declares, rather than being 'escapist' is actually a poem about 'the desire or compulsion to escape',[7] a critical judgement which places it firmly in the thematic territory of the odes ('To a Nightingale' most particularly).

Keats's experimental sonnets are discussed in H. W. Garrod's *Keats*,[8] M. R.

---

3 Walter Jackson Bate argues that Keats's decision to turn to the Shakespearian sonnet is part of his resolution, in early 1818, to cut loose from both his poetic mentors ('I will have no more of Wordsworth or Hunt in particular') and his previous poetic models: 'In turning to the Shakespear-ian pattern [. . .] he was making at least a gesture both of independence and of his new start. For which the exception of the loose heroic couplet – which he had abandoned after *Endymion* – no form was so closely associated with his previous poetry as the Petrarchan sonnet' (*John Keats*, London: Chatto & Windus, 1963, p. 297).
4 The 'Ode to a Grecian Urn' varies the frame slightly.
5 Ian Jack, *English Literature 1815–1832*, Oxford: Clarendon Press, p. 121.
6 Stuart M. Sperry, *Keats the Poet*, Princeton, NJ: Princeton University Press, 1973, p. 228. Sperry's use of 'lords' in his quotation from the sonnet, a word which appeared in the first draft of 'To Sleep' but which Keats later corrected to the more appropriate 'hoards', is idiosyncratic.
7 Morris Dickstein, *Keats and his Poetry: A Study in Development*, Chicago, Ill.: University of Chicago Press, 1971, p. 27.
8 H. W. Garrod, *Keats*, Oxford: Clarendon Press, 1926, pp. 83–90.

Ridley's *Keats' Craftmanship*,[9] Walter Jackson Bate's *The Stylistic Development of Keats* and the same author's *John Keats*.[10] The most extensive study of Keats's sonnets in general is found in Lawrence John Zillman's *John Keats and the Sonnet Tradition*.[11]

O soft embalmer of the still midnight,
Shutting, with careful fingers and benign,
Our gloom-pleas'd eyes, embower'd from the light,
Enshaded in forgetfulness divine:
O soothest[12] Sleep! if so it please thee, close   5
In midst of this thine hymn my willing eyes,
Or wait the "Amen", ere[13] thy poppy[14] throws
Around my bed its lulling charities.
Then save me, or the passèd[15] day will shine
Upon my pillow, breeding many woes,—   10
Save me from curious Conscience, that still hoards
Its strength for darkness, burrowing like a mole;
Turn the key deftly in the oilèd wards,[16]
And seal the hushed Casket of my Soul.

Ode to Psyche

The 'Ode to Psyche' was composed in the spring of 1819, probably between 21–30 April. The poem was first published in *Lamia, Isabella, The Eve of St Agnes, and other Poems* (1820).[1] It is the first of the remarkable series of odes which Keats composed in the spring of that year ('To Psyche', 'To a Nightingale', 'On a Grecian Urn', 'On Melancholy'). In the journal-letter to George and Georgiana

---

9 M. R. Ridley, *Keats' Craftmanship: A Study in Poetic Development*, Oxford: Clarendon Press, 1933, pp. 196–210.
10 Walter Jackson Bate, *The Stylistic Development of Keats*, New York: The Modern Language Association of America, 1945, pp. 125–33; Bate, *John Keats*, pp. 495–8.
11 Lawrence John Zillman, *John Keats and the Sonnet Tradition*, Los Angeles, Calif.: Lymanhouse, 1939. See also John Kerrigan's 'Wordsworth and the Sonnet: Building, Dwelling, Thinking' (*Essays in Criticism*, 35, 1985, pp. 45–75), which contrasts the Keatsian sonnet with that of Wordsworth, and Stuart Curran's *Poetic Form and British Romanticism*, New York: Oxford University Press, 1986, pp. 52–4.
12 Most soothing. A term borrowed, like so much else in Keats, from Milton (see *Comus*, l. 823).
13 Before.
14 A reference to the narcotic properties of the poppy.
15 This, like 'oilèd' below, is an example of a 'wrenched accent', a poetic stress (marked by the grave) on a syllable in a verse line which in everyday speech would be unstressed.
16 Wards are the contours within a lock.

---

1 The source of the present text.

Keats of 14 February – 3 May 1819 in which it is transcribed, the poet calls it 'the first and only one [of my poems] with which I have taken even moderate pains – I have for the most part dash'd off my lines in a hurry – This I have done leisurely – I think it reads the more richly for it.' In Keats's principal source for the ode, The Golden Ass[2] (second century AD) by the Roman author Lucius Apuleius, Psyche (the Greek word for 'soul') is a girl whose beauty rivals even that of Venus. The jealous goddess malevolently sends her son Cupid to torment her. However, Cupid himself falls in love with Psyche. After many tribulations the two are united and Psyche achieves immortality as a goddess. Apuleius calls the story of Cupid and Psyche 'the latest-born of the myths' and, in his letter to his brother and sister-in-law, Keats writes: 'You must recollect that Psyche was not embodied as a a goddess before the time of Apuleius the Platonist who lived after their A[u]gustan age, and consequently the Goddess was never worshipped or sacrificed to with any of the ancient fervour – and perhaps never thought of in the old religion – I am more orthodox tha[n] to let a he[a]then Goddess be so neglected.' The ode sees Keats vowing to become the priest of this neglected goddess and establish a temple to her in his mind. His worship of Psyche takes the form of poetry's 'branched thoughts' and the poem is as concerned with poetic creation as it is with myth. Given that Psyche means 'soul', the poem is unsurprisingly often linked with Keats's meditation on soul-making, which is found earlier in the journal-letter: 'this System of Soul-making – may have been the Parent of all the more palpable and personal Schemes of Redemption, among the Zoroastrians, the Christians and the Hindoos. For as one part of the human species must have their carved Jupiter, so another part must have … their Christ their Oromanes and their Vishnu' (pp. 18–20). Keats must have Psyche.

Though hardly a neglected poem, the 'Ode to Psyche' has not received the deluge of critical attention which has been lavished upon the 'Ode to a Nightingale' and the 'Ode on a Grecian Urn'. Indeed, for some critics, Walter Jackson Bate most notably, the 'principal' value of the poem is that it clears the path forward to its successors: 'through writing it, Keats learned better how to proceed'.[3] Bate sees the first two stanzas as inadequate 'filler', characterised by thematic 'uncertainty' and stylistic clumsiness ('banal phrasing' such as 'happy, happy dove'). Nonetheless, though relatively few commentators rank this ode as highly as the triumphs of later spring, 'Psyche' has had a significant number of partisans. That said, enthusiasts tend to share Bate's unease about the poem's opening,[4] concentrating on the later stanzas and, most particularly, on what

---

2   Which he read in William Adlington's 1566 English translation.
3   Walter Jackson Bate, John Keats, London: Chatto & Windus, 1963, p. 491. Such a view is perhaps lent a certain credence by Keats's own comment in his journal-letter: the 'Ode' 'will I hope encourage me to write other things in even a more peaceable and healthy spirit'.
4   Kenneth Allott concedes that 'the poem opens badly', but argues that it 'warms up rapidly after a weak start' (in Kenneth Muir (ed.), John Keats: A Reassessment, Liverpool: Liverpool University Press, 1958, p. 87). His essay reads the poem in terms of the 'system of soul-making' set out in Keats's journal-letter and its meditation on 'the meaning and function of myth'.

John Barnard calls 'the astonishing final stanza'. To Barnard, the ode 'sees its myth as being at once fictive and true. Feigning is a necessary element in the workings of fancy, but that is compensated for by the imagination's infinite multiplicity, which "breeding flowers, will never breed the same"'.[5] Stuart Sperry's important 1973 account of the poem, which reads it as a meditation upon the poetic imagination and the nature of poetry, is extracted above on **pp. 55–6.** Ian Jack (1967) declares that 'We will not understand the "Ode to Psyche" unless we recognize that it is essentially a pagan act of worship'. For Jack, Keats's protestations of love to his betrothed ('Love is my religion', 'My Creed is Love and you are its only tenet', 'I could build an altar to you') under- pin the poem: 'Fanny Brawne served [. . .] as a sort of model for Psyche.' Jack also reads Keats's erotically charged paganism as a repudiation of contempor- ary religion, 'the affirmation of a young man who had begin to hate parsons, a defiant celebration of the "happy pieties" which had for too long been banished by . . . the "dreadful care" of institutional Christianity'.[6]

Jack's book is useful on the sources of the poem, as is Bate, notably in his account of Keats's handling of Apuleius.[7] H. W. Garrod's *Keats*, and, most com- prehensively, M. R. Ridley's *Keats's Craftsmanship*,[8] examine its metrical form. There is also important recent historicist work on the poem. Jeffrey N. Cox emphasises its eroticism, and traces its 'poetics and politics of pleasure',[9] whilst Daniel P. Watkins (**pp. 66–9**) reads the ode in Marxist terms. Watkins also, provocatively, reads 'Psyche' in terms of gender, discerning a disturbing sexual politics in the poem. Whereas Harold Bloom reads the sexual myth of Psyche in positive terms (she is 'a sexual Goddess who renews consciousness and thus renews the earth'[10]), for Watkins, Keats's text is underpinned by his need to usurp Cupid and 'dominate' Psyche. The poet takes erotic 'pleasure' in that domination; Keats's is a 'masculinist poetic strategy' and the 'Ode to Psyche', it seems, is both 'bourgeois and patriarchal'.

O Goddess! hear these tuneless numbers,[11] wrung   1
  By sweet enforcement and remembrance dear,
And pardon that thy secrets should be sung
  Even into thine own soft-conched[12] ear:

---

5 John Barnard, *John Keats*, Cambridge: Cambridge University Press, 1987, p. 103.
6 Ian Jack, *Keats and the Mirror of Art*, Oxford: Clarendon Press, 1967, p. 213.
7 Bate, *Keats*, pp. 488–90.
8 H. W. Garrod, *Keats*, Oxford: Clarendon Press, 1926, pp. 83–90; M. R. Ridley, *Keats' Craftsman- ship: A Study in Poetic Development*, Oxford: Clarendon Press, 1933, pp. 191–210.
9 Jeffrey N. Cox, *Politics and Poetry in the Cockney School*, Cambridge: Cambridge University Press, 1999, pp. 117–20.
10 Harold Bloom, *The Visionary Company*, Ithaca, NY: Cornell University Press (1st edn 1961), rev. edn 1971, p. 405.
11 Verses. A self-deprecating reference to Keats's own poetry.
12 A conch is a shell. The fleshy spirals of Psyche's ear presumably resemble a conch.

Surely I dreamt to-day, or did I see[13]
    The winged Psyche with awaken'd eyes?[14]
        I wander'd in a forest thoughtlessly,[15]
And, on the sudden, fainting with surprise,
Saw two fair creatures, couched side by side
    In deepest grass, beneath the whisp'ring roof   10
        Of leaves and trembled blossoms, where there ran
            A brooklet, scarce espied:[16]
'Mid hush'd, cool-rooted flowers, fragrant-eyed,
    Blue, silver-white, and budded Tyrian,[17]
They lay calm-breathing, on the bedded grass;
    Their arms embraced, and their pinions[18] too;
    Their lips touch'd not, but had not bade adieu,
As if disjoined by soft-handed slumber,
And ready still past kisses to outnumber
    At tender eye-dawn of aurorean[19] love: 20
        The winged boy[20] I knew;
But who wast thou, O happy, happy dove?[21]
        His Psyche true!

O latest born and loveliest vision far
    Of all Olympus' faded hierarchy![22]
Fairer than Phoebe's sapphire-region'd star,[23]
    Or Vesper,[24] amorous glow-worm of the sky;
Fairer than these, though temple thou hast none,
        Nor altar heap'd with flowers;
Nor virgin-choir to make delicious moan   30
        Upon the midnight hours;
No voice, no lute, no pipe, no incense sweet
        From chain-swung censer[25] teeming;

13 Allott (Miriam Allott (ed.), *The Poems of John Keats*, London: Longman, 1970) compares this line
    to Spenser's *Amoretti*: 'Was it a dreame, or did I see it playne.' Cf. 'Ode to a Nightingale', ll. 79–80:
    'Was it a vision, or a waking dream?/Fled is that music: – Do I wake or sleep?'
14 '[E]yes which were not dreaming, obviously, but also suggests that imaginative perception is a
    heightened form of everyday seeing' (John Barnard (ed.), *John Keats: The Complete Poems*,
    Harmondsworth: Penguin, 1973, p. 645).
15 i.e. without a care.
16 i.e difficult to make out.
17 i.e. purple or crimson, after a dye made at the Middle Eastern city of Tyre.
18 A poetical term for wings.
19 i.e. roseate.
20 Cupid.
21 Psyche is not conventionally portrayed as a dove. The source for this image is probably Mary
    Tighe's *Psyche* (1805), a poem which Keats admired, and one in which the goddess is described as a
    'Pure spotless dove'.
22 Compare Oceanus' remarks on the eclipse of the Titans by the Olympians and the inevitability of
    progress and evolution in *Hyperion*, II. 173–243.
23 i.e the moon. of which Phoebe (one of the synonyms of Artemis) was the goddess.
24 i.e. Hesperus, the evening star.
25 A vessel in which incense is burnt.

No shrine, no grove, no oracle, no heat
　　Of pale-mouth'd prophet[26] dreaming.

O brightest! though too late for antique vows,
　　Too, too late for the fond[27] believing lyre,
When holy were the haunted forest boughs,
　　Holy the air, the water, and the fire;
Yet even in these days so far retir'd   40
　　From happy pieties, thy lucent fans,[28]
　　Fluttering among the faint Olympians,
I see, and sing, by my own eyes inspir'd.[29]
So let me be thy choir, and make a moan
　　　　Upon the midnight hours;
Thy voice, thy lute, thy pipe, thy incense sweet
　　　　From swinged censer teeming;
Thy shrine, thy grove, thy oracle, thy heat
　　Of pale-mouth'd prophet dreaming.

Yes, I will be thy priest, and build a fane[30]   50
　　In some untrodden region of my mind,
Where branched thoughts,[31] new grown with pleasant pain,
　　Instead of pines shall murmur in the wind:
Far, far around shall those dark-cluster'd trees
　　Fledge the wild-ridged mountains steep by steep;
And there by zephyrs,[32] streams, and birds, and bees,
　　The moss-lain dryads[33] shall be lull'd to sleep;
And in the midst of this wide quietness
A rosy sanctuary will I dress
With the wreath'd trellis of a working brain,   60
　　With buds, and bells, and stars without a name,
With all the gardener Fancy e'er could feign,[34]
　　Who breeding flowers, will never breed the same:
And there shall be for thee all soft delight

---

26 The prophet will be pale in his trance but his words will be heated in their inspiration.
27 Devoted, reverend.
28 Shining wings.
29 Rather than by external inspiration as in the trance of the prophet in ll. 34–5.
30 Temple.
31 The poet's thoughts branch out like those of a tree. Sperry finds this image deeply ambiguous: 'the organism of the image is immediately qualified, not merely by the phrase that follows ("new grown with pleasant pain") but by the involution of the whole gardening metaphor, which as it develops gradually suggests more the kind of artifice that leads to forced growth ("wreath'd trellis," "gardener Fancy," "feigns") than cultivation' (Stuart M. Sperry, Keats the Poet, Princeton, NJ: Princeton University Press, 1973, p. 258).
32 Gentle breezes.
33 Wood-nymphs.
34 i.e. invent.

That shadowy thought[35] can win,
A bright torch, and a casement[36] ope at night,
To let the warm Love in![37]

Ode to a Nightingale

'Ode to a Nightingale' was written in May 1819. It was first published in the *Annals of the Fine Arts* in July 1819 and subsequently included in *Lamia, Isabella, The Eve of St. Agnes, and other Poems* (1820).[1] The poem was written when Keats was staying with his friend Charles Armitage Brown at Hampstead, and Brown describes its composition thus:

> In the Spring of 1819 a nightingale had built her nest in my house. K. felt a continual and tranquil joy in her song; and one morning he took a chair from the breakfast-table to the grass-plot under a plum-tree where he sat for two or three hours. When he came into the house, I perceived he had some scraps of paper in his hand, and these he was quietly thrusting behind the books. On inquiry, I found these scraps, four or five in number, contained his poetic feeling on the song of the nightingale. The writing was not well legible; and it was difficult to arrange the stanzas on so many scraps. With his assistance I succeeded, and this was his "Ode to a Nightingale," a poem which has been the delight of everyone.[2]

Whereas 'To Psyche' is an irregular ode[3] in the conventional manner, 'To a Nightingale' is formally innovative in its introduction of the ten-line stanza[4] which Keats used (with minor variations of rhyme and metre) in his subsequent spring odes ('On a Grecian Urn', 'On Melancholy', 'On Indolence'). That said, it is the artistic power and sensuous phrasing of the poem which has made it one of Keats's most celebrated works. However, 'To a Nightingale' is notable for more than just the richness of its language; Keats takes an established poetic convention – the address to the nightingale – and transforms it into a

---

35 'Either musing thought that evolves obscurely or, perhaps, thought that is shadowy as the mere ghost of sensations' (Allott, *The Poems of John Keats*, p. 521).
36 Window.
37 Discussing the final two lines, Gittings makes the biographical point that Keats wrote the ode when he was living at Wentworth Place 'with Fanny Brawne next door [. . .] French windows opened into the garden from her house just as they did from his. Here was the setting for the *Ode to Psyche*, with its hint of love always impending, just round the corner' (Robert Gittings, *John Keats: The Living Year*, London: Heinemann, 1954, p. 128).

---

1 The source of the current text.
2 Charles Armitage Brown,
3 Irregular in terms of number of lines per stanza, or 'strophe'.
4 Here his stanzas begin with cross-rhymed lines (*abab*) and conclude with a sestet (rhymed *cdecde*).

compelling meditation upon art, life and death. As Miriam Allott has written: 'The nightingale was a stock subject for celebration by Romantic and pre-Romantic poets, but Keats's treatment of the subject is individual. The poem traces the inception, nature and decline of the creative mood, and expresses Keats's attempt to understand his feelings about the contrast between the ideal and actual and the close association of pain with pleasure.'[5]

'Ode to a Nightingale' is perhaps the finest expression of the theme which echoes through much of Keats's mature work: the attraction, in a universe of suffering and pain, of an escape into an idealised realm of the imagination, and, simultaneously, the drawbacks of such transcendence: the troubling awareness, most particularly, that the desire to escape earthly imperatives and 'fade away' into the ideal world represented by the nightingale involves losing touch with one's own humanity. The bird has no experience of death, pain and sorrow, those ineluctable aspects of mortal life. This fact raises a number of key critical questions about the poem. Does it endorse an attempt to lose the self in the pleasures of the imagination? Or, on the other hand, does it offer a thinly veiled criticism of art as something which is isolated from the harsh realities of human existence? Whether the bird symbolises art, the imagination, poetry, beauty or the ideal, are its wings always 'viewless'? Or might the poem be more positive, demonstrating that a sense of beauty and the ideal has the power to console, enabling humanity to come to terms with the harsh facts of reality? Can the imagination help one to cope with sickness, sorrow and death, or are its 'deceiving' consolations ultimately illusory?

Much critical writing on the 'Ode to a Nightingale' engages with these issues, as in the important readings by Helen Vendler and Nicholas Roe (**pp. 60–2** and **pp. 69–72**). Roe demonstrates how the perception of the 'ideal' is inextricably intertwined with 'the harsh realities of the present', even serving to heighten our awareness of those realities: 'the "immortal Bird" – which sings beyond the boundaries of human life – brings an intimation of the unescapable facts of existence'. For Vendler, the gap between the ideal and the actual which the poem discusses is large; if it can be bridged, it can only be bridged momentarily: 'between the solipsistic immortal world and our social and mortal one there can be no commerce except by the viewless wings of sensation in Poesy-Fancy, which cannot bear us long aloft.' Some Keatsians, however, have been more optimistic about the capacity of the bird to speak to the mortal world; several early commentators argued that it embodies the possibility of aesthetic consolation in the face of grief, suffering and oppression. In Leigh Hunt's 1820 assessment, the ode deals with the 'imaginative relief, which poetry alone presents us in her "charmed cup"' This is the relief which aesthetic experience can bring to 'real melancholy': melancholy such as that known by Keats himself, with his 'sickened and shaken body' and the psychological wounds caused by 'critical

5   Miriam Allott (ed.), *The Poems of John Keats*, London: Longman, 1970, p. 524.

malignity'. More recent criticism, as per Roe and Vendler, has tended to focus upon the complexity of the poet's position. Cleanth Brooks, ever attuned to Keatsian irony, sees the heart of the poem in the 'following paradox: the world of the imagination offers a release from the painful world of actuality, yet at the same time it renders the world of actuality more painful by contrast'.[6] And for Stuart Sperry, though the ode 'is the supreme example in all Keats's poetry of the impulse to imaginative escape that flies in the face of the knowledge of human limitation, the impulse fully expressed in "Away! away! for I *will* fly to thee" [. . .] the process is far from an unthinking one'.[7] Sperry continues; 'The third stanza openly confronts those "disagreeables" the imagination must somehow deal with – sickness, sorrow, age, and finally death'. And faced with these inescapable realities, the poem can only offer the 'escapist: "*Fade*, far away, dissolve and quite *forget*"'. And even here, the release is temporary, and 'the various different connotations of death cannot long be suppressed'.[8]

There is a significant body of literary criticism on the 'Ode to a Nightingale': individual articles abound and very few general studies of the poet do not offer studies of the ode. For further reading, see Ridley's *Keats' Craftsmanship*,[9] Gittings's *John Keats: The Living Year*,[10] Bate's *John Keats*,[11] Jack's *Keats and the Mirror of Art*,[12] Jones's *John Keats's Dream of Truth*[13] and Barnard's *John Keats*.[14]

1
My heart aches, and a drowsy numbness pains   1
   My sense, as though of hemlock[15] I had drunk,
Or emptied some dull opiate to the drains[16]
   One minute past,[17] and Lethe-wards[18] had sunk:
'Tis not through envy of thy happy lot,
   But being too happy in thine happiness,
      That thou, light-winged Dryad[19] of the trees
      In some melodious plot

---

6 *Modern Poetry and the Tradition*, Chapel Hill, NC: University of North Carolina Press, 1939, p. 31.
7 Stuart M. Sperry, *Keats the Poet*, Princeton, NJ: Princeton University Press, 1973, pp. 263–4.
8 *Ibid.*, p. 265.
9 M. R. Ridley, *Keats' Craftmanship: A Study in Poetic Development*, Oxford: Clarendon Press, 1933, pp. 210–31.
10 Robert Gittings, *John Keats: The Living Year*, London: Heinemann, 1954, pp. 131–41.
11 Walter Jackson Bate, *John Keats*, London: Chatto & Windus, 1963, pp. 498–510.
12 Ian Jack, *Keats and the Mirror of Art*, Oxford: Clarendon Press, 1967, pp. 46–57.
13 John Jones, *John Keats's Dream of Truth*, London: Chatto & Windus, 1969.
14 John Barnard, *John Keats*, Cambridge: Cambridge University Press, 1987, pp. 108–11.
15 A plant which was used medicinally as a powerful sedative. Taken in excessive quantities, hemlock was poisonous (it had caused the death of Socrates), and Keats here introduces the oblivion/death motif which runs through the poem.
16 Dregs.
17 Ago.
18 Lethe was the Hadean river which brought oblivion to all who drank of its waters.
19 Wood-nymph.

Of beechen green, and shadows numberless,
  Singest of summer in full-throated ease.   10

2

O, for a draught of vintage![20] that hath been
  Cool'd a long age in the deep-delved earth,
Tasting of Flora[21] and the country green,[22]
Dance, and Provençal song,[23] and sunburnt mirth!
O for a beaker full of the warm South,[24]
  Full of the true, the blushful Hippocrene,[25]
    With beaded bubbles winking at the brim,
      And purple-stained mouth;
That I might drink, and leave the world unseen,[26]
And with thee fade away into the forest dim: 20

3

Fade far away, dissolve, and quite forget
  What thou among the leaves hast never known,
The weariness, the fever, and the fret
  Here, where men sit and hear each other groan;
Where palsy[27] shakes a few, sad, last gray hairs,
  Where youth grows pale, and spectre-thin, and dies;[28]
    Where but to think is to be full of sorrow
      And leaden-eyed despairs,
Where Beauty cannot keep her lustrous eyes,
  Or new Love pine at them beyond to-morrow.   30

4

Away! Away! for I will fly to thee,
  Not charioted by Bacchus[29] and his pards,[30]

20 i.e. vintage wine.
21 The Roman goddess of flowers. Keats writes to Fanny Keats on 1 May 1819 of his longing for 'a little claret wine out of a cellar a mile deep [. . .] a strawberry bed to say your prayers to Flora in'.
22 If Flora suggests the mythological realms, the country green invokes, in Sperry's phrase, 'the homely, familiar world of commonplace actuality'.
23 Provence was particularly associated with the medieval troubadours.
24 i.e. Mediterranean wine.
25 A periphrastic, i.e. poetically elaborate, reference to wine. The Hippocrene, a fountain on Mount Helicon which was sacred to the Muses, was used allusively in reference to poetic inspiration. 'The fundamental point, clearly, is to intimate a relation between the delights of wine and the delights of poetry' (Christopher Ricks, *Keats and Embarrassment*, Oxford: Oxford University Press, 1974).
26 Unnoticed by the world, but arguably also 'without noticing the world'.
27 An affliction of the nervous system involving the loss of control of the muscles, involuntary tremors or paralysis.
28 Often seen as a reference to the death in December 1818 of Keats's tubercular brother Tom. The line echoes Wordsworth's *The Excursion*, IV, 1760 ('While man grows old, and dwindles and decays').
29 J. Lemprière writes in his *Classical Dictionary* (1788), a work which Keats knew and admired, that Bacchus 'was drawn in a chariot by a lion and a tiger and was accompanied by Pan and all the satyrs'.
30 Leopards.

But on the viewless[31] wings of Poesy,
   Though the dull brain perplexes and retards:
Already with thee! tender is the night,
   And haply[32] the Queen-Moon is on her throne,
      Cluster'd around by all her starry Fays;[33]
      But here there is no light,
Save what from heaven is with the breezes blown
   Through verdurous[34] glooms[35] and winding mossy ways.   40

5

I cannot see what flowers are at my feet,
   Nor what soft incense hangs upon the boughs,
But, in embalmed[36] darkness, guess each sweet
   Wherewith the seasonable month[37] endows
The grass, the thicket, and the fruit-tree wild;
   White hawthorn, and the pastoral eglantine;[38]
      Fast fading violets cover'd up in leaves;
      And mid-May's eldest child,
The coming musk-rose,[39] full of dewy wine,
   The murmurous haunt of flies on summer eves.   50

6

Darkling[40] I listen; and, for many a time
   I have been half in love with easeful Death,
Call'd him soft names in many a mused rhyme,
   To take into the air my quiet breath;
Now more than ever seems it rich to die,
   To cease upon the midnight with no pain,
      While thou art pouring forth thy soul abroad
      In such an ecstasy!
Still wouldst thou sing, and I have ears in vain—
   To thy high requiem become a sod.[41]   60

---

31 Invisible.
32 By chance.
33 Fairies.
34 Flourishing.
35 'Darkness or obscurity, the result of night, clouds, deep shadow' (OED).
36 i.e. balmy, but with overtones of entombment.
37 May.
38 The sweet-briar.
39 The musk-rose normally flowers in June.
40 In darkness.
41 'I wish for death every day and night [. . .] and then I wish death away, for death would destroy even those pains which are better than nothing. Land and Sea, weakness and decline, are great separators, but death is the great divorcer for ever' (Keats to Charles Brown, 30 September 1820).

7
Thou wast not born for death, immortal Bird!
  No hungry generations tread thee down;
The voice I hear this passing night was heard
  In ancient days by emperor and clown:[42]
Perhaps the self-same song that found a path
  Through the sad heart of Ruth,[43] when, sick for home,
    She stood in tears amid the alien corn;
      The same that oft-times hath
Charm'd magic casements,[44] opening on the foam
Of perilous seas, in faery lands forlorn.[45]   70

8
Forlorn![46] the very word is like a bell
  To toll me back from thee to my sole[47] self!
Adieu! the fancy cannot cheat so well
  As she is fam'd to do, deceiving elf.
Adieu! adieu! thy plaintive anthem fades
  Past the near meadows, over the still stream,
    Up the hill-side; and now 'tis buried deep
      In the next valley-glades:
Was it a vision, or a waking dream?
Fled is that music:—Do I wake or sleep?[48]   80

Ode on a Grecian Urn

The 'Ode on a Grecian Urn' is generally seen as dating from May 1819, though its exact position in the composition of the odes of that month is unknown. It was first published in the *Annals of the Fine Arts* in January 1820 and was

---

42 Peasant.
43 In the Old Testament, the Moabitess Ruth had to leave her country to labour in the fields of Boaz at Bethlehem.
44 Windows.
45 Lost, departed.
46 Cleanth Brooks writes in *Modern Poetry and the Tradition* (Chapel Hill, NC: University of North Carolina Press, 1939) that 'in the first instance, "forlorn" is being used primarily in its archaic sense of "utterly lost" [. . .] But the meaning of "forlorn" is definitely shifted as the poet repeats the word [. . .] its meaning "pitiable, left desolate" [. . .] describes the poet's own state.'
47 Solitary.
48 Barnard glosses this question thus: 'Is reality the ecstatic world of the nightingale's song, or the everyday world he has "awakened" to?' (John Barnard (ed.), *John Keats: The Complete Poems*, Harmondsworth: Penguin, 1973). According to Sperry, the poet's final 'questions seek to reduce the life and potentiality of the verse, its continuity and infinite suggestiveness, to the value of a logical abstraction by forcing upon it the alien methodology of "either/or" [. . .] They dramatize the replacement of one kind of comprehension [. . .] by another that is more familiar, the kind of busy common sense' (*Keats the Poet*).

subsequently included in *Lamia, Isabella, The Eve of St Agnes, and other Poems* (1820).[1] If Keats had a particular Grecian urn in mind when he composed the poem, then its identity remains mysterious. It is more likely that the urn is partly his own creation, partly a composite drawn from his reading about and viewing of classical art (Greek urns and vases were enthusiastically collected by contemporary connoisseurs and museums). Ian Jack's *Keats and the Mirror of Art* discusses the probable influences on Keats's urn: the Portland Vase, the Townley Vase and the Elgin Marbles in the British Museum and the Vase of Sosibios in the Louvre. Jack demonstrates 'how common a practice it was to write a poem inspired by a particular work of art' in this period, and for him, the ode 'is the most memorable outcome of the debate about the relations between Poetry and the Visual Arts which was pursued so vigorously at this time'.[2]

The ode reflects the fascination with Greek art and culture evident throughout Keats's career. However, the poet's enthusiasm is not uncritical and here, as in the 'Ode to a Nightingale', there is a central ambivalence about the relationship between the unchanging, ideal world of art and beauty figured by the urn and that of humanity, characterised as it is by suffering, death and decay. Keats's rich descriptions of the pastoral scenes of love, sexual desire, music-making and religious ceremony painted on the urn offer a meditation upon the timeless quality of art. However, this is underpinned by an awareness of the mutability of human life and the fleeting nature of happiness and love and, perhaps, a sense that there is something limiting, even inhuman about the urn's 'cold pastoral'. Whatever the attractions of art, human experience is inextricably involved with sorrow and suffering; perhaps Keats, as Douglas Bush notes, cannot, in the final analysis, 'convince himself that love and beauty on marble are better than flesh-and-blood experience'.[3] Certainly recent scholarship on the poem places great stress upon its ambiguities. John Barnard summarises current critical thought as seeing the urn as 'symbolic of the kind of truth proposed by art, more particularly by poetry and the imagination, but one whose order of knowing is implicitly criticised by the speaker as a limited one which denies humanity. Although intense, the figures on the urn can never consummate their desire, and belong to an ominous world of coldness and fixity.'[4] Opinion about Keats's handling of art and the imagination has not also been so equivocal. Writing in 1953, Earl R. Wasserman saw the ode as straightforwardly idealistic: 'the intention of the poem must be to hold up art as the source of the highest form of wisdom',[5]

---

1 The source of the present text.
2 Ian Jack, *Keats and the Mirror of Art*, Oxford: Clarendon Press, 1967, p. 215.
3 Quoted in John Barnard (ed.), *John Keats: The Complete Poems*, Harmondsworth: Penguin, 1973, p. 649.
4 John Barnard, *John Keats*, Cambridge: Cambridge University Press, 1987, p. 104.
5 Earl R. Wasserman, *The Finer Tone: Keats' Major Poems*, Baltimore, Md.: Johns Hopkins University Press, 1953, p. 60.

whilst John Middleton Murry, writing in 1926, though aware of the poem's attention to suffering, argued that such agonies allow a richer humanity to emerge: the poem offers 'deep wisdom purchased at the full price of deep suffering'.[6]

Much discussion of the poem has focused on its last two lines, in which the urn speaks directly to mankind. The urn's address may echo the inscriptions sometimes found on Greek and Roman vases; as Jack writes: 'If Keats knew the introduction to Henry Moses's *Collection of Antique Vases*, he will have read there that inscriptions "are often found" on painted vases, and they sometimes contain "a moral sentiment". And so Keats decided to give his urn "a moral sentiment", and to make this sentiment an affirmation of the profound significance of Beauty'.[7] Keats's 'moral sentiment' is contained in the most contentious lines in his work. Matters are not helped by the textual problems associated with the verses. In the poem's first publication in January 1820, they are printed thus:

> Beauty is Truth, Truth Beauty. – That is all
> Ye know on Earth, and all ye need to know.

However, in the July publication in the *Lamia* volume (the text used here), inverted commas have been added thus:

> "Beauty is truth, truth beauty," – that is all
> Ye know on earth, and all ye need to know.

The original manuscripts of the poem serve to confuse rather than clarify matters, having neither full stop nor quotation marks after 'truth beauty':

> Beauty is truth, – truth beauty, – that is all
> Ye know on earth, and all ye need to know.

And in the standard edition of Keats's poetry, Jack Stillinger's, the lines are given in a way that supports the editor's conviction that the lines are addressed to man by the urn:

> 'Beauty is truth, truth beauty, – that is all
> Ye know on earth, and all ye need to know.'

So how are we to read these lines? Are both lines addressed to man by the urn? Or are the words after 'Beauty is truth, truth beauty' addressed by the poet to the urn? Or by the poet to the reader? Keats's most notable recent editors,

---

6   John Middleton Murry, *Keats and Shakespeare*, London: Oxford University Press, Humphrey Milward, 1925, p. 130.
7   Jack, *Keats and the Mirror of Art*, p. 223.

Allott, Barnard and Stillinger, have favoured the first suggestion, with qualifications, but the case remains unsettled and each reading has critical validity. This question is but part of the discussion of the lines' meaning, which has generated intense debate. To some critics (such as Ian Jack, who considered Keats's decision to mimic the moral inscriptions on Greek vases ill-advised[8]) their aphoristic nature works against the ambiguity found elsewhere in the poem; whilst for others their complexity encapsulates the paradoxes embedded in the poem as a whole (as in Cleanth Brooks's 'Keats's Sylvan Historian; History without Footnotes' (1947), which is extracted on **pp. 46–7**). T. S. Eliot declared that 'The statement [. . .] seems to me meaningless; or perhaps, the fact that it is grammatically meaningless conceals another meaning from me',[9] and Arthur Quiller-Couch, who read the lines as demonstrating that Keats was a pure aesthete, 'a young apostle of poetry for poetry's sake', chides the poet for his 'vague observation': 'to anyone whom life has taught to face facts and define his terms, [this is] actually an uneducated conclusion, albeit most pardonable in one so young.'[10] On the other hand, I. A. Richards sees Keats's lines as 'a pseudo-statement'; for him, those who seek in it 'the quintessence of an aesthetic philosophy' mistake the poem, which is actually expressive of feeling rather than systematic philosophy, 'the expression of a certain blend of feelings'.[11] F. W. Bateson's *English Poetry* (1950) sees their message as over-simplified, but necessarily so, part of Keats's project of 'uniting Romanticism ("beauty") and realism ("truth") [. . .] the feeling with the concept, poetry and philosophy'.[12] And for Barnard (1987), the urn's statement is 'at best a partial truth. If the urn claims too much for itself, the ode nevertheless admits the measure of consolation which it can offer'.[13] However important the poem's conclusion might be, the reader might also bear in mind Bate's remark that there are dangers in an over-concentration on the final lines and in separating them 'from the context of the poem' as whole.[14] Stuart Sperry is also worth citing in this context. Sperry spends eight pages of *Keats the Poet* examining the lines without reaching any clear conclusion, and, indeed, argues that those who impose a single meaning on them destroy their power. We must be negatively capable in our reading: 'What the ode expresses is the difficulty and yet the necessity of remaining content with the way art speaks to us, with the kind of "half knowledge" it offers. Once we demand the "Urn" to speak to us definitively, in a way commensurable with "fact & reason", we find we have destroyed its life.'[15]

8 Jack, *Keats and the Mirror of Art*.
9 T. S. Eliot, *Selected Essays*, New York: Harcourt, Brace, 1950, p. 231.
10 Quoted in Murry, *Keats and Shakespeare*.
11 I. A. Richards, *Practical Criticism*, London: Routledge, 1929, pp. 186–7.
12 See F. W. Bateson, *English Poetry: A Critical Introduction*, London: Longmans, Green, 1950, pp. 217–22.
13 Barnard, *John Keats*, p. 108.
14 Walter Jackson Bate, *John Keats*, London: Chatto & Windus, 1963, p. 517.
15 Stuart M. Sperry, *Keats the Poet*, Princeton, NJ: Princeton University Press, 1973, p. 278.

For further reading, see William Empson's *The Structure of Complex Words*,[16] Helen Vendler's *The Odes of John Keats*[17] and Susan Wolfson's *The Questioning Presence*.[18] Recent politically charged readings of the poem are to be found in Daniel P. Watkins's *Keats's Poetry and the Politics of the Imagination*,[19] Theresa M. Kelley's 'Keats, Ekphrasis, and History'[20] and Jeffrey N. Cox's fine account in *Poetry and Politics in the Cockney School* (extracted on **pp. 74–5**).

1

Thou still unravish'd[21] bride of quietness,   1
    Thou foster-child[22] of silence and slow time,
Sylvan[23] historian,[24] who canst thus express
    A flowery tale[25] more sweetly than our rhyme:
What leaf-fring'd legend haunts about thy shape
    Of deities or mortals, or of both,
        In Tempe[26] or the dales of Arcady?[27]
    What men or gods are these? What maidens loth?
What mad pursuit? What struggle to escape?
    What pipes and timbrels?[28] What wild ecstasy?[29]   10

2

Heard melodies are sweet, but those unheard
    Are sweeter; therefore, ye soft pipes, play on;
Not to the sensual[30] ear, but, more endear'd,
    Pipe to the spirit ditties of no tone:

16 Wiliam Empson, *The Structure of Complex Words*, London: Chatto & Windus, 1951.
17 Helen Vendler, *The Odes of John Keats*, Cambridge, Mass.: The Belknap Press of the Harvard University Press, 1983.
18 Susan J. Wolfson, *The Questioning Presence*, Ithaca, NY: Cornell University Press, 1986.
19 Daniel P. Watkins, *Keats's Poetry and the Politics of the Imagination*, Rutherford, NJ: Fairleigh Dickinson University Press, 1989.
20 In Nicholas Roe (ed.), *Keats and History*, Cambridge: Cambridge University Press, 1995, pp. 31–32.
21 (Literally) virginal.
22 Because the potter who made the urn is dead.
23 Woody. A sylvan is a deity or spirit of the woods.
24 The vase is an historian because it tells tales of the past.
25 The tale could be 'flowery' inasmuch as it offers a bucolic, pastoral story, or 'flowery' in the sense of over-ornate or over-elaborate.
26 Tempe was a valley in Thessaly. The term is used by association as a generic name for a delightful rural spot.
27 A poetic term for Arcadia, which according to Lemprière's *Classical Dictionary* was 'much celebrated by the poets, and famous for its mountains'. By association, 'Arcadian' means ideally rustic or rural.
28 Tambourines.
29 William Walsh writes of the first stanza: 'The double nature of the urn, blending the serenity of utter peace and the violence of passion – which is the pivot of the first stanza and the source for the rest of the poem – is powerfully confirmed by the deep and varied natural movement of the rhythm: calm, slow and full in the first half, but broken and agitated in the six peremptory and Dionysiac questions with which the stanza concludes' (*Introduction to Keats*, London: Methuen, 1989).
30 Physical.

Fair youth, beneath the trees, thou canst not leave
  Thy song, nor ever can those trees be bare;
    Bold Lover, never, never canst thou kiss,
Though winning near the goal yet, do not grieve;
  She cannot fade, though thou hast not thy bliss,
    For ever wilt thou love, and she be fair!   20

3
Ah, happy, happy boughs! that cannot shed
  Your leaves, nor ever bid the Spring adieu;
And, happy melodist, unwearied,
    For ever piping songs for ever new;
More happy love! more happy, happy love!
  For ever warm and still to be enjoy'd,
    For ever panting, and for ever young;
All breathing human passion far above,[31]
  That leaves a heart high-sorrowful and cloy'd,
    A burning forehead, and a parching tongue.[32]   30

4
Who are these coming to the sacrifice?
  To what green altar, O mysterious priest,
Lead'st thou that heifer lowing at the skies,
    And all her silken flanks with garlands drest?
What little town by river or sea shore,
  Or mountain-built with peaceful citadel,
    Is emptied of this folk, this pious morn?
And, little town, thy streets for evermore
  Will silent be; and not a soul to tell
    Why thou art desolate, can e'er return.   40

5
O Attic[33] shape! Fair attitude! with brede[34]
  Of marble men and maidens overwrought,
With forest branches and the trodden weed;
  Thou, silent form, dost tease us out of thought[35]

---

31 Compare Hazlitt: 'Greek statues are marble to the touch and to the heart [...] In their faultless
   excellence they appear sufficient to themselves. By their beauty they are raised above the frailties of
   passion or suffering.'
32 Bate comments: 'More is being deprived the figures on the urn than is bestowed. They are now
   conceived negatively, through what they lack; and in only the weak final line does their lack suggest
   much advantage. "All breathing human passion" is a weighted phrase: "above", half-ironic, loses
   its evaluative force and begins to connote unawareness. "Cloy'd" at least implies fulfilment.
   Finally, a heart "high-sorrowful" is able to experience the mystery of sorrow' (*John Keats*).
33 Grecian.
34 (Used metaphorically) embroidery.
35 '[T]wo, not necessarily exclusive, readings are possible: either, defeats our attempts to reason, or,
   raises us beyond merely intellectual speculation to an intuitive level' (Barnard, *John Keats: The
   Complete Poems*).

As doth eternity: Cold Pastoral!
  When old age shall this generation waste,
    Thou shalt remain, in midst of other woe
  Than ours, a friend to man, to whom thou say'st,
    "Beauty is truth, truth beauty,"—that is all
  Ye know on earth, and all ye need to know.   50

Ode on Melancholy

The 'Ode on Melancholy' was first published in Keats's 1820 volume, *Lamia, Isabella, The Eve of St Agnes, and other Poems.*[1] The poem's manuscripts are marked '1819', and Keats's editors generally see the poem as dating from May of that year.[2] This claim is principally based on thematic rather than any other kind of evidence, for the poem shares the preoccupations of the great odes written in May 1819, 'Ode to a Nightingale' and 'Ode on a Grecian Urn'. Certainly the 'Ode on Melancholy' is best understood as a poem which addresses the quint-essentially Keatsian theme of the close association between melancholy and joy. Nicholas Roe summarises the ode as a work which 'rejects the conventional trappings of a macabre, gothic imagination, in favour of a meditation on themes which had preoccupied Keats in *Ode to a Nightingale* and *Ode on a Grecian Urn*: beauty and its transience, and the interpenetration of melancholy and delight'.[3]

Miriam Allott offers a useful thematic summary of the poem's three stanzas: 'The poem is a characteristic Keatsian statement about the necessary relationship between joy and sorrow. True Melancholy is not to be found among thoughts of oblivion, death and gloom (stanza 1); it descends suddenly and is linked with the perception of beauty and its transience (stanza 2); it is associated with beauty, joy, pleasure and delight and is felt by only those who can experience these intensely (stanza 3).'[4] According to Walter Jackson Bate, the first stanza offers a protest 'against the conventional symbols of oblivion, death, and melancholy'.[5] Douglas Bush, on the other hand, dismisses it as manifesting 'a purely and thinly sensuous aestheticism' which 'support[s] the old notion of Keats as an epicure of voluptuous sensation'.[6] However, Bush seems to mis-read the playful opening of the poem, which actually offers a dismissal of over-stretched and attitudinising sensibility, and assumes an ironic distance from an

---

1 The source of the present text.
2 See, for instance, Miriam Allott (ed.), *The Poems of John Keats*, London: Longman, 1970, p. 538 and John Barnard (ed.), *John Keats: The Complete Poems*, Harmondsworth: Penguin, 1973, p. 658.
3 John Keats, *Selected Poems*, ed. Nicholas Roe, London: Dent, 1995, p. 322.
4 Allott, *Keats*, p. 538.
5 Walter Jackson Bate, *John Keats*, London: Chatto & Windus, 1963, p. 522. John Barnard reads the first stanza as a wittily ironic rejection of a sentimental contemplation of suicide (*John Keats*, Cambridge: Cambridge University Press, 1987, p. 113).
6 Douglas Bush, *John Keats: His Life and Writings*, New York: Macmillan, 1966, p. 147.

affected, even luxurious, indulgence in melancholy. In the second stanza, real, rather than posturing, melancholy arrives, suddenly and unprompted. It dwells constantly with 'Beauty', 'Joy' and 'Pleasure' and the theme of 'the interpenetration of melancholy and delight' in the second and third stanzas is the one which has most preoccupied critics of the poem.[7] For Barnard, 'Keats's essential experience is the oxymoronic realisation that pain is indivisible from joy' and that paradox 'receives its most memorable formulation'[8] in the 'Ode on Melancholy'.

For further reading, see Bloom's *The Visionary Company*,[9] Helen Vendler's *The Odes of John Keats*[10] and Robert Cummings's 'Keats's Melancholy in the Temple of Delight'.[11]

1

No, no, go not to Lethe,[12] neither twist   1
  Wolf's-bane,[13] tight-rooted, for its poisonous wine;
Nor suffer thy pale forehead to be kiss'd
  By nightshade, ruby grape[14] of Proserpine;[15]
Make not your rosary of yew-berries,[16]
  Nor let the beetle, nor the death-moth[17] be
    Your mournful Psyche,[18] nor the downy owl
A partner in your sorrow's mysteries;
  For shade to shade will come too drowsily,
    And drown the wakeful anguish of the soul.   10

2

But when the melancholy fit shall fall
  Sudden from heaven like a weeping cloud,

---

7 See Bate, *John Keats*, pp. 520–4 and Barnard, *John Keats*, pp. 112–16. Sperry, however, sees the theme of the interpenetration of joy and melancholy as 'actually subordinate' to Keats's preoccupation with poetic creativity, part of his analysis throughout the odes of the 'process of imaginative intuition' and the 'nature of the creative process' (Stuart M. Sperry, *Keats the Poet*, Princeton, NJ: Princeton University Press, 1973, pp. 283 and 243).
8 Barnard, *John Keats*, p. 112.
9 Harold Bloom, *The Visionary Company*, Ithaca, NY: Cornell University Press (1st edn 1961), rev. edn 1971, pp. 413–16.
10 Helen Vendler, *The Odes of John Keats*, Cambridge, Mass.: The Belknap Press of the Harvard University Press, 1983, pp. 157–90.
11 Robert Cummings, 'Keats's Melancholy in the Temple of Delight', *Keats–Shelley Journal*, 36, 1987, pp. 50–62.
12 The Hadean waters of oblivion.
13 A yellow-leaved plant which had sinister overtones in the popular imagination, as it was associated with witches' potions.
14 The deadly nightshade has red berries.
15 The Queen of the Underworld.
16 Yew trees were seen as symbolic of sadness.
17 i.e. the death's head moth, which has skull-like markings on its wings.
18 The personification of the soul (see the headnote to 'Ode to Psyche'). In Greek, 'psyche' also means 'butterfly'. Keats's punning jest warns against one's butterfly soul becoming a death's head moth.

That fosters the droop-headed flowers all,
　　And hides the green hill in an April shroud;
Then glut thy sorrow[19] on a morning rose,[20]
　　Or on the rainbow of the salt sand-wave,
　　　Or on the wealth of globed peonies;[21]
Or if thy mistress some rich anger shows,
　　Imprison her soft hand, and let her rave,
　　　And feed deep, deep upon her peerless eyes.　　　　　20

3
She dwells with Beauty—Beauty that must die;
　　And Joy, whose hand is ever at his lips
Bidding adieu; and aching Pleasure nigh,
　　Turning to poison while the bee-mouth sips:
Aye, in the very temple of Delight
　　Veil'd Melancholy has her sovran shrine,
　　　Though seen of none save him whose strenuous tongue
Can burst Joy's grape against his palate fine;
　　His soul shalt taste the sadness of her might,
　　　And be among her cloudy trophies[22] hung.[23]　　　　30

From 'Lamia'

'Lamia' tells the tragic story, derived from a tale found in Robert Burton's *The Anatomy of Melancholy* (which is itself based upon a story told by the Greek author Philostratus), of a sorceress who is transformed from a serpent into a beautiful woman. In Part I, the serpentine enchantress Lamia, who is enamoured of the earnest young Corinthian Lycius, is granted her new nymph-like shape by the god Hermes, in return for assisting in one of his romantic intrigues. Arriving at Corinth, Lycius is instantly enamoured of Lamia and the couple retire to her enchanted palace. In Part II, against Lamia's promptings, Lycius organises a great wedding feast. At the nuptials, Lycius's old tutor Apollonius recognises Lamia as 'a serpent'. Hermes' spell evaporates, Lamia reverts to her old shape and expires with a scream of agony, and Lycius dies of grief soon after. Keats drafted Part I of 'Lamia' between 28 June and 11 July 1819 and completed the poem between 12 August and early September of the same year. It was first published

---

19 i.e. indulge your sorrow to the full.
20 i.e. a rose which flowers and withers in the same day.
21 Red flowers.
22 As per the trophies of martial victory displayed in classical temples.
23 In *A Survey of English Literature 1780–1830*, London: Edward Arnold, 1912, Oliver Elton argues that 'the conclusion [...] is a sublime sort of Epicureanism; for it is the enjoyer who knows Melancholy best'.

in his 1820 collection, *Lamia, Isabella, The Eve of St Agnes, and other Poems.*[1] In September 1819, Keats writes of 'Lamia' that 'I am certain there is that sort of fire in it which must take hold of people in some way – give them either pleasant or unpleasant sensations. What they want is a sensation of some sort'. Keats's optimism that the poem would catch his readers' attention is reflected in his decision to position it first in the 1820 volume, and several of the poet's most significant contemporaries caught the bait: Charles Lamb argued that 'Lamia' was 'of gorgeous stuff as ever romance was composed of' and Leigh Hunt found it 'the very quintessence of the romantic'. Hunt was Keats's best early critic, and most subsequent accounts have engaged with 'Lamia' on similar terms to his. For Hunt, the poem dramatises the division between reality, philosophy and science (encapsulated in the figure of Apollonius) on one side, and poetry, idealism and dreaming (symbolised by Lamia and Lycius) on the other. Keats's sympathies are with Lamia and what she represents: 'He would see fair play to the serpent, and makes the power of the philosopher an ill-natured and disturbing thing. Lamia though liable to be turned into painful shapes had a soul of humanity, and the poet does not see why she should not have her pleasures accordingly, merely because a philosopher saw that she was not a mathematical truth.' Hunt goes on to lament Keats's emphasis upon the division between philosophy and poetry ('Do not all charms fly/At the mere touch of cold philosophy?'), arguing that it is a 'learned vulgarism' to emphasise their incompatibility.

Twentieth-century critics have debated the same issues. Some, with Hunt, see Keats's portrayal of Apollonius as an attack upon a sour rationalism at the touch of which poetry and the imagination is destroyed, whilst others take a diametrically opposed position: that it is the world-view of Lamia and Lycius (here seen as self-delusion, the empty dreaming condemned in 'The Fall of Hyperion') which is the subject of Keats's criticism. David Perkins exemplifies the latter approach, seeing Keats's sympathies as being, in the final analysis, with philosophy and 'reality' rather than poetry and 'illusion'. He offers a bleak account of the poem which sees it as a 'condemnation' of 'the visionary imagination': 'the vision deceives. The lover of vision may be only the innocent victim of his own quest for happiness, or he may be a fool as well. In any case, he is certain to become a "wretched wight".'[2] Though Apollonius might be 'crabbed, that is also partly the attitude of the poem to what he represents': 'the important point is that within the poem Apollonius is penetrating and Lycius deceived

1 The source of the present text.
2 David A. Perkins, *The Quest for Permanence: The Symbolism of Wordsworth, Shelley and Keats*, Cambridge, Mass.: Harvard University Press, 1959, p. 264.

[. . .] Apollonius, then, represents a clear though perhaps a single-eyed view of reality.' Lycius, on the other hand, 'cannot bear mortal life as it is, and crumples at the impact'.³ Miriam Allott encapsulates the opposite perspective; for her 'Lamia'

> makes on its own imaginative terms a successful statement of the idea which Keats tried to expound – superfluously perhaps – in conceptual language towards the end of his story ('Do not all charms fly at the mere touch of cold philosophy'): What Keats's poem as a whole communicates to us with great emotional honesty is his angry exasperation with Apollonius, his pity for Lamia [. . .] his self-identification [. . .] with Lycius, and his distressed sense that the final catastrophe is inevitable. He has no 'answer' to this: no answer is possible. He cannot banish the dream: in describing he asserts its value. [. . .] He cannot ignore the philosopher, an unbidden guest who insists on making his unbidden presence felt. All that is left for him to do is express his pain and to utter his bitter protest against Apollonius – that is, against the kind of approach to life which seems to him to endanger the poetic imagination.⁴

For further reading, see Gittings's *John Keats: The Living Year*,⁵ Bate's *John Keats*⁶ and Barnard's *John Keats*.⁷ See also John Jones's *John Keats' Dream of Truth*, which reads 'Lamia' as a 'cruel comedy' in which Keats adopts a detached attitude to all of his protagonists, and sees the poem as the tonal opposite of 'Isabella' (about which Keats had declared 'I enter *fully* into the feeling'): '*Lamia* stands at the opposite pole to 'Isabella' [. . .] in this matter of Negative Capability: entering fully into the feeling is what that poem wittingly avoids.'⁸ J. Middleton Murry offers a strained reading of the poem as autobiography: 'Keats is Lycius, Fanny Brawne is Lamia, and Apollonius is Charles Brown the realist trying to break Fanny's spell over Keats by insisting upon her as the female animal.'⁹ M. R. Ridley reads the poem against one of its principal influences, Coleridge's portrayal of the mysterious Geraldine in 'Christabel'.¹⁰ And Marjorie Levinson sees the poem as a 'contemporary satire' on money and

3 *Ibid.*, pp. 271–2.
4 In Kenneth Muir (ed.), *Keats: A Reassessment*, Liverpool: Liverpool University Press, 1958, pp. 59–60.
5 Robert Gittings, *John Keats: The Living Year*, London: Heinemann, 1954, pp. 147–50.
6 Walter Jackson Bate, *John Keats*, London: Chatto & Windus, 1963, pp. 57–81.
7 John Barnard, *John Keats*, Cambridge: Cambridge University Press, 1987, pp. 119–27.
8 John Jones, *John Keats's Dream of Truth*, London: Chatto & Windus, 1969, p. 245.
9 John Middleton Murry, *Keats and Shakespeare*, London: Oxford University Press, Humphrey Milward, 1925, p. 157.
10 M. R. Ridley, *Keats' Craftsmanship: A Study in Poetic Development*, Oxford: Clarendon Press, 1933.

a commercial culture within which women (not only the the prostitutes for which Corinth was infamous, but Lamia herself) are 'commodified'.[11]

Part I

Upon a time, before the faery broods[12]   1
Drove Nymph and Satyr[13] from the prosperous woods,[14]
Before King Oberon's[15] bright diadem,[16]
Sceptre, and mantle, clasp'd with dewy gem,
Frighted away[17] the Dryads[18] and the Fauns[19]
From rushes green, and brakes,[20] and cowslip'd lawns,
The ever-smitten Hermes[21] empty left
His golden throne, bent warm on amorous theft:
From high Olympus had he stolen light,
On this side of Jove's clouds, to escape the sight   10
Of his great summoner, and made retreat
Into a forest on the shores of Crete.
For somewhere in that sacred island[22] dwelt
A nymph, to whom all hoofed Satyrs knelt;
At whose white feet the languid Tritons[23] poured
Pearls, while on land they wither'd and adored.
Fast by the springs where she to bathe was wont,
And in those meads where sometime she might haunt,
Were strewn rich gifts, unknown to any Muse,[24]
Though Fancy's casket were unlock'd to choose.   20
Ah, what a world of love was at her feet!
So Hermes thought, and a celestial heat
Burnt from his winged heels to either ear,

11 See Marjorie Levinson, *Keats's Life of Allegory: The Origins of a Style*, Oxford: Blackwell, 1988, pp. 254–95.
12 Lines 1–5: Keats declares that his poem utilises classical myth rather than the later folklore of the fairy.
13 Mythological woodland creatures, part human and part beast (sometimes a horse. but more usually a goat).
14 The woods are richer in the sense of being denser and more extensive than in modern times.
15 The king of the fairies.
16 Crown.
17 i.e. before classical myth was displaced by legends of the fairy world.
18 Wood-nymphs.
19 Mythological rural creatures, half-man, half-goat.
20 Bracken.
21 The Greek messenger god, son of Zeus and Maia. The 'ever-smitten' Hermes was renowned for his amorous nature.
22 Sacred because of its status as the birthplace of Zeus.
23 Mermen.
24 i.e. beyond the poetic imagination.

That from a whiteness, as the lily clear,
Blush'd into roses 'mid his golden hair,
Fallen in jealous curls about his shoulders bare.
From vale to vale, from wood to wood, he flew,
Breathing upon the flowers his passion new,
And wound with many a river to its head,
To find where this sweet nymph prepar'd her secret bed: 30
In vain; the sweet nymph might nowhere be found,
And so he rested, on the lonely ground,
Pensive, and full of painful jealousies
Of the Wood-Gods, and even the very trees.
There as he stood, he heard a mournful voice,
Such as once heard, in gentle heart, destroys
All pain but pity: thus the lone voice spake:
"When from this wreathed tomb[25] shall I awake!
When move in a sweet body fit for life,
And love, and pleasure, and the ruddy strife[26]   40
Of hearts and lips! Ah, miserable me!"
The God, dove-footed, glided silently
Round bush and tree, soft-brushing, in his speed,
The taller grasses and full-flowering weed,
Until he found a palpitating snake,
Bright, and cirque-couchant[27] in a dusky brake.

She was a gordian[28] shape of dazzling hue,
Vermilion-spotted,[29] golden, green, and blue;
Striped like a zebra, freckled like a pard,[30]
Eyed like a peacock,[31] and all crimson barred;   50
And full of silver moons, that, as she breathed,
Dissolv'd, or brighter shone, or interwreathed
Their lustres with the gloomier tapestries—
So rainbow-sided, touch'd with miseries,
She seem'd, at once, some penanced lady elf,[32]
Some demon's mistress, or the demon's self.
Upon her crest she wore a wannish[33] fire
Sprinkled with stars, like Ariadne's tiar:[34]

---

25 Lamia is lamenting her serpentine appearance.
26 Lamia wants human blood to flow through her veins.
27 Lying coiled up in circles. The word was coined by Keats.
28 Intricately knotted (after the knot supposedly tied by the Phrygian king Gordius).
29 i.e. scarlet-spotted.
30 Leopard.
31 The circles on a peacock's plumage are known as 'eyes'.
32 i.e. an elf who has been punished for some misadventure by metamorphosis.
33 Pale.
34 Tiara. Bacchus gave Ariadne a seven-starred crown which, after her death, was transformed into a constellation.

Her head was serpent, but ah, bitter-sweet!
She had a woman's mouth with all its pearls complete: 60
And for her eyes: what could such eyes do there
But weep, and weep, that they were born so fair?
As Proserpine[35] still weeps for her Sicilian air.
Her throat was serpent, but the words she spake
Came, as through bubbling honey, for Love's sake,
And thus; while Hermes on his pinions[36] lay,
Like a stoop'd falcon ere he takes his prey.

"Fair Hermes, crown'd with feathers, fluttering light,
I had a splendid dream of thee last night:
I saw thee sitting, on a throne of gold,   70
Among the Gods, upon Olympus old,
The only sad one; for thou didst not hear
The soft, lute-finger'd Muses chaunting clear,
Nor even Apollo when he sang alone,
Deaf to his throbbing throat's long, long melodious moan.
I dreamt I saw thee, robed in purple flakes,[37]
Break amorous through the clouds, as morning breaks,
And, swiftly as a bright Phoebean dart,[38]
Strike for the Cretan isle; and here thou art!
Too gentle Hermes, hast thou found the maid?"   80
Whereat the star of Lethe[39] not delay'd
His rosy eloquence, and thus inquired:
"Thou smooth-lipp'd serpent, surely high inspired!
Thou beauteous wreath,[40] with melancholy eyes,
Possess whatever bliss thou canst devise,
Telling me only where my nymph is fled,—
Where she doth breathe!" "Bright planet, thou hast said,"
Return'd the snake, "but seal with oaths, fair God!"
"I swear," said Hermes, "by my serpent rod,
And by thine eyes, and by thy starry crown!"   90

Lamia tells Hermes how to procure the nymph and the god leaves.
Lamia is rewarded by her metamorphosis into a woman.

Left to herself, the serpent now began
To change; her elfin blood in madness ran,

35 Proserpine was carried away from Sicily by Pluto, to become the queen of the Underworld.
36 Wings.
37 Fleecy clouds, tinted by the sun.
38 i.e. a sunbeam (after Phoebus the god of light, another guise of Apollo).
39 Hermes led the souls of the dead over the river Lethe.
40 Lamia's serpentine body is curled.

Her mouth foam'd, and the grass, therewith besprent,[41]
Wither'd at dew so sweet and virulent;
Her eyes in torture fix'd, and anguish drear,   150
Hot, glaz'd, and wide, with lid-lashes all sear,[42]
Flash'd phosphor and sharp sparks, without one cooling tear.
The colours all inflam'd throughout her train,
She writh'd about, convuls'd with scarlet pain:
A deep volcanian yellow took the place
Of all her milder-mooned body's grace;
And, as the lava ravishes the mead,
Spoilt all her silver mail, and golden brede;[43]
Made gloom of all her frecklings, streaks and bars,
Eclips'd her crescents, and lick'd up her stars: 160
So that, in moments few, she was undrest
Of all her sapphires, greens, and amethyst,
And rubious-argent:[44] of all these bereft,
Nothing but pain and ugliness were left.
Still shone her crown; that vanish'd, also she
Melted and disappear'd as suddenly;
And in the air, her new voice luting soft,
Cried, "Lycius! gentle Lycius!"—Borne aloft
With the bright mists about the mountains hoar
These words dissolv'd: Crete's forests heard no more.   170

Lamia arrives at Corinth, meets Lycius and 'entices' him.

Let the mad poets say whate'er they please
Of the sweets of Fairies, Peris,[45] Goddesses,
There is not such a treat among them all,   330
Haunters of cavern, lake, and waterfall,
As a real woman, lineal indeed
From Pyrrha's pebbles[46] or old Adam's seed.
Thus gentle Lamia judg'd, and judg'd aright,
That Lycius could not love in half a fright,
So threw the goddess off, and won his heart
More pleasantly by playing woman's part,
With no more awe than what her beauty gave,
That, while it smote, still guaranteed to save.

41 Sprinkled. A Spenserian archaism.
42 Scorched.
43 Embroidery, patterning.
44 Ruby-embedded silver.
45 Angelic beings in Persian mythology.
46 After an angry Zeus sent a great flood, Pyrrha and Deucalion repopulated the world by throwing
    stones which were transformed into men and women.

Lycius to all made eloquent reply,   340
Marrying to every word a twinborn sigh;
And last, pointing to Corinth, ask'd her sweet,
If 'twas too far that night for her soft feet.
The way was short, for Lamia's eagerness
Made, by a spell, the triple league decrease
To a few paces; not at all surmised
By blinded Lycius, so in her comprized.[47]
They pass'd the city gates, he knew not how
So noiseless, and he never thought to know.

    As men talk in a dream, so Corinth all,   350
Throughout her palaces imperial,
And all her populous streets and temples lewd,[48]
Mutter'd, like tempest in the distance brew'd,
To the wide-spreaded night above her towers.
Men, women, rich and poor, in the cool hours,
Shuffled their sandals o'er the pavement white,
Companion'd or alone; while many a light
Flared, here and there, from wealthy festivals,
And threw their moving shadows on the walls,
Or found them cluster'd in the corniced shade   360
Of some arch'd temple door, or dusky colonnade.[49]

    Muffling his face, of greeting friends in fear,
Her fingers he press'd hard, as one came near
With curl'd gray beard, sharp eyes, and smooth bald crown,
Slow-stepp'd, and robed in philosophic gown:
Lycius shrank closer, as they met and past,
Into his mantle, adding wings to haste,
While hurried Lamia trembled: "Ah," said he,
"Why do you shudder, love, so ruefully?
Why does your tender palm dissolve in dew?"—   370
"I'm wearied," said fair Lamia: "tell me who
Is that old man? I cannot bring to mind
His features:—Lycius! wherefore did you blind
Yourself from his quick eyes?" Lycius replied,
"'Tis Apollonius[50] sage, my trusty guide
And good instructor; but to-night he seems
The ghost of folly haunting my sweet dreams."

---

47 Absorbed, preoccupied.
48 Corinthian temples were supposed to have held sexual ceremonials. In Keats's source for 'Lamia',
    Burton writes: 'In that one temple of Venus, a thousand whores did prostitute themselves.'
49 Column.
50 The first-century Corinthian philosopher.

While yet he spake they had arrived before
A pillar'd porch, with lofty portal door,
Where hung a silver lamp, whose phosphor[51] glow   380
Reflected in the slabbed steps below,
Mild as a star in water; for so new,
And so unsullied was the marble hue,
So through the crystal polish, liquid fine,
Ran the dark veins, that none but feet divine
Could e'er have touch'd there. Sounds Aeolian[52]
Breath'd from the hinges, as the ample span
Of the wide doors disclos'd a place unknown
Some time to any, but those two alone,
And a few Persian mutes, who that same year   390
Were seen about the markets: none knew where
They could inhabit; the most curious
Were foil'd, who watch'd to trace them to their house:
And but the flitter-winged verse must tell,
For truth's sake, what woe afterwards befel,
'Twould humour many a heart to leave them thus,
Shut from the busy world of more incredulous.

Part II

Love in a hut,[53] with water and a crust,   1
Is—Love, forgive us!—cinders, ashes, dust;
Love in a palace is perhaps at last
More grievous torment than a hermit's fast:—
That is a doubtful tale from faery land,
Hard for the non-elect to understand.
Had Lycius liv'd to hand his story down,
He might have given the moral a fresh frown,
Or clench'd it quite:[54] but too short was their bliss
To breed distrust and hate, that make the soft voice hiss.   10
Besides, there, nightly, with terrific glare,
Love,[55] jealous grown of so complete a pair,
Hover'd and buzz'd his wings, with fearful roar,
Above the lintel of their chamber door,
And down the passage cast a glow upon the floor.

---

51 Phosphorous.
52 Like the sounds produced by the Aeolian harp, a stringed instrument adapted to produce musical sounds when exposed to the wind.
53 i.e. a humble cottage.
54 Proved it conclusively. Lycius does not live long enough to reflect upon love in a palace.
55 i.e. Cupid. Cupid is 'jealous', i.e. protective, though it might be argued that he ultimately aims to bring down the lovers on account of his envy of the 'complete' initial perfection of their love.

For all this[56] came a ruin: side by side
They were enthroned, in the even tide,
Upon a couch, near to a curtaining
Whose airy texture, from a golden string,
Floated into the room, and let appear   20
Unveil'd the summer heaven, blue and clear,
Betwixt two marble shafts:—there they reposed,
Where use had made it sweet, with eyelids closed,
Saving a tythe which love still open kept,
That they might see each other while they almost slept;
When from the slope side of a suburb hill,
Deafening the swallow's twitter, came a thrill
Of trumpets—Lycius started—the sounds fled,
But left a thought, a buzzing in his head.
For the first time, since first he harbour'd in   30
That purple-lined palace of sweet sin,
His spirit pass'd beyond its golden bourn[57]
Into the noisy world almost forsworn.
The lady, ever watchful, penetrant,[58]
Saw this with pain, so arguing a want
Of something more, more than her empery[59]
Of joys; and she began to moan and sigh
Because he mused beyond her, knowing well
That but a moment's thought is passion's passing bell.
"Why do you sigh, fair creature?" whisper'd he: 40
"Why do you think?" return'd she tenderly:
"You have deserted me;—where am I now?
Not in your heart while care weighs on your brow:
No, no, you have dismiss'd me; and I go
From your breast houseless: ay, it must be so."
He answer'd, bending to her open eyes,
Where he was mirror'd small in paradise,
"My silver planet, both of eve and morn!
Why will you plead yourself so sad forlorn,
While I am striving how to fill my heart   50
With deeper crimson, and a double smart?
How to entangle, trammel up[60] and snare
Your soul in mine, and labyrinth you there
Like the hid scent in an unbudded rose?
Ay, a sweet kiss—you see your mighty woes.

56 In spite of this.
57 Realm.
58 Penetrating.
59 Empire.
60 Enmesh.

My thoughts! shall I unveil them? Listen then!
What mortal hath a prize, that other men
May be confounded and abash'd withal,
But lets it sometimes pace abroad majestical,
And triumph, as in thee I should rejoice   60
Amid the hoarse alarm of Corinth's voice.
Let my foes choke, and my friends shout afar,
While through the thronged streets your bridal car
Wheels round its dazzling spokes."—The lady's cheek
Trembled; she nothing said, but, pale and meek,
Arose and knelt before him, wept a rain
Of sorrows at his words; at last with pain
Beseeching him, the while his hand she wrung,
To change his purpose. He thereat was stung,
Perverse, with stronger fancy to reclaim   70
Her wild and timid nature to his aim:
Besides, for all his love, in self despite,
Against his better self, he took delight
Luxurious in her sorrows, soft and new.
His passion, cruel grown, took on a hue
Fierce and sanguineous⁶¹ as 'twas possible
In one whose brow had no dark veins to swell.
Fine was the mitigated⁶² fury, like
Apollo's presence when in act to strike
The serpent⁶³—Ha, the serpent! certes,⁶⁴ she   80
Was none. She burnt, she lov'd the tyranny,⁶⁵
And, all subdued, consented to the hour
When to the bridal he should lead his paramour.⁶⁶
Whispering in midnight silence, said the youth,
"Sure some sweet name thou hast, though, by my truth,
I have not ask'd it, ever thinking thee
Not mortal, but of heavenly progeny,
As still I do. Hast any mortal name,
Fit appellation⁶⁷ for this dazzling frame?
Or friends or kinsfolk on the citied earth,   90
To share our marriage feast and nuptial mirth?"
"I have no friends," said Lamia, "no, not one;
My presence in wide Corinth hardly known:

---

61 Red or inflamed with anger.
62 Moderated, controlled.
63 Apollo destroyed the huge Python which guarded the oracular shrine at Delphi.
64 Certainly.
65 There is, perhaps, a certain erotic wish-fulfilment on Keats's part here. Commenting on this pas-
    sage, the poet wrote: 'Women love to be forced to do a thing, by a fine fellow – *such* as this.'
66 Lover.
67 Label.

My parents' bones are in their dusty urns
Sepulchred, where no kindled incense burns,
Seeing all their luckless race are dead, save me,
And I neglect the holy rite for thee.
Even as you list invite your many guests;
But if, as now it seems, your vision rests
With any pleasure on me, do not bid   100
Old Apollonius—from him keep me hid."
Lycius, perplex'd at words so blind and blank,[68]
Made close inquiry; from whose touch she shrank,
Feigning a sleep; and he to the dull shade
Of deep sleep in a moment was betray'd.[69]

Lycius makes preparations for the wedding feast.

The day appear'd, and all the gossip rout.
O senseless Lycius! Madman! wherefore flout
The silent-blessing fate, warm cloister'd hours,
And show to common eyes these secret bowers?
The herd approach'd; each guest, with busy brain,   150
Arriving at the portal, gaz'd amain,[70]
And enter'd marveling: for they knew the street,
Remember'd it from childhood all complete
Without a gap, yet ne'er before had seen
That royal porch, that high-built fair demesne;[71]
So in they hurried all, maz'd,[72] curious and keen:
Save one, who look'd thereon with eye severe,
And with calm-planted steps walk'd in austere;
'Twas Apollonius: something too he laugh'd,
As though some knotty problem, that had daft[73]   160
His patient thought, had now begun to thaw,
And solve and melt:—'twas just as he foresaw.

He met within the murmurous[74] vestibule
His young disciple. " 'Tis no common rule,
Lycius," said he, "for uninvited guest
To force himself upon you, and infest

68 Incomprehensible (to Lycius).
69 Lycius' sleep is induced by Lamia's magic.
70 Intently.
71 Domain.
72 Amazed.
73 Baffled.
74 The guests in the vestibule are murmuring.

With an unbidden presence the bright throng
Of younger friends; yet must I do this wrong,
And you forgive me." Lycius blush'd, and led
The old man through the inner doors broad-spread;   170
With reconciling words and courteous mien
Turning into sweet milk the sophist's[75] spleen.

The wedding feast begins.

Soon was God Bacchus at meridian height;[76]
Flush'd were their cheeks, and bright eyes double bright:
Garlands of every green, and every scent
From vales deflower'd, or forest-trees branch rent,
In baskets of bright osier'd[77] gold were brought
High as the handles heap'd, to suit the thought
Of every guest; that each, as he did please,
Might fancy-fit his brows, silk-pillow'd at his ease.   220

 What wreath for Lamia? What for Lycius?
What for the sage, old Apollonius?
Upon her aching forehead be there hung
The leaves of willow and of adder's tongue;
And for the youth, quick, let us strip for him
The thyrsus,[78] that his watching eyes may swim
Into forgetfulness; and, for the sage,
Let spear-grass and the spiteful thistle wage
War on his temples. Do not all charms fly
At the mere touch of cold philosophy?   230
There was an awful[79] rainbow once in heaven:
We know her woof, her texture; she is given
In the dull catalogue of common things.[80]
Philosophy will clip an Angel's wings,
Conquer all mysteries by rule and line,
Empty the haunted air, and gnomed mine—

---

75 Philosopher, though the word has negative overtones of cold-hearted pedantry, which are reinforced at ll. 227–30.
76 i.e. the revelry was at its height.
77 Woven.
78 The wand of Bacchus.
79 Awe-inspiring.
80 The imaginative perception of the rainbow is threatened by the reductive, scientific analysis of such sublime natural phenomena. Keats endorsed Charles Lamb's remark (made at a party which both attended at B. R. Haydon's in December 1817) that Isaac Newton had 'destroyed all the Poetry of the rainbow, by reducing it to a prism'.

Unweave a rainbow, as it erewhile made
The tender-person'd Lamia melt into a shade.

   By her glad Lycius sitting, in chief place,
Scarce saw in all the room another face,   240
Till, checking his love trance, a cup he took
Full brimm'd, and opposite sent forth a look
'Cross the broad table, to beseech a glance
From his old teacher's wrinkled countenance,
And pledge him. The bald-head philosopher
Had fix'd his eye,[81] without a twinkle or stir
Full on the alarmed beauty of the bride,
Brow-beating her fair form, and troubling her sweet pride.
Lycius then press'd her hand, with devout touch,
As pale it lay upon the rosy couch: 250
'Twas icy, and the cold ran through his veins;
Then sudden it grew hot, and all the pains
Of an unnatural heat shot to his heart.
"Lamia, what means this? Wherefore dost thou start?
Know'st thou that man?" Poor Lamia answer'd not.
He gaz'd into her eyes, and not a jot
Own'd they the lovelorn piteous appeal:
More, more he gaz'd: his human senses reel:
Some hungry spell that loveliness absorbs;
There was no recognition in those orbs.   260
"Lamia!" he cried—and no soft-toned reply.
The many heard, and the loud revelry
Grew hush; the stately music no more breathes;
The myrtle sicken'd in a thousand wreaths.
By faint degrees, voice, lute, and pleasure ceased;
A deadly silence step by step increased,
Until it seem'd a horrid presence there,
And not a man but felt the terror in his hair.
"Lamia!" he shriek'd; and nothing but the shriek
With its sad echo did the silence break.   270
"Begone, foul dream!" he cried, gazing again
In the bride's face, where now no azure[82] vein
Wander'd on fair-spaced temples; no soft bloom
Misted the cheek; no passion to illume
The deep-recessed vision:—all was blight;
Lamia, no longer fair, there sat a deadly white.

---

81 Barnard points out that 'Apollonius is now like a snake' (John Barnard (ed.), *John Keats: The Complete Poems*, Harmondsworth: Penguin, 1973).
82 Blue.

"Shut, shut those juggling[83] eyes, thou ruthless man!
Turn them aside, wretch! or the righteous ban[84]
Of all the Gods, whose dreadful images
Here represent their shadowy presences,   280
May pierce them on the sudden with the thorn
Of painful blindness; leaving thee forlorn,
In trembling dotage to the feeblest fright
Of conscience, for their long offended might,
For all thine impious proud-heart sophistries,
Unlawful magic, and enticing lies.
Corinthians! look upon that gray-beard wretch!
Mark how, possess'd, his lashless eyelids stretch
Around his demon eyes! Corinthians, see!
My sweet bride withers at their potency."   290
"Fool!" said the sophist, in an under-tone
Gruff with contempt; which a death-nighing[85] moan
From Lycius answer'd, as heart-struck and lost,
He sank supine beside the aching ghost.
"Fool! Fool!" repeated he, while his eyes still
Relented not, nor mov'd; "from every ill
Of life have I preserv'd thee to this day,
And shall I see thee made a serpent's prey?"
Then Lamia breath'd death breath; the sophist's eye,
Like a sharp spear, went through her utterly,   300
Keen, cruel, perceant,[86] stinging: she, as well
As her weak hand could any meaning tell,
Motion'd him to be silent; vainly so,
He look'd and look'd again a level—No!
"A Serpent!" echoed he; no sooner said,
Than with a frightful scream she vanished:
And Lycius' arms were empty of delight,
As were his limbs of life, from that same night.
On the high couch he lay!—his friends came round—
Supported him—no pulse, or breath they found,   310
And, in its marriage robe, the heavy body wound.

---

83 Spell-binding.
84 Edict.
85 Death-nearing.
86 Piercing.

To Autumn

It is likely that this poem, the last of Keats's great lyrics, was composed on Sunday 19 September 1819 after the poet had returned from a country walk near Winchester in Hampshire. On the following Tuesday, he writes to J. H. Reynolds: 'How beautiful the season is now – How fine the air. A temperate sharpness about it. Really, without joking, chaste weather – Dian skies – I never lik'd stubble fields so much as now – Aye better than the chilly green of the spring. Somehow a stubble plain looks warm – in the same way that some pictures look warm – this struck me so much in my [S]unday's walk that I composed upon it.' 'To Autumn' is generally included in critical discussion of Keats's odes, though the poet did not explicitly label it as such. The poem simultaneously celebrates the fruitfulness of the season and offers an elegiac lament for the passing of spring and summer. Indeed, because of its status as Keats's final major lyric, it has also been read as a deeply poignant poem,[1] as if its eulogy of autumn, the season which heralds the 'cold threshold'[2] of winter, betokens an awareness, arguably even an acceptance, of physical decay and impending death.

Before the 1980s, most commentaries dwelt on the formal excellence of the poem: 'each generation,' declares Walter Jackson Bate, 'has found it one of the most nearly perfect poems in English'; '[F]or no other poem of the last two centuries does the classical critical vocabulary prove so satisfying'.[3] For M. R. Ridley, 'To Autumn' is 'the most serenely flawless poem in our language',[4] whilst for Stuart Sperry, the 'perfection of the ode' lies in its status as 'Keats's last and most mature comment on the poetic process'. To Sperry, the poem's description of autumn is actually a veiled, metaphorical meditation on creativity: 'its whole development, from the imagery of ripening and storing in the first stanza, through that of winnowing and slow extraction in the second, to the subtle, thin, and tenuous music with which the poem rises to its close, represents his final adaptation of his favourite metaphor for poetic creation.'[5] M. H. Abrams considered 'To Autumn' Keats's 'highest achievement' and argued that its power lies in attention to the subject of human mortality: 'The poem is about a season of the year, but [. . .] its ostensible subject [. . .] turns out to be the occasion for engaging with the multiple dilemmas of being human in the material world, in

---

1 See Harold Bloom, *The Visionary Company*, Ithaca, NY: Cornell University Press (1st edn 1961), rev. edn 1971, pp. 434–5. See also M. H. Abrams's 'Keats's Poems: The Material Dimensions', in Robert Ryan and Ronald A. Sharp (eds), *The Persistence of Poetry: Bicentennial Essays on Keats*, Amherst, Mass.: University of Massachusetts Press, 1998. Arnold Davenport reads the poem as one of 'sorrow, loss and bereavement' ('A Note on *To Autumn*', in Kenneth Muir (ed.), *Keats: A Reassessment*, Liverpool: Liverpool University Press, 1958, pp. 96–102). Christopher Ricks writes of the 'poignancy [. . .] in the deep pain and deep serenity of "To Autumn"' (*Keats and Embarrassment*, Oxford: Oxford University Press, 1974, p. 205).
2 The term is Geoffrey H. Hartman's.
3 Walter Jackson Bate, *John Keats*, London: Chatto & Windus, 1963.
4 M. R. Ridley, *Keats' Craftmanship: A Study in Poetic Development*, Oxford: Clarendon Press, 1933, p. 289.
5 Stuart M. Sperry, *Keats the Poet*, Princeton, NJ: Princeton University Press, 1973, p. 337.

which nothing can stay.'⁶ For Abrams, '"To Autumn" was the last work of artistic consequence that Keats completed [. . .] he achieved this celebratory poem, with its calm acquiescence to time, transience and mortality, at a time when he was possessed by a premonition, little short of conviction, that he had himself less than two years to live'.⁷ Douglas Bush, on the other hand, reads the poem as manifesting Keatsian 'escapism' rather than 'acquiescence': 'To Autumn' is 'less a resolution of the perplexities of life and poetic ambition than an escape into the luxury of pure – though now sober – sensation'.⁸ Against readings such as those of Abrams and Bush, Ian Jack bluntly repudiates biographical interpretations which see the poem as a meditation on impending death: 'This is not a poem about Keats: it is a poem about autumn.'⁹ According to Jack, Keats 'regarded autumn as the season of harvest and achievement, disregarding its other role as the herald of winter and of death',¹⁰ and the 'remarkable success' of 'To Autumn' actually lies in the fact that 'the poet himself makes no appearance' in the poem: 'Like a painter he loses himself in the contemplation of what he is describing.'¹¹ Jack's sense that Keats erases himself completely from his poem is shared by Aileen Ward. For her, Keats is 'completely lost in his images, and the images are presented as meaning simply themselves: Keats's richest utterance is the barest of metaphor'.¹² Such a reading does not allow the possibility that 'To Autumn' might be read in terms of the historical and social context in which it appeared. Indeed, in his important, if difficult, essay 'Poem and Ideology: A Study of Keats's "To Autumn"', Geoffrey H. Hartman calls 'To Autumn' 'a poem without explicit social context' which manifests a 'true impersonality'. For Hartman, 'the poem starts on enchanted ground and never leaves it'.¹³

Jerome J. McGann, in his important and provocative New Historicist essay 'Keats and the Historical Method in Literary Criticism' (1979), which is extracted on **pp. 57–60**, prompted a series of sociohistorical readings of 'To Autumn'. McGann agrees with Hartman that the poem seeks to avoid the political, exemplifying 'a charmed world far removed from [. . .] the dangerous political tensions of [Keats's] society'. However, McGann, unlike Hartman, faults

---

6 Abrams, 'Keats's Poems', p. 45.

7 *Ibid.*, pp. 51–2.

8 Douglas Bush, 'Keats and His Ideas', in M. H. Abrams (ed.), *English Romantic Poets: Modern Essays in Criticism*, New York: Oxford University Press, 1960, p. 337.

9 Ian Jack, *Keats and the Mirror of Art*, Oxford: Clarendon Press, 1967, p. 235.

10 *Ibid.*, p. 234.

11 Ian Jack, *English Literature 1815–1832*, Oxford: Oxford University Press, p. 119. Jack later published a detailed account of Keats's 'painterly' vision in 'To Autumn' in *Keats and the Mirror of Art*, pp. 232–43.

12 Aileen Ward, *John Keats: The Making of a Poet*, London: Secker & Warburg, 1963, p. 322.

13 'Poem and Ideology: A Study of Keats's "To Autumn"', in Geoffrey H. Hartman, *The Fate of Reading and Other Essays*, Chicago, Ill.: University of Chicago Press, 1975, pp. 124–46. Hartman's essay argues for the historical and ideological status of 'To Autumn', but only in terms of its status as a meditation on poetics: 'Keats's poem is indeed an event in history: not in world-history, however, but simply in the history of fiction' (p. 126).

the poem for its inattention to, or attempted transcendence of, politics. In the month after the yeomanry had killed six people attending a radical meeting at St Peter's Fields, Manchester, in the 'Peterloo massacre', Keats ignores the political turmoil in English society and devotes himself to the idealised world of nature. The 'escapism' which Bush sees in Keats's poem is echoed here as a charge of political bad faith. Keats's 1820 volume, says McGann, is 'great' but 'politically reactionary', and 'To Autumn' 'attempt[s] to "escape" the period which provides the poem with its context'. This argument initiated a series of historical interpretations of 'To Autumn' (by such critics as Paul Fry,[14] Andrew Bennett and Nicholas Roe), many of which repudiate McGann's position and attempt to read the poem in explicitly political terms. Bennett's Keats, Narrative, and Audience argues that the 'perfected language of pastoral description is invaded by political questions of lawful exchange, agricultural boundaries and labour relations',[15] whilst Roe's 'Keats's Commonwealth' offers a riposte to McGann which reads 'To Autumn' in the light of the 'discourses of political and social justice after the outrage at Peterloo'.[16] Roe's argument is detailed and nuanced, and should be read in full. However, it can be exemplified by his argument that the massacre at Manchester is hinted at in the imagery of the poem: 'in the "reaping hook", the "last oozings" of the "cyder-press", the "soft-dying day", and the "rosy hue" of the "stubble-plains". Through such verbal details the apocalyptic harvest of the fields of St Peter is quietly acknowledged.'[17] Here the Keatsian lyricism of 'To Autumn', rather than attempting escape from personal suffering or political turmoil, is seen as subtly engaged with sociopolitical reality.[18]

1
Season of mists and mellow fruitfulness,   1
    Close bosom-friend of the maturing sun;[19]
Conspiring with him how to load and bless
    With fruit the vines that round the thatch-eves run;
To bend with apples the moss'd cottage-trees,
    And fill all fruit with ripeness to the core;
        To swell the gourd,[20] and plump the hazel shells

14 See Paul Fry, 'History, Existence, and "To Autumn"', in 'Keats and Politics: A Forum', in Studies in Romanticism, 25, 1985, pp. 211–19. Fry's essay explicitly repudiates McGann's. See also David Worrall, Radical Culture. Discourse, Resistance and Surveillance, 1790–1820, Hemel Hempstead: Harvester Wheatsheaf, 1992, pp. 201–2.
15 See Andrew Bennett, Keats, Narrative, and Audience, Cambridge: Cambridge University Press, 1994, pp. 162–4.
16 'Keats's Commonwealth', in Nicholas Roe, Keats and History, Cambridge: Cambridge University Press, 1995, pp. 194–211.
17 Ibid., p. 207.
18 The source of the present text is the poem's first publication in Lamia, Isabella, The Eve of St. Agnes, and other Poems (1820).
19 The sun ripens the earth's produce, though it itself might also be seen as maturing as the year wanes.
20 i.e. the flesh of the fruit.

With a sweet kernel; to set budding more,
   And still more, later flowers for the bees,
   Until they think warm days will never cease,   10
      For Summer has o'er-brimm'd their clammy cells.

2

Who hath not seen thee oft amid thy store?
   Sometimes whoever seeks abroad may find
Thee sitting careless[21] on a granary floor,
   Thy hair soft-lifted by the winnowing wind;
Or on a half-reap'd furrow sound asleep,
   Drows'd with the fume of poppies,[22] while thy hook[23]
      Spares the next swath and all its twined flowers:
And sometimes like a gleaner thou dost keep
   Steady thy laden head across a brook;   20
   Or by a cyder-press, with patient look,
      Thou watchest the last oozings hours by hours.

3

Where are the songs of Spring? Ay, where are they?
   Think not of them, thou hast thy music too,—
While barred clouds bloom the soft-dying day,
   And touch the stubble-plains with rosy hue;
Then in a wailful choir the small gnats mourn
   Among the river sallows,[24] borne aloft
      Or sinking as the light wind lives or dies;
And full-grown lambs loud bleat from hilly bourn;[25]   30
   Hedge-crickets sing; and now with treble soft
   The red-breast whistles from a garden-croft;
      And gathering swallows twitter in the skies.

From 'The Fall of Hyperion. A Dream'

In late July 1819, when he was staying at Shanklin on the Isle of Wight, Keats decided to recast his fragmentary epic *Hyperion*, which he had abandoned three months earlier. The most significant innovation in 'The Fall of Hyperion' is the

21 Carefree.
22 A reference to the poppy's narcotic properties.
23 Reaping blade.
24 Willows.
25 Boundary. Keats's elegiac tone here also suggests an echo of *Hamlet*: 'The dread of something after death,/The undiscovered Country, from whose Borne No Traveller returns' (III. i. 79–80).

introduction of a framing narrative in the form of a dream vision.[1] The initial setting is a mysterious forest bower, where the narrator, a poet, discovers a feast laid out near an arbour and drinks from a 'cool vessel' which, unbeknown to him, has narcotic properties (lines 19–60). Waking, he finds the arbour gone, replaced by the enormous temple of Saturn, within which is an altar tended by the goddess Moneta (61–106). The poet then undergoes a trial in which he must climb the altar's steps or 'die on that marble' (107–36). There ensues a discourse (136–290) between the poet and the priestess about the varieties of human experience. Seeking insight into the sorrow which torments Moneta, the poet is granted god-like (though tormenting) powers of perception which allow him to view the torments of Saturn and the Titans (an adapted version of the existing narrative of Hyperion. A Fragment begins at line 294). 'The Fall of Hyperion', like its predecessor, was never completed, and breaks off early in its second canto. Tinkering apart, Keats had ceased composition by 21 September 1819, on which date he writes to Reynolds that 'I have given up Hyperion'. Though ill-health has been cited as a cause for his decision to give up the poem,[2] Keats's letter gives poetical reasons: 'there were too many Miltonic inversions in it – Miltonic verse cannot be written but in an artful or rather artist's humour.' 'I wish to give myself up to other sensations,' Keats declares; the 'true voice of feeling' rather than 'the false beauty proceeding from art'. 'The Fall of Hyperion' remained unpublished until 1848,[3] and was little read until the turn of the twentieth century. The poet Robert Bridges, writing in 1895, was one of the first to argue for its importance, seeing the fragment as Keats's 'most mature attempt [. . .] to express his own convictions concerning human life'. Since then, the poem has grown in critical estimation. For M. R. Ridley, it sees its author 'climb[ing] to a higher point than he had ever reached in poetry',[4] whilst for Harold Bloom it is 'the culmination of Keats's work'.[5]

Perhaps paradoxically, 'The Fall of Hyperion' is a dream vision which attacks dreaming. The key dialogue between the poet and Moneta draws a distinction between the humanitarian 'poet' and the self-indulgent 'dreamer'. 'Dreamers weak' are lost in escapist fantasy, ignoring the sufferings of their fellow men. The

---

1   An allegorical narrative poem which tells a story which was experienced by the narrator in a dream. The most notable European example is Dante's *Divine Comedy*, which Keats knew intimately and which, according to J. L. Lowes, provided an important model for the first section of 'The Fall of Hyperion' (J. L. Lowes, 'Moneta's Temple', *Proceedings of the Modern Language Association*, 1936, pp. 1098–13).
2   By Walter Jackson Bate most particularly. See Bate, *John Keats*, London: Chatto & Windus, 1963, p. 614.
3   In Richard Monckton Milnes's *Life, Letters, and Literary Remains of John Keats*, 2 vols, London: E. Moxon, 1848. The textual base here is that found in *John Keats: The Poetical Works*, ed. H. B. Forman, Oxford: Clarendon Press, 1906.
4   M. R. Ridley, *Keats' Craftsmanship: A Study in Poetic Development*, Oxford: Clarendon Press, 1933, p. 280.
5   Harold Bloom, *The Visionary Company*, Ithaca, NY: Cornell University Press (1st edn 1961), rev. edn 1971, p. 427.

'poet' on the other hand is more empathetic, being one of 'those to whom the miseries of the world/Are misery and will not let them rest'. This concept of suffering is vital within the poem, and the recycled *Hyperion* story of the agonies of the Titans is pressed into service as an example. For Harold Bloom, 'The Fall of Hyperion' is 'a very harsh and purgatorial poem, written with the heart's blood of a poet who senses that death is all but upon him'.[6] The insistent questionings of Moneta as to the nature and utility of poetry and the protagonist's sense of self-doubt might well betoken, in Miriam Allott's words, a work where 'Keats also faces the general question of the poet's value to humanity and the particular question of his own poetic achievement'.[7] John Barnard sees the 'narrator's nightmare-like encounter with the goddess Moneta' as 'the imaginative centre of *The Fall of Hyperion*'; for him, its substance is 'the realisation that the modern poet's burden is the pain of consciousness [. . .] Keats's dream-vision describes a prolonged rite of passage, initiating the self-conscious poet into painful maturity'.[8] Barnard also draws parallels between this poem and the 'vale of soul-making' passage of the journal-letter to George and Georgiana Keats of 21 April 1819 (see pp. 19–20): 'Keats's answer to Christianity [in the journal-letter] is profoundly humanist, a humanism embodied in *The Fall of Hyperion*. Moneta is the narrator's "mediator", and her demand that the "dreamer" suffer begins the process by which the heart is educated.'[9]

For further critical discussion of the poem, see Ridley's *Keats' Craftmanship*;[10] Robert Gittings's *John Keats: The Living Year*;[11] Kenneth Muir's 'The Meaning of Hyperion';[12] Bate's *John Keats*;[13] John Jones's *John Keats's Dream of Truth*;[14] Stuart Sperry's *Keats the Poet*;[15] and Michael O'Neill's '"When this warm scribe my hand": Writing and History in *Hyperion* and *The Fall of Hyperion*'.[16] There are useful commentaries on the poem in Bloom's *The Visionary Company*[17] and Barnard's *John Keats*.[18]

---

6 *Ibid.*, p. 430. Bloom reads l. 107–17 as a 'reference to Keats's own approaching death' (p. 425).
7 Miriam Allott, 1973, p. 656.
8 John Barnard, *John Keats*, Cambridge: Cambridge University Press, 1987, pp. 129–30.
9 *Ibid.*, p. 135.
10 Ridley, *Keats' Craftmanship*, pp. 256–60.
11 Robert Gittings, *John Keats: The Living Year*, London: Heinemann, 1954, pp. 176–85.
12 Kenneth Muir (ed.), *Keats: A Reassessment*, Liverpool: Liverpool University Press, 1958, pp. 103–23.
13 Bate, *John Keats*, pp. 585–605.
14 John Jones, *John Keats's Dream of Truth*, London: Chatto & Windus, 1969, pp. 91–114.
15 Stuart M. Sperry, *Keats the Poet*, Princeton, NJ: Princeton University Press, 1973, pp. 10–23.
16 O'Neill in Nicholas Roe (ed.), *Keats and History*, Cambridge: Cambridge University Press, 1995, pp. 143–62.
17 Bloom, *The Visionary Company*, pp. 421–33.
18 Barnard, *John Keats*, pp. 129–37.

Canto I

Fanatics have their dreams, wherewith they weave   1
A paradise for a sect; the savage too
From forth the loftiest fashion of his sleep[19]
Guesses at Heaven; pity these have not
Trac'd upon vellum or wild Indian leaf
The shadows of melodious utterance.[20]
But bare of laurel[21] they live, dream, and die;
For Poesy alone can tell her dreams,
With the fine spell of words alone can save
Imagination from the sable[22] chain   10
And dumb enchantment. Who alive can say,
"Thou art no Poet—may'st not tell thy dreams?"
Since every man whose soul is not a clod
Hath visions, and would speak, if he had loved,
And been well nurtured in his mother tongue.
Whether the dream now purpos'd to rehearse
Be poet's or fanatic's will be known
When this warm scribe my hand is in the grave.

Methought I stood where trees of every clime,
Palm, myrtle, oak, and sycamore, and beech,   20
With plantain,[23] and spice-blossoms, made a screen;
In neighbourhood of fountains (by the noise
Soft-showering in my ears), and, (by the touch
Of scent,) not far from roses. Turning round
I saw an arbour with a drooping roof
Of trellis vines, and bells, and larger blooms,
Like floral censers,[24] swinging light in air;
Before its wreathed doorway, on a mound
Of moss, was spread a feast of summer fruits,
Which, nearer seen, seem'd refuse of a meal   30
By angel tasted or our Mother Eve;
For empty shells were scattered on the grass,
And grape-stalks but half bare, and remnants more,
Sweet-smelling, whose pure kinds I could not know.
Still was more plenty than the fabled horn[25]

---

19 i.e. in his most exalted dreams.
20 i.e. they have not written down their dreams.
21 The laurel wreath awarded to poets.
22 Black, dark.
23 A tree-like tropical plant.
24 Incense-burning vessels.
25 Ceres' cornucopia, or horn of plenty. Cf. 'Lamia', I. 187.

Thrice emptied could pour forth, at banqueting
For Proserpine[26] return'd to her own fields,
Where the white heifers low. And appetite
More yearning than on Earth I ever felt
Growing within, I ate deliciously;   40
And, after not long, thirsted, for thereby
Stood a cool vessel of transparent juice
Sipp'd by the wander'd bee, the which I took,
And, pledging all the mortals of the world,
And all the dead whose names are in our lips,
Drank. That full draught is parent of my theme.
No Asian poppy[27] nor elixir fine
Of the soon-fading jealous Caliphat;[28]
No poison gender'd in close monkish cell,[29]
To thin the scarlet conclave of old men,[30]   50
Could so have rapt unwilling life away.
Among the fragrant husks and berries crush'd,
Upon the grass I struggled hard against
The domineering potion; but in vain:
The cloudy swoon came on, and down I sank,
Like a Silenus[31] on an antique vase.
How long I slumber'd 'tis a chance to guess.
When sense of life return'd, I started up
As if with wings; but the fair trees were gone,
The mossy mound and arbour were no more: 60
I look'd around upon the carved sides
Of an old sanctuary with roof august,[32]
Builded so high, it seem'd that filmed clouds
Might spread beneath, as o'er the stars of heaven;
So old the place was, I remember'd none
The like upon the Earth: what I had seen
Of grey cathedrals, buttress'd walls, rent towers,[33]
The superannuations of sunk realms,[34]
Or Nature's rocks toil'd hard in waves and winds,
Seem'd but the faulture[35] of decrepit things   70

---

26 Pluto carried off Ceres' daughter, Proserpine, to be queen of the Underworld. To placate her grief, Jupiter allowed her to spend half the year in Hades, half the year on earth.
27 With its narcotic properties.
28 Caliphs were Muslim potentates who were, to the Western imagination, manipulative and murderous tyrants. The 'elixir[s] fine' are poisons used by these dignitaries in their political intrigues.
29 Catholic priests also had a lurid appeal to the English Protestant imagination.
30 The conclave of cardinals which elects the Pope.
31 The father of the satyrs.
32 Noble.
33 i.e. ruined towers.
34 i.e. ancient sunken cities, such as the legendary Atlantis.
35 Decayed remnants. A Keatsian nonce word.

To that eternal domed Monument.—
Upon the marble at my feet there lay
Store of strange vessels and large draperies,
Which needs had been of dyed asbestos wove,
Or in that place the moth could not corrupt,[36]
So white the linen, so, in some, distinct
Ran imageries[37] from a sombre loom.
All in a mingled heap confus'd there lay
Robes, golden tongs, censer and chafing-dish,[38]
Girdles, and chains, and holy jewelries.   80

Turning from these with awe, once more I rais'd
My eyes to fathom the space every way;
The embossed roof, the silent massy range
Of columns north and south, ending in mist
Of nothing, then to eastward, where black gates
Were shut against the sunrise evermore.—
Then to the west I look'd, and saw far off
An image,[39] huge of feature as a cloud,
At level of whose feet an altar slept,
To be approach'd on either side by steps,   90
And marble balustrade,[40] and patient travail
To count with toil the innumerable degrees.
Towards the altar sober-paced I went,
Repressing haste, as too unholy there;
And, coming nearer, saw beside the shrine
One minist'ring;[41] and there arose a flame.—
When in mid-way the sickening East wind
Shifts sudden to the south, the small warm rain
Melts out the frozen incense from all flowers,
And fills the air with so much pleasant health   100
That even the dying man forgets his shroud;—
Even so that lofty sacrificial fire,
Sending forth Maian incense,[42] spread around
Forgetfulness of everything but bliss,
And clouded all the altar with soft smoke;
From whose white fragrant curtains thus I heard

---

36 A Biblical reference. Cf. Matthew 6:19–20: 'Lay not up for yourselves treasures upon earth, where
   moth and rust doth corrupt and where thieves break through and steal.'
37 Patterns.
38 A vessel used to burn incense.
39 This is the temple of the priestess Moneta.
40 Banister.
41 Moneta.
42 i.e. incense which smells like the flowers of May. Keats wrote a fragmentary 'Ode to May' in May
   1818 which hymned the 'Mother of Hermes! and still youthful Maia!'.

Language pronounc'd: "If thou canst not ascend
These steps, die on that marble where thou art.
Thy flesh, near cousin to the common dust,
Will parch for lack of nutriment—thy bones   110
Will wither in few years, and vanish so
That not the quickest eye could find a grain
Of what thou now art on that pavement cold.
The sands of thy short life are spent this hour,
And no hand in the universe can turn
Thy hourglass, if these gummed leaves[43] be burnt
Ere thou canst mount up these immortal steps."
I heard, I look'd: two senses both at once,
So fine, so subtle, felt the tyranny
Of that fierce threat and the hard task proposed.   120
Prodigious seem'd the toil; the leaves were yet
Burning—when suddenly a palsied[44] chill
Struck from the paved level up my limbs,
And was ascending quick to put cold grasp
Upon those streams that pulse beside the throat:[45]
I shriek'd, and the sharp anguish of my shriek
Stung my own ears—I strove hard to escape
The numbness; strove to gain the lowest step.
Slow, heavy, deadly was my pace: the cold
Grew stifling, suffocating, at the heart;   130
And when I clasp'd my hands I felt them not.
One minute before death, my iced foot touch'd
The lowest stair; and as it touch'd, life seem'd
To pour in at the toes: I mounted up,
As once fair angels on a ladder flew
From the green turf to Heaven[46]—"Holy Power,"
Cried I, approaching near the horned shrine,
"What am I that should so be saved from death?
What am I that another death come not
To choke my utterance sacrilegious, here?"   140
Then said the veiled shadow—"Thou hast felt
What 'tis to die[47] and live again before
Thy fated hour, that thou hadst power to do so
Is thy own safety; thou hast dated on
Thy doom."—"High Prophetess," said I, "purge off,

---

43 i.e. the leaves from a gum tree.
44 Paralysing.
45 Arteries.
46 A reference to the story of Jacob's ladder in Genesis 28.
47 Keats had first-hand knowledge of premature death, most notably in his experience of the last days
    of his mother and brother. His description at ll. 122–35 may draw on these dark recollections.

Benign, if so it please thee, my mind's film."[48]—
"None can usurp this height," return'd that shade,
"But those to whom the miseries of the world
Are misery,[49] and will not let them rest.
All else who find a haven in the world,   150
Where they may thoughtless sleep away their days,
If by a chance into this fane[50] they come,
Rot on the pavement where thou rottedst half."—
"Are there not thousands in the world," said I,
Encourag'd by the sooth[51] voice of the shade,
"Who love their fellows even to the death,
Who feel the giant agony of the world,
And more, like slaves to poor humanity,
Labour for mortal good? I sure should see
Other men here; but I am here alone."   160
"Those whom thou spak'st of are no vision'ries,"
Rejoin'd that voice—"They are no dreamers weak,
They seek no wonder but the human face;
No music but a happy-noted voice—
They come not here, they have no thought to come—
And thou art here, for thou art less than they—
What benefit canst thou, or all thy tribe,
To the great world? Thou art a dreaming thing,
A fever of thyself[52]—think of the Earth;
What bliss even in hope is there for thee?   170
What haven? every creature hath its home;
Every sole[53] man hath days of joy and pain,
Whether his labours be sublime or low—
The pain alone; the joy alone; distinct:
Only the dreamer venoms[54] all his days,
Bearing more woe than all his sins deserve.[55]
Therefore, that happiness be somewhat shar'd,
Such things as thou art are admitted oft
Into like gardens thou didst pass erewhile,
And suffer'd in these temples: for that cause   180
Thou standest safe beneath this statue's knees."
"That I am favour'd for unworthiness,

---

48 i.e. make my understanding clear.
49 i.e those with a benevolent and fellow-feeling cast of mind.
50 Temple.
51 Jones calls 'sooth' a 'private Keatsian adjective [which] appears to conflate "smooth" and
    "soothing" ' (John Jones, *John Keats's Dream of Truth*, London: Chatto & Windus, 1969).
52 The fever of poetic composition, a metaphor found several times in Keats's correspondence.
53 Single.
54 The dreamer is aware of human misery on a daily basis.
55 The poet suffers more than the normal person as 'his' experiences of joy and sorrow are com-
    mingled; the ordinary man's are compartmentalised or discrete.

By such propitious parley medicin'd
In sickness not ignoble,[56] I rejoice,
Aye, and could weep for love of such award."
So answer'd I, continuing, "If it please,
Majestic shadow, tell me: sure not all
Those melodies sung into the World's ear
Are useless: sure a poet is a sage;
A humanist,[57] physician to all men.   190
That I am none I feel, as vultures feel
They are no birds when eagles are abroad.
What am I then: Thou spakest of my tribe:
What tribe?" The tall shade veil'd in drooping white
Then spake, so much more earnest, that the breath
Moved the thin linen folds that drooping hung
About a golden censer from the hand
Pendent[58]—"Art thou not of the dreamer tribe?
The poet and the dreamer are distinct,
Diverse, sheer opposite, antipodes.   200
The one pours out a balm upon the World,
The other vexes it."[59] Then shouted I
Spite of myself, and with a Pythia's spleen[60]
"Apollo! faded! O far flown Apollo!"[61]
Where is thy misty pestilence to creep
Into the dwellings, through the door crannies
Of all mock lyrists, large self worshipers
And careless hectorers in proud bad verse.[62]
Though I breathe death with them it wil be life
To see them sprawl before me into graves.   210
Majestic shadow, tell me where I am,
Whose altar this; for whom this incense curls;
What image this whose face I cannot see,
For the broad marble knees; and who thou art,
Of accent feminine so courteous?"

Then the tall shade, in drooping linens veil'd,
Spoke out, so much more earnest, that her breath

---

56 The poetic fever is not ignoble as it involves an empathetic awareness of humanity's woes.
57 Humanitarian.
58 Suspended.
59 Here the poet is seen as humanitarian, pouring out a balm upon the world, whilst the dreamer is
    seen as self-indulgent.
60 The Pythia was the high priestess of the Delphic Oracle, and delivered her prophecies in a fevered
    and incoherent chant.
61 Apollo is the patron of poetic composition. The poet is lamenting the corrupt state of modern
    poetry.
62 This may be a diatribe against the state of contemporary poetry in general, but individual targets
    have been identified: Byron most particularly, but also Wordsworth and Thomas Moore.

Stirr'd the thin folds of gauze that drooping hung
About a golden censer from her hand
Pendent; and by her voice I knew she shed   220
Long-treasured tears. "This temple, sad and lone,
Is all spar'd[63] from the thunder of a war[64]
Foughten long since by giant hierarchy
Against rebellion: this old image here,
Whose carved features wrinkled as he fell,
Is Saturn's; I Moneta,[65] left supreme
Sole Priestess of this desolation."—
I had no words to answer, for my tongue,
Useless, could find about its roofed home
No syllable of a fit majesty   230
To make rejoinder to Moneta's mourn.[66]
There was a silence, while the altar's blaze
Was fainting for sweet food: I look'd thereon,
And on the paved floor, where nigh were piled
Faggots of cinnamon, and many heaps
Of other crisped spice-wood—then again
I look'd upon the altar, and its horns
Whiten'd with ashes, and its lang'rous flame,
And then upon the offerings again;
And so by turns—till sad Moneta cried,   240
"The sacrifice is done, but not the less
Will I be kind to thee for thy good will.
My power, which to me is still a curse,
Shall be to thee a wonder; for the scenes
Still swooning[67] vivid through my globed[68] brain,
With an electral[69] changing misery,
Thou shalt with these dull mortal eyes behold,
Free from all pain, if wonder pain thee not."
As near as an immortal's sphered[70] words
Could to a mother's soften, were these last: 250
And yet I had a terror of her robes,
And chiefly of the veils, that from her brow
Hung pale, and curtain'd her in mysteries,
That made my heart too small to hold its blood.
This saw that Goddess, and with sacred hand

---

63 Is all that is left.
64 The war of the Olympians against the Titans, the subject of *Hyperion. A Fragment.*
65 Moneta has been identified with Mnemosyne ('memory'), the mother of the muses.
66 Lament.
67 Moneta's visions are powerful enough to induce fainting.
68 Having the form of a globe. A Keatsian coinage. See 'Ode on Melancholy', l. 17.
69 Electrically, i.e. charged as if by electricity.
70 i.e. all-compassing.

Parted the veils. Then saw I a wan face,
Not pin'd by human sorrows, but bright-blanch'd[71]
By an immortal sickness which kills not;
It works a constant change, which happy death
Can put no end to; deathwards progressing   260
To no death was that visage; it had past
The lilly and the snow; and beyond these
I must not think now, though I saw that face—
But for her eyes I should have fled away.
They held me back, with a benignant light,
Soft mitigated by divinest lids
Half-closed, and visionless entire[72] they seem'd
Of all external things;—they saw me not,
But in blank splendor, beam'd like the mild moon,
Who comforts those she sees not, who knows not   270
What eyes are upward cast. As I had found
A grain of gold upon a mountain's side,
And twing'd with avarice strain'd out my eyes
To search its sullen entrails rich with ore,
So at the view of sad Moneta's brow,
I ask'd to see what things the hollow brain
Behind environed: what high tragedy
In the dark secret chambers of her skull
Was acting, that could give so dread a stress
To her cold lips, and fill with such a light   280
Her planetary eyes; and touch her voice
With such a sorrow—"Shade of Memory!"[73]—
Cried I, with act adorant at her feet,
"By all the gloom hung round thy fallen house,
By this last temple, by the golden age,[74]
By great Apollo, thy dear Foster Child,[75]
And by thyself, forlorn divinity,
The pale Omega[76] of a withered race,
Let me behold, according as thou saidst,
What in thy brain so ferments to and fro!"   290
No sooner had this conjuration[77] pass'd
My devout lips, than side by side we stood
(Like a stunt bramble by a solemn pine)
Deep in the shady sadness of a vale,[78]

---

71 White, bleached.
72 i.e. inattentive of external things. Moneta's attention is solely focused upon her inner visions.
73 Moneta is identified with Mnemosyne, goddess of memory.
74 The time of Titanic rule.
75 Mnemosyne has been identified with Juno, wife of Jupiter. Apollo was Jupiter's son by Latona.
76 Remnant. Omega is the last letter of the Greek alphabet.
77 Invocation, prayer.
78 The first line of *Hyperion. A Fragment.* 'The Fall of Hyperion' breaks off at this point.

4

Further Reading

Further Reading

Recommended Editions

There are several excellent complete editions of Keats's poetry. The standard scholarly edition is Jack Stillinger's *The Poems of John Keats* (Cambridge, Mass.: Belknap Press of Harvard University Press, 1978), which distils many years of work on Keats and includes textual variants, publication history and detailed attention to the manuscripts of each poem. However, this edition is principally concerned with the textual nuance of Keats's work and offers little in the way of explanatory footnotes. Consequently, the student reader of Keats in search of a complete edition is best advised to work with one of the reliable annotated editions: Miriam Allott's *The Poems of John Keats* (London: Longman, 1970), which has the most comprehensive explanatory footnotes, or John Barnard's *John Keats: The Complete Poems* (Harmondsworth: Penguin, 1973). The best selection of Keats's poetry currently available is Nicholas Roe's *John Keats: Selected Poems* (London: Dent, 1995), whilst Elisabeth Cook's *John Keats* (Oxford: Oxford University Press, 1990) offers a valuable selection from both the poetry and prose. The standard edition of the letters is *Letters of John Keats* (Cambridge, Mass.: Harvard University Press, 1958), edited, in two volumes, by Hyder E. Rollins, and the best selection from the correspondence is Robert Gittings's *The Letters of John Keats: A Selection* (Oxford: Oxford University Press, 1970).

Biographies

Keats has also been fortunate in the quality of his biographers. The student looking for an accessible account of the poet's life might begin with Aileen Ward's enjoyable *John Keats: The Making of a Poet* (London: Secker & Warburg, 1963), which is written with verve and panache, though its attempts at psychobiographical analysis are sometimes questionable. The standard life remains Walter Jackson Bate's magisterial *John Keats* (Cambridge, Mass.: Belknap Press of Harvard University Press, 1963), which combines biography with acute critical assessment of the poetry and letters and deserves the superlatives which have been heaped upon it by Keatsians. Robert Gittings's full biography *John Keats* (London: Heinemann, 1968) is entertaining and opinionated, and is especially valuable for its attention to the social context of Keats's work.

Top Ten Critical Studies

These are ten of the most significant books published on Keats during the twentieth century. Extracts from all of them appear in Section 2, Interpretations, in this volume.

Bate, Walter Jackson, *John Keats* (Cambridge, Mass.: Belknap Press of Harvard University Press, 1963). Combines a life with perceptive critical commentary. Perhaps the most valuable single book on Keats.

Garrod, H. W., *Keats* (Oxford: Clarendon Press, 1926). Arguably the best prewar study on Keats.

Jones, John, *John Keats's Dream of Truth* (London: Chatto & Windus, 1969). An idiosyncratic and eloquent account of Keats's 'sensual humanism'.

Levinson, Marjorie, *Keats's Life of Allegory: The Origins of a Style* (Oxford: Basil Blackwell, 1988). Fuses New Historicism, post-structuralism, Marxism and gender studies in a provocative, highly original, if sometimes opaque, study.

Ricks, Christopher, *Keats and Embarrassment* (Oxford: Clarendon Press, 1974). A brilliant meditation on the importance of embarrassment to 'the shape of [Keats's] imagination'.

Roe, Nicholas (ed.), *Keats and History* (Cambridge: Cambridge University Press, 1995). The best collection of essays to deal with the sociohistorical significance of Keats's poetry.

Roe, Nicholas, *John Keats and the Culture of Dissent* (Oxford: Clarendon Press, 1997). Combines close reading techniques and a detailed attention to poetic form with historical enquiry. The best book on Keats's politics.

Sperry, Stuart M., *Keats the Poet* (Princeton, NJ: Princeton University Press, 1973). A landmark volume which addresses Keats's preoccupation with the poetic imagination and the nature of poetry, and which stresses the indeterminacy of meaning evident in his poetry.

Vendler, Helen, *The Odes of John Keats* (Cambridge, Mass.: Belknap Press of Harvard University Press, 1983). Detailed close readings of the great odes allied to an account of the poems' coherence as an organic whole.

Wasserman, Earl R., *The Finer Tone: Keats' Major Poems* (Baltimore, Md.: Johns Hopkins University Press, 1953). Though Wasserman's allegorical approach and bejewelled prose have few imitators these days, his book remains a significant moment in post-war Keatsian criticism.

Further Reading

Barnard, John, *John Keats* (Cambridge: Cambridge University Press, 1987). An excellent introduction to Keats's poetry. Highly recommended to the student reader.

Bennett, Andrew, *Keats, Narrative and Audience: The Posthumous Life of Writing* (Cambridge: Cambridge University Press, 1994). A sophisticated discussion of both Keats's narrative poetry and the reception of the poet's work.

de Almeida, Hermione, *Romantic Medicine and John Keats* (New York and Oxford: Oxford University Press, 1991). A specialised but valuable study which deals with the way in which Keats's first profession resounds through his poetry.

Finney, Claude Lee, *The Evolution of Keats's Poetry* (Cambridge, Mass.: Harvard University Press, 1936). A comprehensive account of the principal influences upon Keats's work, both biographical and literary.

Jack, Ian, *Keats and the Mirror of Art* (Oxford: Clarendon Press, 1967). A learned and entertaining study of the influence of painting and sculpture upon Keats's work.

Murry, John Middleton, *Keats and Shakespeare: A Study of Keats's Poetic Life from 1860 to 1820* (1925). A study of Keats's relationship with Shakespeare, highly partisan in its account of the poet's 'miraculous' genius.

Ridley, M. R., *Keats's Craftsmanship: A Study in Poetic Development* (Oxford: Clarendon Press, 1933). An opinionated, detailed and provocative study of Keats's progress from poetic 'apprentice' to poetic 'master'.

Stillinger, Jack, *The Hoodwinking of Madeline and Other Essays on Keats's Poems* (Urbana, Ill.: University of Illinois Press, 1971). Walter Jackson Bate apart, Jack Stillinger is the doyen of modern Keatsian studies: the editor of the standard edition of Keats's work and author of many significant books and articles on the poet.

Watkins, Daniel P., *Keats's Poetry and the Politics of the Imagination* (Rutherford, NJ: Fairleigh Dickinson University Press, 1989). An earnest and politically committed Marxist account of Keats's major poetry.

Wolfson, Susan J., *The Questioning Presence: Wordsworth, Keats, and the Interrogative Mode in Romantic Poetry* (Ithaca, NY: Cornell University Press, 1988). An account of Keats's interactions with his great contemporary.

Index

'History, Self, and Gender in "Ode to Psyche"' (Watkins 1995) 30, 31, 66–9

Homans, Margaret 31

'The Hoodwinking of Madeline: Scepticism in "The Eve of St. Agnes"' (Stillinger 1961) 27–8, 73, 120

Howitt, William 2, 33, 42–3

humanism 29, 51, 178

Hunt, James Henry Leigh 6, 7, 8, 37, 59, 72; anti-conservatism 74, 75; Croker critique 34; effeminacy of *Hyperion* 30; *The Eve of St. Agnes'* 119; *Indicator* 40, 58, 134, 136; influence of 1, 25, 54, 82–3; Keats's repudiation of 15; 'Lamia' 159; letter from 12, 20–1; Lockhart critique 36; 'Ode to a Nightingale' 146; 'On First Looking into Chapman's Homer' 79; reputation of Keats 26; 'The Young Poets' 6, 10, 32, 33–4, 79

'Hymn to Pan' 74, 84–6

Hyperion 7, 10, 45–6, 96–118; depersonalised notion of Keats 49, 50, 97; gender criticism 31; grand march of intellect 16, 98; *Indicator* review 40; Shelley praise for 41, *see also* 'The Fall of Hyperion'

'I stood tiptoe' 10

identity 12, 17–18, 19–20, 48, 50–1, 63; gender criticism 65, 66, 67, 68, 73, 74; masculine 121, *see also* self

ideological criticism 29, 30, *see also* politics

the imagination 10, 12, 13, 29, 55; 'Lamia' 159, 160; 'Ode on a Grecian Urn' 151; 'Ode to a Nightingale' 146, 147

'Imitation of Spenser' 9

imperialism 54, 80–1, 88

indeterminacy of meaning 29, 55–6

Indicator (journal) 6, 40, 58, 134, 136

irony 28, 55, 56, 147

'Isabella; or, The Pot of Basil' 7, 10, 86–96, 160; political passages 54; sensuality 51–3, 97; vulgarity 49, 50

Jack, Ian 87, 98, 147; 'Ode on a Grecian Urn' 151, 152, 153; 'Ode to Psyche' 142; 'To Autumn' 174; 'To Sleep' 139

Jeffrey, Francis 8, 32, 38

John Keats: His Life and Writings (Bush 1966) 98

John Keats: The Complete Poems (Barnard 1973) 29, 147, 160, 178

John Keats: The Living Year (Gittings 1954) 28–9, 136, 147, 160, 178

John Keats: The Making of a Poet (Ward 1963) 28

John Keats (Bate 1963) 28, 50–1, 81, 98, 136, 140, 147, 160, 178

John Keats and the Culture of Dissent (Roe 1997) 30, 69–72, 81

John Keats (Gittings 1968) 28, 98

John Keats and the Sonnet Tradition (Zillman 1939) 140

John Keats's Dream of Truth (Jones 1969) 29, 51–3, 88, 147, 160, 178

Jones, John 19, 29, 147, 178; 'La Belle Dame Sans Merci' 136; *Hyperion* 97; 'Isabella' 88, 160; sensuousness 43, 51–3

Jong, Erica 30–1

'Keats, Ekphrasis, and History' (Kelley 1995) 154

Keats and Embarrassment (Ricks 1974) 29, 56–7

Keats (Garrod 1926) 27, 45–6, 96–7, 139, 142

'Keats and Gender Criticism' (Wolfson 1998) 31, 72–4

Keats, George 6, 7, 9, 10, 26; defence of John 39, 44; letters to 14, 18–20, 66, 134, 138, 140–1, 178

'Keats and the Historical Method in Literary Criticism' (McGann 1979) 30, 57–60, 174

Keats and History (ed. Roe 1995) 30

Keats and the Mirror of Art (Jack 1967) 98, 147, 151

Keats, Narrative, and Audience (Bennett 1994) 175

Keats the Poet (Sperry 1973) 29, 55–6, 153, 178

'Keats and Politics' (Wolfson 1986) 30

'Keats Reading Women: Women Reading Keats' (Homans 1990) 31

'Keats and Reality' (Bayley 1962) 29, 49–50, 88, 97

Keats and Shakespeare (Murry 1925) 27, 81

Keats, Tom 6, 7, 9, 10, 14, 64–5, 70

Lightning Source UK Ltd.
Milton Keynes UK
UKOW04f2054200314

228541UK00001B/19/P